SOLARO

STUDY GUIDE

Mathematics of Data Management

12 (MDM4U)

SOLARO Study Guide is designed to help students achieve success in school. The content in each study guide is 100% curriculum aligned and serves as an excellent source of material for review and practice. To create this book, teachers, curriculum specialists, and assessment experts have worked closely to develop the instructional pieces that explain each of the key concepts for the course. The practice questions and sample tests have detailed solutions that show problem-solving methods, highlight concepts that are likely to be tested, and point out potential sources of errors. ***SOLARO Study Guide*** is a complete guide to be used by students throughout the school year for reviewing and understanding course content, and to prepare for assessments.

Canadian Cataloguing in Publication Data

Rao, Gautam, 1961 –

SOLARO Study Guide – Mathematics of Data Management, Grade 12 Ontario

1. Mathematics – Juvenile Literature. I. Title

Published by
Castle Rock Research Corp.
2410 Manulife Place
10180 – 101 Street
Edmonton, AB T5J 3S4

2 3 4 FP 13 10 09

Publisher
Gautam Rao

Contributors
Jasmin Benevides
Monica Dhamrait
Mary Fiore
Bob Frizzell
Jane Gannon
Pat Sill
Kathy Stevens

CASTLE ROCK
RESEARCH CORP

Dedicated to the memory of Dr. V. S. Rao

SOLARO STUDY GUIDE—Mathematics of Data Management Grade 12 (MDM4U)

SOLARO STUDY GUIDE consists of the following sections:

Key Tips for Being Successful at School gives examples of study and review strategies. It includes information about learning styles, study schedules, and note taking for test preparation.

Class Focus includes a unit on each area of the curriculum. Units are divided into sections, each focusing on one of the specific expectations, or main ideas, that students must learn about in that unit. Examples, definitions, and visuals help to explain each main idea. Practice questions on the main ideas are also included. At the end of each unit is a test on the important ideas covered. The practice questions and unit tests help students identify areas they know and those they need to study more. They can also be used as preparation for tests and quizzes. Most questions are of average difficulty, though some are easy and some are hard—the harder questions are called *Challenger Questions*. Each unit is prefaced by a ***Table of Correlations***, which correlates questions in the unit (and in the practice tests at the end of the book) to the specific curriculum expectations. Answers and solutions are found at the end of each unit.

Key Strategies for Success on Tests helps students get ready for tests. It shows students different types of questions they might see, word clues to look for when reading them, and hints for answering them.

Practice Tests includes one to three tests based on the entire course. They are very similar to the format and level of difficulty that students may encounter on final tests. In some regions, these tests may be reprinted versions of official tests, or reflect the same difficulty levels and formats as official versions. This gives students the chance to practice using real-world examples. Answers and complete solutions are provided at the end of the section.

For the complete curriculum document (including specific expectations along with examples and sample problems), visit http://www.edu.gov.on.ca/eng/curriculum/

SOLARO STUDY GUIDE *Study Guides* are available for many courses. Check www.castlerockresearch.com for a complete listing of books available for your area.

For information about any of our resources or services, please call Castle Rock Research at 1.800.840.6224 or visit our website at http://www.castlerockresearch.com.

At Castle Rock Research, we strive to produce an error-free resource. If you should find an error, please contact us so that future editions can be corrected.

TABLE OF CONTENTS

Key Tips for being Successful at School

KEY TIPS FOR BEING SUCCESSFUL AT SCHOOL

KEY FACTORS CONTRIBUTING TO SCHOOL SUCCESS

In addition to learning the content of your courses, there are some other things that you can do to help you do your best at school. You can try some of the following strategies:

- **Keep a positive attitude:** Always reflect on what you can already do and what you already know.
- **Be prepared to learn:** Have the necessary pencils, pens, notebooks, and other required materials for participating in class ready.
- **Complete all of your assignments:** Do your best to finish all of your assignments. Even if you know the material well, practice will reinforce your knowledge. If an assignment or question is difficult for you, work through it as far as you can so that your teacher can see exactly where you are having difficulty.
- **Set small goals for yourself when you are learning new material:** For example, when learning the parts of speech, do not try to learn everything in one night. Work on only one part or section each study session. When you have memorized one particular part of speech and understand it, move on to another one. Continue this process until you have memorized and learned all the parts of speech.
- **Review your classroom work regularly at home:** Review to make sure you understand the material you learned in class.

- **Ask your teacher for help:** Your teacher will help you if you do not understand something or if you are having a difficult time completing your assignments.
- **Get plenty of rest and exercise:** Concentrating in class is hard work. It is important to be well-rested and have time to relax and socialize with your friends. This helps you keep a positive attitude about your schoolwork.
- **Eat healthy meals:** A balanced diet keeps you healthy and gives you the energy you need for studying at school and at home.

HOW TO FIND YOUR LEARNING STYLE

Every student learns differently. The manner in which you learn best is called your learning style. By knowing your learning style, you can increase your success at school. Most students use a combination of learning styles. Do you know what type of learner you are? Read the following descriptions. Which of these common learning styles do you use most often?

- **Linguistic Learner:** You may learn best by saying, hearing, and seeing words. You are probably really good at memorizing things such as dates, places, names, and facts. You may need to write down the steps in a process, a formula, or the actions that lead up to a significant event, and then say them out loud.
- **Spatial Learner:** You may learn best by looking at and working with pictures. You are probably really good at puzzles, imagining things, and reading maps and charts. You may need to use strategies like mind mapping and webbing to organize your information and study notes.
- **Kinesthetic Learner:** You may learn best by touching, moving, and figuring things out using manipulatives. You are probably really good at physical activities and learning through movement. You may need to draw your finger over a diagram to remember it, tap out the steps needed to solve a problem, or feel yourself writing or typing a formula.

SCHEDULING STUDY TIME

You should review your class notes regularly to ensure that you have a clear understanding of all the new material you learned. Reviewing your lessons on a regular basis helps you to learn and remember ideas and concepts. It also reduces the quantity of material that you need to study prior to a test. Establishing a study schedule will help you to make the best use of your time.

Regardless of the type of study schedule you use, you may want to consider the following suggestions to maximize your study time and effort:

- Organize your work so that you begin with the most challenging material first.
- Divide the subject's content into small, manageable chunks.
- Alternate regularly between your different subjects and types of study activities in order to maintain your interest and motivation.
- Make a daily list with headings like "Must Do," "Should Do," and "Could Do."
- Begin each study session by quickly reviewing what you studied the day before.
- Maintain your usual routine of eating, sleeping, and exercising to help you concentrate better for extended periods of time.

CREATING STUDY NOTES

MIND-MAPPING OR WEBBING

Use the key words, ideas, or concepts from your reading or class notes to create a mind map or web (a diagram or visual representation of the given information). A mind map or web is sometimes referred to as a knowledge map. Use the following steps to create a mind map or web:

1. Write the key word, concept, theory, or formula in the centre of your page.
2. Write down related facts, ideas, events, and information, and link them to the central concept with lines.
3. Use coloured markers, underlining, or symbols to emphasize things such as relationships, timelines, and important information.

The following examples of a Frayer Model illustrate how this technique can be used to study vocabulary.

Definition • Perimeter is the distance around the outside of a polygon.	**Notes** • Perimeter is measured in linear units (e.g., metres, centimetres, and so on).
Perimeter	
Examples • The length of a fence around a yard • The distance around a circle (circumference)	**Non-Examples** • The area of grass covering a lawn • The size of a rug lying on a floor

Definition • A cube is a solid 3-D object with six faces.	**Notes** • A cube is different from other shapes because it has six equally-sized square faces, eight vertices, and twelve equal edges.
Cube	
Examples 	**Non-Examples** 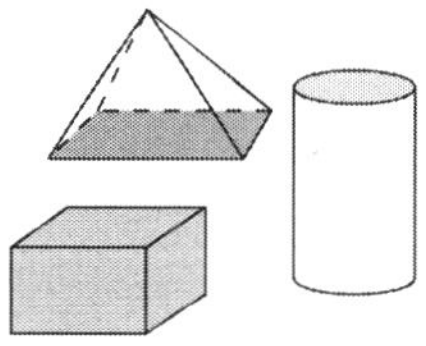

Index Cards

To use index cards while studying, follow these steps:

1. Write a key word or question on one side of an index card.
2. On the reverse side, write the definition of the word, answer to the question, or any other important information that you want to remember.

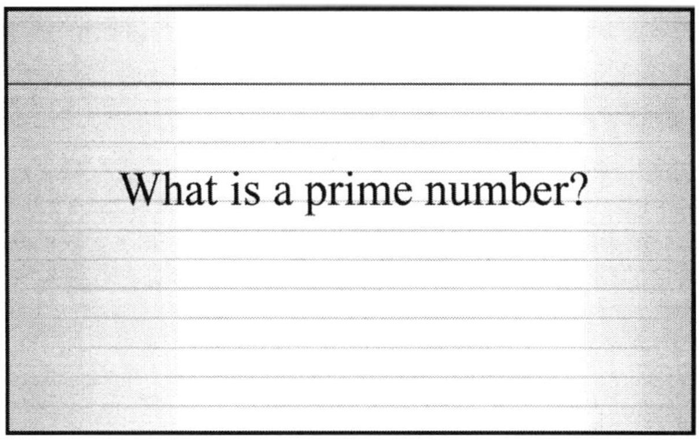

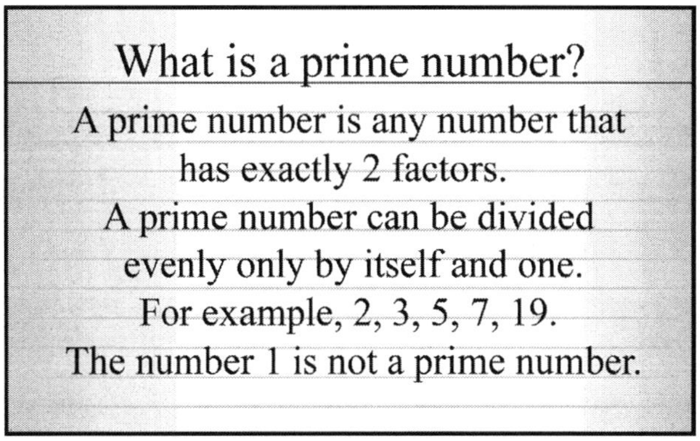

Symbols and Sticky Notes—Identifying Important Information

Use symbols to mark your class notes. The following are some examples:

- An exclamation mark (!) might be used to point out something that must be learned well because it is a very important idea.
- A question mark (?) may highlight something you are not certain about
- A diamond (◊) or asterisk (*) could highlight interesting information that you want to remember.

Sticky notes are useful in the following situations:

- Use sticky notes when you are not allowed to put marks in books.
- Use sticky notes to mark a page in a book that contains an important diagram, formula, explanation, or other information.
- Use sticky notes to mark important facts in research books.

Memorization Techniques

- **Association** relates new learning to something you already know. For example, to remember the spelling difference between dessert and desert, recall that the word *sand* has only one *s*. So, because there is sand in a desert, the word *desert* has only one *s*.
- **Mnemonic** devices are sentences that you create to remember a list or group of items. For example, the first letter of each word in the phrase "Every Good Boy Deserves Fudge" helps you to remember the names of the lines on the treble-clef staff (E, G, B, D, and F) in music.

- **Acronyms** are words that are formed from the first letters or parts of the words in a group. For example, RADAR is actually an acronym for Radio Detecting and Ranging, and MASH is an acronym for Mobile Army Surgical Hospital. HOMES helps you to remember the names of the five Great Lakes (Huron, Ontario, Michigan, Erie, and Superior).
- **Visualizing** requires you to use your mind's eye to "see" a chart, list, map, diagram, or sentence as it is in your textbook or notes, on the chalkboard or computer screen, or in a display.
- **Initialisms** are abbreviations that are formed from the first letters or parts of the words in a group. Unlike acronyms, an initialism cannot be pronounced as a word itself. For example, GCF is an initialism for **G**reatest **C**ommon **F**actor.

Key Strategies for Reviewing

Reviewing textbook material, class notes, and handouts should be an ongoing activity. Spending time reviewing becomes more critical when you are preparing for a test. You may find some of the following review strategies useful when studying during your scheduled study time:

- Before reading a selection, preview it by noting the headings, charts, graphs, and chapter questions.
- Before reviewing a unit, note the headings, charts, graphs, and chapter questions.
- Highlight key concepts, vocabulary, definitions, and formulas.
- Skim the paragraph, and note the key words, phrases, and information.
- Carefully read over each step in a procedure.
- Draw a picture or diagram to help make the concept clearer.

KEY STRATEGIES FOR SUCCESS: A CHECKLIST

Reviewing is a huge part of doing well at school and preparing for tests. Here is a checklist for you to keep track of how many suggested strategies for success you are using. Read each question, and put a check mark (✓) in the correct column. Look at the questions where you have checked the "No" column. Think about how you might try using some of these strategies to help you do your best at school.

Key Strategies for Success	Yes	No
Do you attend school regularly?		
Do you know your personal learning style—how you learn best?		
Do you spend 15 to 30 minutes a day reviewing your notes?		
Do you study in a quiet place at home?		
Do you clearly mark the most important ideas in your study notes?		
Do you use sticky notes to mark texts and research books?		
Do you practise answering multiple-choice and written-response questions?		
Do you ask your teacher for help when you need it?		
Are you maintaining a healthy diet and sleep routine?		
Are you participating in regular physical activity?		

Counting Probability

COUNTING AND PROBABILITY

Table of Correlations		
Specific Expectation	**Practice Questions**	**Unit Test Questions**
By the end of this course, students will:		
CP1.1 *recognize and describe how probabilities are used to represent the likelihood of a result of an experiment and the likelihood of a real-world event*	1	1
CP1.2 *describe a sample space as a set that contains all possible outcomes of an experiment, and distinguish between a discrete sample space as one whose outcomes can be counted and a continuous sample space as one whose outcomes can be measured*	2	2
CP1.3 *determine the theoretical probability,* P_i *(i.e., a value from 0 to 1), of each outcome of a discrete sample space, recognize that the sum of the probabilities of the outcomes is 1 (i.e., for* n *outcomes,* $P1 + P2 + P3 + \ldots + Pn = 1$*), recognize that the probabilities* P_i *form the probability distribution associated with the sample space, and solve related problems*	3, 4, NR1	3, NR1
CP1.4 *determine, through investigation using class-generated data and technology-based simulation models, the tendency of experimental probability to approach theoretical probability as the number of trials in an experiment increases*	5, OR1	4, NR2
CP1.5 *recognize and describe an event as a set of outcomes and as a subset of a sample space, determine the complement of an event, determine whether two or more events are mutually exclusive or non-mutually exclusive, and solve related probability problem using a variety of strategies*	6, NR2	5, NR3
CP1.6 *determine whether two events are independent or dependent and whether one event is conditional on another event, and solve related probability problems using a variety of strategies*	7, 8, NR3	6, OR 1
CP2.1 *recognize the use of permutations and combinations as counting techniques with advantages over other counting techniques, distinguish between situations that involve the use of permutations and those that involve the use of combinations, and make connections between, and calculate, permutations and combinations*	9, 10	7, 8
CP2.2 *solve simple problems using techniques for counting permutations and combinations, where all objects are distinct, and express the solutions using standard combinatorial notation*	11, NR4	9, NR4
CP2.3 *solve introductory counting problems involving the additive counting principle and the multiplicative counting principle*	12, NR5, OR2	10, NR5, NR6

CP2.4	*make connections, through investigation, between combinations (i.e.,* n *choose* r*) and Pascal's triangle*	13	11
CP2.5	*solve probability problems using counting principles for situations involving equally likely outcomes*	14, NR6	12, NR7

COUNTING AND PROBABILITY

CP1.1 *recognize and describe how probabilities are used to represent the likelihood of a result of an experiment (e.g., spinning spinners; drawing block from a bag that contains different coloured blocks; playing a game with number cubes; playing Aboriginal stick-and-stone games) and the likelihood of a real-world event (e.g., that it will rain tomorrow, that an accident will occur, that a product will be defective)*

PROBABILITIES

Probabilities can be used to make predictions about everyday occurrences. These predictions are often based on data that has been collected over a certain time period. Sometimes, you can only predict what might happen. For example, if a weather report forecasts a 90% chance of snow tomorrow, there is still that slight chance (10%) that it will not snow. Although there is no guarantee, a 90% probability of snow suggests that it will probably snow tomorrow.

A prediction can also be made on the results of an experiment. Several trials are performed, and the outcome of each trial is recorded. The resulting data is used to calculate the probability that a particular outcome will occur.

An example of a prediction made from the results of an experiment would be counting the number of successful free throws made by a basketball player. In today's practice a player successfully makes 15 out of 20 shots. The coach may predict that in tomorrow's game the same player will make 75% of her free throws. However, the result of the experiment in the practice does not guarantee the result in the game.

The experimental probability or empirical probability of a particular outcome is determined by dividing the number of times the outcome occurred during an experiment by the number of trials (or attempts) performed. The probability, P_i of an event, E, is calculated as shown below.

$$P(E) = \frac{\text{Number of times the desired outcome occurred}}{\text{Total number of trials}}$$

The probability of an event is expressed as a ratio or decimal between 0 and 1, inclusive. The closer the value is to 1, the more likely the event will occur.

Example

Data from a survey about home ownership was collected regarding the residents of a town. The given table shows the results of the survey.

Residents	**At address less than two years**	**At address more than two years**	**Total for category**
Owners	1000	9000	10 000
Renters	3500	1500	5000
Total	4500	10 500	15 000

A mail carrier is walking down one of the town's streets. Determine the probability that the resident at the next home she delivers to

a) is an owner

b) is a renter and has lived at that address for less than two years

c) is a renter and has lived at that address for more than two years

Solution

a) P(resident is an owner)

$$= \frac{\text{number of owners}}{\text{total number of houses}}$$

$$= \frac{10\ 000}{15\ 000} \approx 0.67$$

b) P(resident is a renter and has lived at the address less than two years

$$= \frac{3500}{15\ 000} \approx 0.23$$

c) P(resident is an owner and has lived at the address more than two years

$= \frac{9000}{15\,000} \approx 0.6$

Related Question: 1

CP1.2 *describe a sample space and distinguish between a discrete sample space as one whose outcomes can be counted (e.g., all possible outcomes of drawing a card or tossing a coin) and a continuous sample space as one whose outcomes can be measured (e.g., all possible outcomes of the time it takes to complete a task or the maximum distance a ball can be thrown)*

Sample Space

A **sample space** is a data set that contains all possible outcomes of an experiment. A **discrete sample space** is one whose outcomes can be counted. A discrete sample space has a *finite* number of possible outcomes.

Example

The chart below illustrates the possible outcomes when two standard six-sided dice are rolled together.

		Die A					
		1	2	3	4	5	6
Die B	1	(1, 1)	(1, 2)	(1, 3)	(1, 4)	(1, 5)	(1, 6)
	2	(2, 1)	(2, 2)	(2, 3)	(2, 4)	(2, 5)	(2, 6)
	3	(3, 1)	(3, 2)	(3, 3)	(3, 4)	(3, 5)	(3, 6)
	4	(4, 1)	(4, 2)	(4, 3)	(4, 4)	(4, 5)	(4, 6)
	5	(5, 1)	(5, 2)	(5, 3)	(5, 4)	(5, 5)	(5, 6)
	6	(6, 1)	(6, 2)	(6, 3)	(6, 4)	(6, 5)	(6, 6)

a) How many possible outcomes are in the sample space?

b) Classify this sample space as discrete or continuous.

Solution

a) The outcomes are the ordered pairs, so there are 36 outcomes.

b) The sample space is discrete because the outcomes can be counted.

A **continuous sample space** is one whose outcomes must be **measured**.

Example

The chart below illustrates the outcomes from the City Finals Female Shot Put Event.

Participant	**Sarah**	**Leah**	**Melissa**	**Suri**
Distance (m)	5.65	6.53	4.98	6.01

a) How many possible outcomes are in the sample space?

b) Classify this sample space as discrete or continuous.

Solution

a) The number of possible outcomes is infinite because the four girls could have thrown their shot puts any number of distances.

b) The sample space is continuous because the number of possible outcomes cannot be defined. This inability to give a finite number is because the outcomes are measured (such as distance, time, etc.), rather than counted (number of colour combinations, number of visitors to a museum, etc.).

Example

Are the sample spaces for the following sets of data discrete or continuous? Explain.

Data Set I

The given table shows the different running shoe sizes worn by the students in a physical education class and the number of students who wear each size.

Shoe Size	Number of Students
6	3
7	5
8	8
9	4
10	2

Data Set II

The table below shows the heights of five girls on a junior high school basketball team.

Player	Mary	Gail	Wendy	Karen	Betty
Height (m)	1.65	1.72	1.66	1.54	1.82

Data Set III

The given chart shows the possible outcomes of painting a toy three different colours using the colours specified.

Top colour: red (R), green (G) or white (W)

Middle colour: blue (B) or orange (O)

Bottom colour: yellow (Y) or purple (P)

Top	Middle	Bottom	Outcome
R	B	Y	RBY
		P	RBP
	O	Y	ROY
		P	ROP
G	B	Y	GBY
		P	GBP
	O	Y	GOY
		P	GOP
W	B	Y	WBY
		P	WBP
	O	Y	WOY
		P	WOP

Solution

Data Set I

The sample space is discrete because there are 22 possible outcomes. There are 22 students in the class. The actual outcomes are 6, 6, 6, 7, 7, 7, 7, 7, 8, 8, 8, 8, 8, 8, 8, 8, 9, 9, 9, 9, 10, and 10.

Data Set II

The sample space is continuous because the outcomes are measured.

Data Set III

The sample space is discrete because there are 12 outcomes. The outcomes can be counted.

Related Question: 2

CP1.3 *determine the theoretical probability, P_i (i.e., a value from 0 to 1), of each outcome of a discrete sample space (e.g., in situations in which all outcomes are equally likely), recognize that the sum of the probabilities of the outcomes is 1 (i.e., for n outcomes, $P_1 + P_2 + P_3 + \ldots + P_n = 1$) recognize that the probabilities P_i form the probability distribution associated with the sample space, and solve related problems*

THEORETICAL PROBABILITY OF AN OUTCOME OF A DISCRETE SAMPLE SPACE

Where outcomes are equally likely in a discrete sample space, the probability of each individual outcome is given by $P_i = \frac{1}{n(S)}$, where $n(S)$ is the total number of outcomes in the sample space. It follows that $0 \le P_i \le 1$ and that the sum of the probabilities of all the distinct outcomes from a given sample space is 1. If an individual outcome occurs *f* times (*f* = frequency), then the probability of that outcome is $P = f \times \frac{1}{n(S)} = \frac{f}{n(S)}$

A probability distribution shows all possible outcomes in an experiment and their associated probabilities. A probability distribution can be expressed in a list or table of values, in a graph such as a histogram, or, in some cases, by a formula. For discrete sample spaces we often express the probability distribution as a list or table.

Example 1

Determine the probability distribution for an experiment in which a student rolls two standard six-sided number cube and records their sum.

Solution

Create a sample space table in which you record the sum of the two dice.

Sums	**1**	**2**	**3**	**4**	**5**	**6**
1	2	3	4	5	6	7
2	3	4	5	6	7	8
3	4	5	6	7	8	9
4	5	6	7	8	9	10
5	6	7	8	9	10	11
6	7	8	9	10	11	12

There are 36 equally likely outcomes and 11 different sums. The probability of a particular sum is based on the frequency of that sum (the number of times it occurs in the sample space). The table below shows the probability distribution of all the possible outcomes.

Outcome (Sum)	**Frequency**	**Probability**
2	1	$\frac{1}{36} = 0.028$
3	2	$\frac{2}{36} = 0.056$
4	3	$\frac{3}{36} = 0.083$
5	4	$\frac{4}{36} = 0.111$
6	5	$\frac{5}{36} = 0.139$
8	5	$\frac{5}{36} = 0.139$
9	4	$\frac{4}{36} = 0.111$
10	3	$\frac{3}{36} = 0.083$
11	2	$\frac{2}{36} = 0.056$
12	1	$\frac{1}{36} = 0.028$
Total	36	$\frac{36}{36} = 1$

Notice that the sum of the probabilities of all possible outcomes is equal to 1.

Example 2

Draw a histogram that shows the probability distribution of the sums produced when two standard six-sided number cubes are rolled. Use the data from the table in Example 1.

Solution

Probability Distribution for the Sum of Two Standard Number Cubes

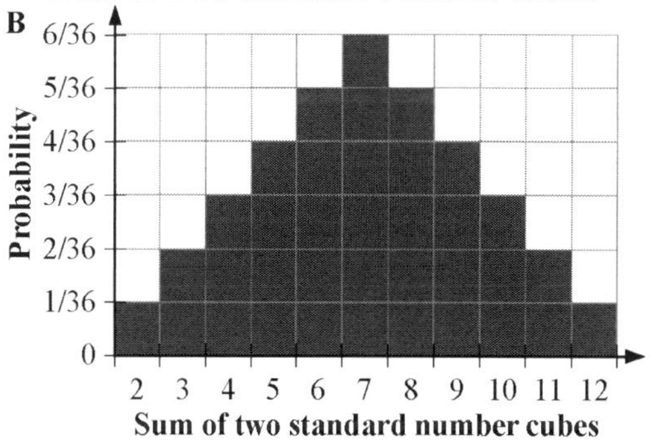

The use of a tool, such as a Histogram, makes the most likely and least likely outcomes very easy to see. In this case, the most likely outcome is a sum of 7, shown by the peak in the middle. The histogram is symmetrical about this value.

Example 3

Using the data from the example 1, determine

a) $P(\text{sum} = 7)$

b) $P(\text{sum} < 5)$

c) $P(\text{sum} \geq 7)$

Solution

a) $P(\text{sum} = 7) = \frac{6}{36} = \frac{1}{6} \approx 0.167$

b) Since you are looking for the probability of the sum being less than 5, you find the total number of favourable outcomes with sums of 2, 3, and 4, which total to 6 and divide by the total number of possible outcomes (36).

$$P(\text{sum} < 5) = \frac{1+2+3}{36} = \frac{6}{36} = \frac{1}{6} \approx 0.167$$

c) For the probability of the sum being greater than or equal to 7, find the total number of favourable outcomes with sums of 7, 8 , 9, 10, 11, and 12, which total 21, and divide by the total number of possible outcomes.

$$P(\text{sum} \geq 7) = \frac{6+5+4+3+2+1}{36}$$

$$= \frac{21}{36} = \frac{7}{12} \approx 0.583$$

Related Question: 3, NR1, 4

CP1.4 *determine, through investigation using class-generated data and technology-based simulation models (e.g., using a random-number generator on a spreadsheet or on a graphing calculator; using dynamic statistical software to simulate repeated trials in an experiment), the tendency of experimental probability to approach theoretical probability as the number of trials in an experiment increases (e.g., "If I simulate tossing two coins 1000 times using technology, the experimental probability that I calculate for getting two tails on the two tosses is likely to be closer to the theoretical probability of* $\frac{1}{4}$ *than if I simulate tossing the coins only 10 times")*

Experimental Probability and Theoretical Probability

When conducting an experiment, your **predicted** outcome is the theoretical probability and your **actual** outcome is the experimental probability.

For many problems, mathematical techniques can be used to calculate (predict) probabilities precisely (theoretical probability). However, in many situations, good estimates of probabilities can be obtained through the compilation of actual outcomes from an experiment that is repeated over and over again, or through the use of technology. This technique of estimating probabilities is called **simulation**. Data generating simulations may be performed by flipping coins, rolling number cubes, drawing cards, and making spinners. Technology based simulations may be performed by generating random numbers using technology.

Example

Janet is taking a test in which each question has 4 possible answers: A, B, C, and D. Only one answer is correct for each question and the test consists of 5 questions.

a) Describe a data-generating simulation model that Janet could use to estimate the probability of getting exactly 3 questions correct strictly by guessing.

b) Use a technology-based simulation model to determine the probability of getting exactly 3 questions correct strictly by guessing.

Solution

a) One data-generation simulation model Janet could use is to build a round spinner with 4 equal sections labelled A, B, C, and D that represent the 4 possible answers for each question. Since it is equally likely that the correct answer is assigned to any one of the 4 choices (A, B, C, and D) for each question, Janet can randomly choose the letter that will represent the correct answer for each of the 5 questions.

Janet chooses A, D, C, B, and D, in that order, as the correct answers for the 5 questions. She then spins the spinner 5 times, since there are 5 questions on the test. She records the outcome of each spin and then compares the outcome to the letters she chose as the correct answer to the 5 questions. She repeats this procedure (trial) several times. She can then estimate the probability of getting exactly 3 questions correct using

$$P = \frac{\text{Number of trials in which exactly 3 correct answers were spun}}{\text{Total number of trials}}$$

b) One technology-based simulation model that Janet could use is the randInt(command on a TI calculator.

The command randInt(1,4,5) generates a list of 5 random integer values (5 questions on the test) between 1 and 4, inclusive (4 choices for each question). To access the command randInt(on the TI-83 input MATH, scroll left once to PRB and press 5. Entering the values 1, 4, 5, close the bracket, and press ENTER. Associate 1 with answer A, 2 with answer B, 3 with answer C, and 4 with answer D. The assigned correct answers A, D, C, B, and D (stated above in part a) are therefore represented by the number sequence 1 4 3 2 4.

Sample results for 10 trials are recorded in the given table.

	Questions				
Trial	**# 1**	**# 2**	**# 3**	**# 4**	**#5**
1	3	1	3	3	2
2	2	2	1	2	3
3	4	3	2	1	2
4	1	2	3	1	3
5	2	2	4	2	1
6	1	4	3	1	3
7	2	1	1	1	1
8	4	1	2	1	2
9	2	3	4	2	3
10	4	3	1	4	3

Trial 6 is the only trial in the table that has exactly 3 questions correct.
Based on the results of this simulation, the experimental probability of guessing exactly 3 answers correctly is $\frac{1}{10} = 0.10$.

To get a better estimate of the probability of guessing exactly 3 answers correctly, more trials should be generated. Generally, the experimental probability tends to approach the theoretical probability as the number of trials increases. Spreadsheets can also be used to quickly generate more trials.

Example

a) What is the theoretical probability of tossing a coin with a result of HEADS?

b) Perform a simulation of tossing a coin 10 times and record the result of each toss. Based on your results, calculate the experimental probability of tossing a coin and getting HEADS.

c) Perform a simulation of tossing a coin 100 times and record the result of each toss. Based on your result, calculate the experimental probability of tossing a coin and getting HEADS.

d) What do you notice about how your result from parts b and c compare to the theoretical probability calculated in part a)?

Solution

a) $P(\text{Heads}) = \frac{1}{2} = 0.5$

b) Because only 10 trials are required, you could either actually flip a coin 10 times and record the answer OR use randInt (0, 1, 1), where the 0 represents heads, the first 1 represents trials and the last 1 represent a single coin being tossed. One possible set of result are as follows:
1, 0, 1, 0, 0, 1, 1, 0, 1, 1

Based on the simulation, the experimental probability of tossing Heads is as follows:

$$P(\text{Heads}) = \frac{4}{10} = \frac{2}{5} = 0.4$$

c) For a simulation requiring 100 trials a spreadsheet may be more time effective. The table below summarizes one such simulation of 100 trials.

Heads	Tails
48	52

Based on this simulation, the experimental probability of tossing HEADS is as follows:

$$P(\text{Heads}) = \frac{48}{100} = \frac{12}{25} = 0.48$$

d) The experimental probability of 0.48 acquired from 100 trials is closer to the theoretical probability of 0.5 compared to the experimental probability of 0.40 acquired from 10 trials. As such, these two simulations confirm the notion that with more trials, experimental probability will approach theoretical probability.

Related Questions: 5, OR1

CP1.5 *recognize and describe an event as a set of outcomes and as a subset of a sample space, determine the complement of an event, determine whether two or more events are mutually exclusive or non-mutually exclusive (e.g., the events of getting an even number or getting an odd number of heads from tossing a coin 5 times are mutually exclusive), and solve related probability problems [e.g., calculate* $P(\sim A)$, $P(A \text{ and } B)$, . $P(A \text{ or } B)$ *using a variety of strategies (e.g., Venn diagrams, lists, formulas)*

DESCRIBING AN EVENT

An **event** is a set of outcomes that is a subset of the sample space. For example, if a single six-sided number cube is rolled, the sample space contains the numbers {1, 2, 3, 4, 5, 6}. The event A of rolling a number that is divisible by 3 contains the outcomes {3, 6}, which is a subset of the sample space.

Sample Space

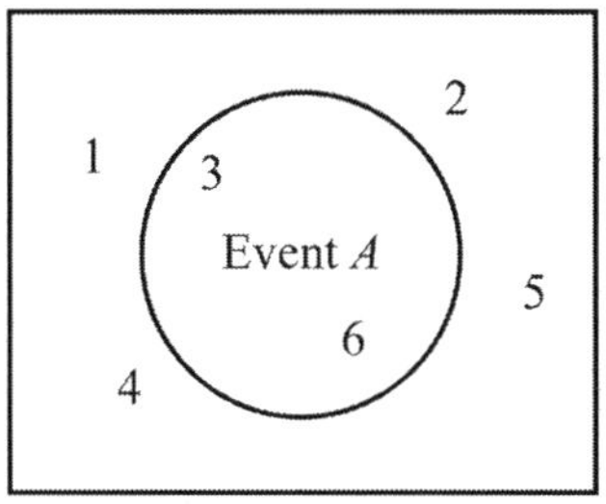

Therefore,

$$P(\text{A}) = \frac{\text{Number of outcomes divisible by 3}}{\text{Number of possible outcomes}}$$

$$= \frac{2}{6} = \frac{1}{3}$$

The **complement** of an event A, denoted by the symbol $\bar{A}$, consists of all outcomes in the sample space that are not in event A. In the example above, $\bar{A}$ consists of the set $\{1, 2, 4, 5\}$, all the outcomes from rolling a single die that are not divisible by 3.

Sample Space

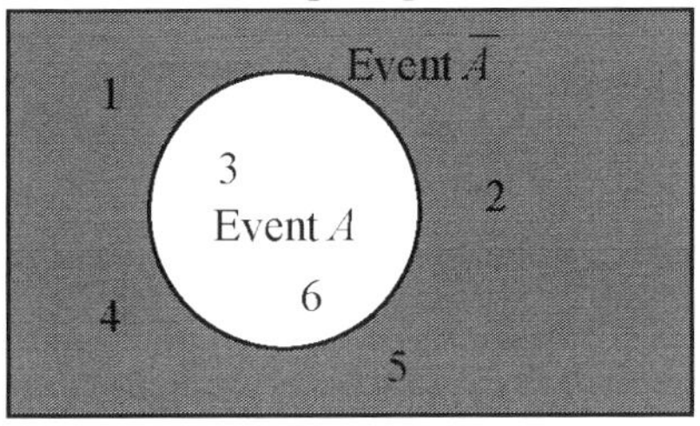

$$P(\bar{A}) = \frac{4}{6} = \frac{2}{3}$$

The sum of the probabilities of complementary events is 1.

$P(A) + P(\bar{A}) = 1$ or $P(\bar{A}) = 1 - P(A)$

Mutually exclusive events are events that do not have any common outcomes. For example, in a standard deck of 52 cards, the set of hearts and the set of diamonds are mutually exclusive because there is no card that is both a heart and a diamond.

The set of hearts and the set of queens are not mutually exclusive because the queen of hearts is both a heart and a queen. Events that do have outcomes in common are non-mutually-exclusive. Both types of events can be represented by Venn diagrams, as illustrate below.

Mutually Exclusive Events

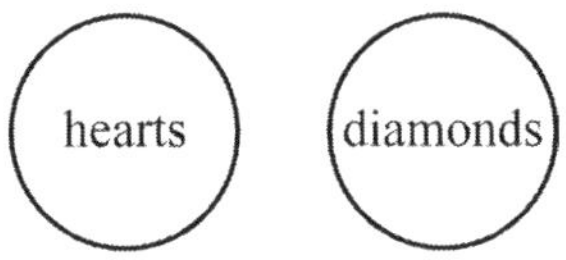

Non-Mutually Exclusive Events

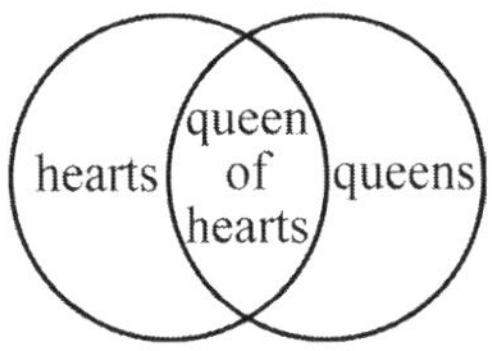

Related questions typically ask for the probability of event A **or** event B happening. To calculate probabilities of mutually exclusive events, use the formula,

$$P(\text{A or B}) = P(\text{A}) + P(\text{B})$$

To calculate probabilities of non-mutually exclusive events, use the formula,

$$P(\text{A or B}) = P(\text{A}) + P(\text{B}) - P(\text{A and B})$$

Sometimes the formula for determining the probability of non-mutually exclusive events can be confusing

Consider being asked to determine the probability of drawing a queen or a heart from a standard deck of 52 cards. You know that there are 4 queens and 13 hearts in a deck of cards.

One of those 4 queens is a queen of hearts and one of the 13 hearts is the queen of hearts. Therefore, without subtracting $P(A \text{ and } B)$, you would actually be counting the queen of hearts twice, which is incorrect because in the sample space of a deck of 52 cards, there is only one queen of hearts.

Related Questions: NR2, 6

CP1.6 *determine whether two events are independent or dependent and whether one event is conditional on another event, and solve related probability problems [e.g., calculate P(A and B), P(A or B), P(A given B)]using a variety of strategies (e.g., tree diagram, lists, formulas)*

Independent and Dependent Events

Two events are independent if the occurrence of one event does not affect the probability of the occurrence of the other event. For example, when two cards are successively drawn from a deck with the first card **replaced** before the second is drawn, the events of drawing each card are independent because for each card that is drawn, the deck is complete (52 cards = sample space for each event).

Two events A and B, are independent if and only if $P(\text{A and B}) = P(\text{A}) \times P(\text{B})$, where $P(\text{A and B})$ is the probability that both events occur simultaneously.

When events are dependent, the occurrence of one event affects the probability of the other. In the example of drawing two cards from a deck, if the first card drawn is not replaced before the second card is drawn, then the two events are dependent. The second card is drawn from 51 cards, so the sample space has been altered.

When the probability of event B depends directly on the outcome of event A, then the conditional probability of B, denoted by $P(\text{B/A})$, is the probability that event B occurs given that event A has already occurred.

To calculate probabilities of dependent events A and B, use the formula

$P(\text{A and B}) = P(\text{A}) \times P(\text{B/A})$, if event *A* occurs first, or $P(\text{B and A}) = P(\text{B}) \times P(\text{A/B})$, if event *B* occurs first.

Example

A card player successively draws two cards at random from a standard deck of 52 cards. Determine the following probabilities with and without the replacement of the first card before the second draw:

a) Probability that both cards are black

b) Probability that the first card is a queen and the second card is a four

c) Probability that one of the cards is a queen and the other is a four

d) Probability that neither card is a heart

Solution

a) With replacement:

$$P(\text{B}_1 \text{ and B}_2) = P(\text{B}_1) \times P(\text{B}_2)$$
$$= \frac{26}{52} \times \frac{26}{52}$$
$$= \frac{1}{2} \times \frac{1}{2} = \frac{1}{4}$$

Without replacement:

$$P(\text{B}_1 \text{ and B}_2) = P(\text{B}_1) \times P(\text{B}_2 | \text{B}_1)$$
$$= \frac{26}{52} \times \frac{25}{51}$$
$$= \frac{1}{2} \times \frac{25}{51} = \frac{25}{102}$$

b) Let Q be the event of drawing a queen and F the event of drawing a four.

With replacement:

$$P(\text{Q}_1 \text{ and F}_2) = P(\text{Q}_1) \times P(\text{F}_2)$$
$$= \frac{4}{52} \times \frac{4}{52}$$
$$= \frac{1}{13} \times \frac{1}{13} = \frac{1}{169}$$

Without replacement:

$$P(\text{Q}_1 \text{ and F}_2) = P(\text{Q}_1) \times P(\text{F}_2 | \text{Q}_1)$$
$$= \frac{4}{52} \times \frac{3}{51}$$
$$= \frac{1}{13} \times \frac{3}{51} = \frac{3}{663} = \frac{1}{221}$$

c) **Note** that in this case, there are actually two different sets of outcomes: either the first card could be a 4 and the second card could be a queen **or** the first card could be a queen and the second card could be a 4. The presence of the word **or** in the previous sentence suggests that the probability of the two separate events must be added.

With replacement:

$$P(\text{Q or F}) = P(\text{Q}_1 \text{and F}_2) + P(\text{F}_1 \text{and Q}_2)$$
$$= P(\text{Q}_1) \times P(\text{F}_2) + P(\text{F}_1) \times P(\text{Q}_2)$$
$$= \frac{4}{52} \times \frac{4}{52} + \frac{4}{52} \times \frac{4}{52}$$
$$= \frac{1}{13} \times \frac{1}{13} + \frac{1}{13} \times \frac{1}{13}$$
$$= \frac{1}{169} + \frac{1}{169}$$
$$= \frac{2}{169}$$

Without replacement:

The probability that the first card is a queen and the second is a four given that the first is a queen is $\frac{1}{221}$ [see the solution to b)].

Similarly, the probability that the first card is a four and the second is a queen given the first card is a four is also $\frac{1}{221}$.

$$P(Q \text{ or } F) = P(Q_1) \times P(F_2 / Q_1) + P(F_1) \times P(Q_2 / F_1)$$
$$= \frac{1}{221} + \frac{1}{221} = \frac{2}{221}$$

d) With replacement:

$$P(\overline{\text{H}_1} \text{ and } \overline{\text{H}_2}) = P(\overline{\text{H}_1}) \times P(\overline{\text{H}_2})$$
$$= \frac{39}{52} \times \frac{39}{52}$$
$$= \frac{3}{4} \times \frac{3}{4} = \frac{9}{16}$$

Without replacement:

$$P(\overline{\text{H}_1} \text{ and } \overline{\text{H}_2}) = P(\overline{\text{H}_1}) \times P(\overline{\text{H}_2} | \text{H}_1)$$
$$= \frac{39}{52} \times \frac{38}{51}$$
$$= \frac{3}{4} \times \frac{38}{51} = \frac{19}{34}$$

Related Questions: 7, NR3, 8

CP2.1 recognize the use of permutations and combinations as counting techniques with advantages over other counting techniques (e.g., making a list; using a tree diagram; making a chart; drawing a Venn diagram), distinguish between situations that involve the use of permutations and those that involve the use of combinations, and make connections between, and calculate, permutations and combinations (e.g., by considering whether or not order matters).

PERMUTATIONS AND COMBINATIONS

A **permutation** is an *arrangement* of a set of objects in which the order of the objects is important.

The number of permutations of all the objects in a group of n objects is $n!$

$$n! = (n)(n-1)(n-2)(n-3)\ldots(3)(2)(1)$$

The number of permutations of a group of n objects taken r at a time, $n \geq r$, is given by

$${}_nP_r = \frac{n!}{(n-r)!}$$

The notation $P(n, r)$ is equivalent to ${}_nP_r$.

A **combination** is a *selection* from a set of objects in which the order of the selection is not important. The number of combinations from a group of n objects taken r at a time is given by

$${}_nC_r = \frac{n!}{(n-r)!r!}$$

The notations ${}_nC_r$, $C(n, r)$, and $\binom{n}{r}$ are all equivalent.

Note that $0! = 1$.

Example

A two-digit number is formed using the digits 1, 3, and 5 without repetition.

a) Draw a tree diagram that illustrates the possible numbers that can be formed.

b) Use permutations to determine the number of possible two-digit numbers.

Solution

a)

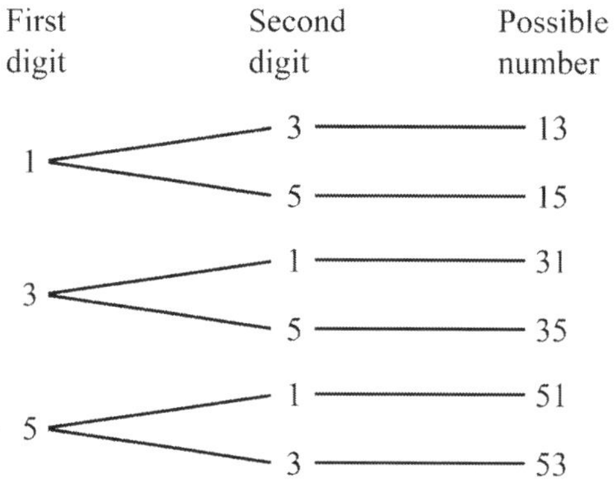

There are 6 possible numbers, as listed in the third column.

b) There are 3 digits available, and you must arrange 2 of them. Using permutation notation,

$${}_3P_2 = \frac{3!}{(3-2)!} = 6$$

There are 6 possible two-digit numbers.

Example

A ballet choreographer wants to use 12 dancers in a scene. The dance company has 20 dancers. How many different groups of dancers can he choose for the scene?

Solution

There are 20 dancers, from which 12 need to be chosen. Since the order is not important, this is a combinations problem.

$${}_{20}C_{12} = \frac{20!}{(20-12)!12!} = \frac{20!}{8!12!} = 125\,970$$

The choreographer can choose from 125 970 different possible groupings of 12 dancers for the scene.

Related Questions: 9, 10

CP2.2 solve simple problems using techniques for counting permutations and combinations, where all the objects are distinct, and express the solutions using standard combinatorial notation

SOLVING PROBLEMS USING TECHNIQUES FOR COUNTING PERMUTATIONS AND COMBINATIONS

Example

At Rossdale High School, 12 students have signed up to serve on the student council.

a) What is the number of arrangements in which the students could be seated in 2 rows to have their picture taken for the yearbook? Leave the answer in factorial notation.

b) A teacher advisor must select 3 of the 12 students to serve as president, vice president, and secretary of the student council. How many different arrangements of council members does she have to choose from?

c) The grad committee is composed of 7 members of the council. How many different selections of members are possible if the president, vice president, and secretary must be on the committee?

Solution

a) The 12 students will sit in 12 seats, where each seating position is unique. This is a permutation of all 12 objects, so there are 12! possible arrangements.

b) Since the 3 students will fill different positions, permutations must be used to solve this problem. Out of the 12 students on the council, 3 must be selected and arranged; therefore,
there are
${}_{12}P_3 = 1320$ different arrangements.

c) The president, vice president, and secretary are already chosen as members of the grad committee, so 4 more students must be chosen from the 9 remaining council members. For this committee, order is not important, so this is a combinations problem. There are ${}_9C_4 = 126$ different arrangements.

Related Questions: 1, NR4

12CP2.3 solve introductory counting problems involving the additive counting principle (e.g., determining the number of ways of selecting 2 boys or 2 girls from a group of 4 boys and 5 girls) and the multiplicative counting principle (e.g., determining the number of ways of selecting 2 boys and 2 girls from a group of 4 boys and 5 girls)

SOLVING COUNTING PROBLEMS

Sometimes, solving a counting problem requires the application of the additive counting principle or the multiplicative counting principle.

The **additive counting principle**:

$$\begin{aligned}&(\text{Number of events in A or B}) = \\ &(\text{Number of events in A}) + \\ &(\text{Number of events in B}) - \\ &(\text{Number of events in A and B})\end{aligned}$$

The **multiplicative counting principle**:

$$\begin{aligned}&(\text{Number of events in A and B}) = \\ &(\text{Number of events in A}) \times \\ &(\text{Number of events in B})\end{aligned}$$

Example

Determine the number of different 5-person groups that can be formed from a family of 4 adults and 8 children if the group must

a) consist of 2 adults and 3 children

b) consist of either 2 adults and 3 children or 3 adults and 2 children

c) include at least 1 adult

Solution

These are combinations problems because the order in which the group members are chosen is not important.

a) There are ${}_4C_2$ groups of 2 adults that can be formed from the 4 adults in the family. There are ${}_8C_3$ groups of 3 children that can be formed from the 8 children in the family. Since the adults and the children are both chosen in order to form a 5-person group, the multiplicative counting principle applies. The total number of different 5-person groups that can be formed is

$$\begin{aligned}{}_4C_2 \times {}_8C_3 &= 6 \times 56 \\ &= 336\end{aligned}$$

b) The number of different groups composed of 2 adults and 3 children is the result from the previous question, ${}_4C_2 \times {}_8C_3$. Using the same approach, the number of different groups composed of 3 adults and 2 children is ${}_4C_3 \times {}_8C_2$. Since either one or the other 5-person group is formed (not both), the additive counting principle applies.

Thus, the total number of possible 5-person groups is

$$\begin{aligned}{}_4C_2 \times {}_8C_3 + {}_4C_3 \times {}_8C_2 &= 6 \times 56 + 4 \times 28 \\ &= 336 + 112 \\ &= 448\end{aligned}$$

In this situation of the additive counting principle, it would not be possible for the groups formed with 2 adults and 3 children to be identical to the groups formed with 3 adults and 2 children. Therefore, nothing needs to be subtracted from the total of 448 five-person groups. The two different grouping techniques will yield **mutually exclusive** groups.

c) "At least 1 adult" means that the group **must** include 1, 2, 3, or all 4 adults. One method for solving the problem is to find the number of different groups with 1 adult, the number with 2 adults, the number with 3 adults, and the number with 4 adults, and then apply the additive counting principle to find the total number of groups.

$${}_4C_1 \times {}_8C_4 + {}_4C_2 \times {}_8C_3 + {}_4C_3 \times {}_8C_2 + {}_4C_4 \times {}_8C_1$$
$$= 4\times 70 + 6\times 56 + 4\times 28 + 1\times 8$$
$$= 280 + 336 + 112 + 8$$
$$= 736$$

An alternative and more efficient method is to determine the number of groups with no adults and subtract this number from the total number of possible groups.

The total number of 5-person groups that can be formed is
$${}_{12}C_5 = 792$$

The number of groups that can be formed with no adults, and therefore 5 children, is
$${}_8C_5 = 56$$

Therefore, the number of groups that can be formed with at least 1 adult is
$${}_{12}C_5 - {}_8C_5 = 736$$

Related Questions: 12, NR5, OR2

CP2.4 *make connections, through investigation, between combinations (i.e., n choose r) and Pascal's triangle [e.g., between* $\binom{2}{r}$ *and row 3 of Pascal's triangle, between* $\binom{n}{2}$ *and diagonal 3 of Pascal's triangle]*

COMBINATIONS AND PASCAL'S TRIANGLE

1
1 1
1 2 1
1 3 3 1
1 4 6 4 1
1 5 10 10 5 1
1 6 15 20 15 6 1
⋮

The numbers that form the pattern in Pascal's triangle (as shown above) can be found using combinations. The combination ${}_{n-1}C_{k-1}$ gives the value for the element number k in row n of the triangle. For example, the fourth number in the sixth row is ${}_{6-1}C_{4-1} = {}_5C_3 = 10$

The process of adding the two numbers directly above a given number, that generates the numbers in any row of Pascal's triangle can be applied to counting paths or routes between two points.
The number of possible pathways can also be determined from the number of possible directions that can be travelled.

Example

How many different paths can be travelled from A to B, in the grid below, if the path must always go either right or upward?

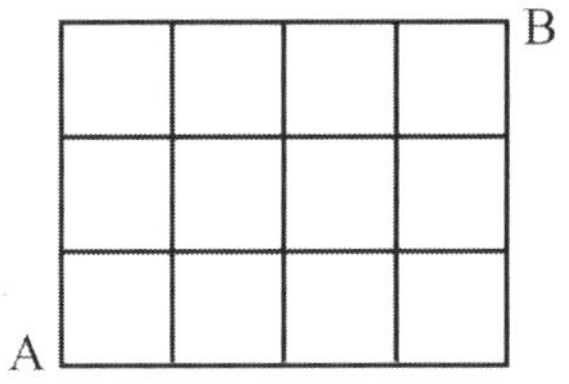

Solution

A pathway from A to B consists of 3 segments travelled upward and 4 segments travelled to the right; thus, out of 7 segments, 3 must be travelled upward.
The number of possible pathways is therefore

$${}_7C_3 = \frac{7!}{3!(7-3)!} = \frac{7!}{3!4!} = 35$$

or

Out of 7 segments, 4 must be travelled to the right; therefore the number of possible pathways is ${}_7C_4 = 35$

or

We can simply count the number of pathways, using the method similar to generating successive rows of Pascal's triangle:

Step 1: Starting from *A*, we must either go up or right. There is only 1 way of getting to the next square, so we denote the path taken by a 1.

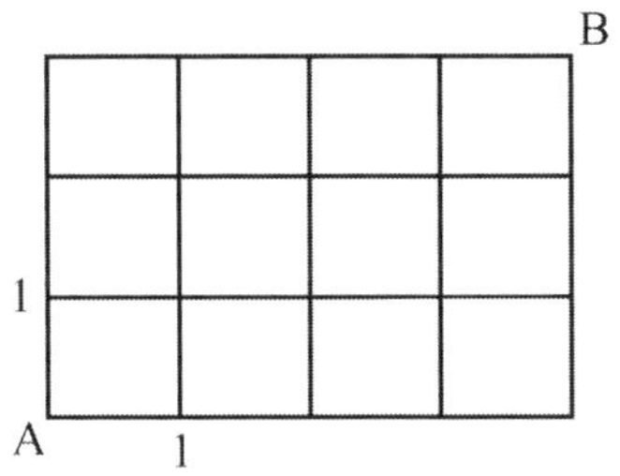

Step 2: Now, we can either move up or right from either point labelled with a 1. That leaves us with the following number of pathway options to the next locations.

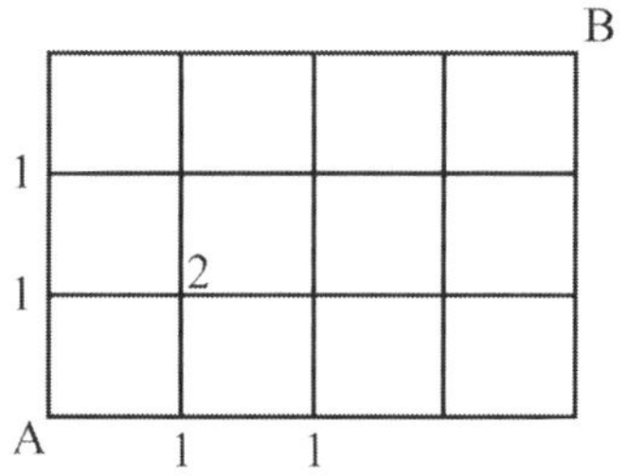

Step 3: Continue the pattern all the way to *B*.

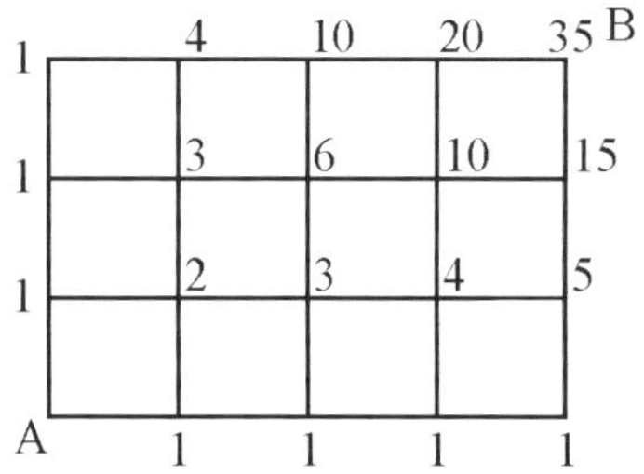

Therefore, this method confirms the 35 pathways calculated using the previous two strategies.

Example

If a pathway diagram is attached to one or more successive diagrams, the multiplicative counting principle can be used to determine the number of pathways through all the diagrams.

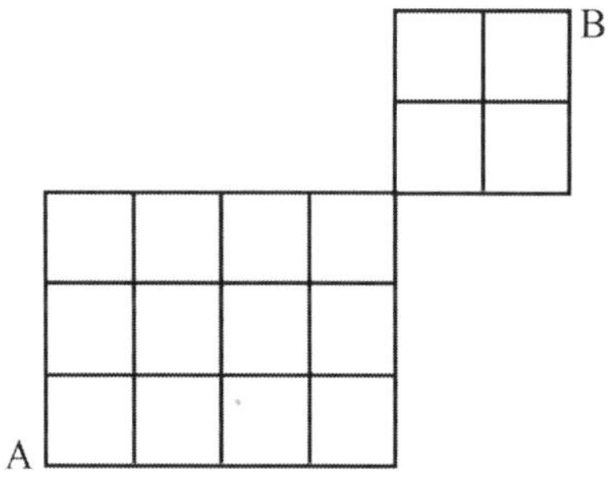

The number of possible pathways from A to B, if a pathway must go only right or upward, is

$${}_7C_3 \times {}_4C_2 = 35 \times 6 = 210$$

Related Question: 13

CP2.5 solve probability problems using counting principles for situations involving equally likely outcomes.

SOLVING PROBABILITY PROBLEMS USING COUNTING

Sometimes, when solving theoretical probability problems, the possible outcomes are not easy to count individually. In these cases, the counting techniques of permutations and combinations can be helpful for calculating the probabilities.

The probability of an event is defined by

$$P(\text{event}) = \frac{\text{Number of favourable outcomes}}{\text{Total number of possible outcomes}}$$

The methods given for solving the following example problems are not unique. In many cases, alternative methods are possible, but the more common methods have been provided.

Example

Alexandra spelled the word COURTING using lettered game tiles. She randomly chose 2 tiles from the word one at a time and placed them left to right in the order in which she chose them. Determine the probability that the tiles she chose

a) spelled CO

b) were both vowels

Solution

a) The number of possible outcomes is the number of two letter permutations of the 8 letters in the word COURTING. This is ${}_8P_2$. There is only 1 favourable outcome: choosing CO, in that order. Thus,

$$P(\text{letters are CO}) = \frac{1}{{}_8P_2} = \frac{1}{56}$$

b) You can solve this problem by determining the number of permutations of the 2 vowels selected from the 3 vowels in the word COURTING, which is ${}_3P_2$. Thus,

$$P(\text{letters are vowels}) = \frac{{}_3P_2}{{}_8P_2} = \frac{6}{56} = \frac{3}{28}$$

Alternatively, you can consider this problem as one involving combinations because the order of the letters is not important. The number of different selections of 2 letters from 8 is ${}_8C_2$, and the number of different selections of 2 vowels from 3 is ${}_3C_2$.

Thus, $P(\text{letters are vowels}) = \frac{{}_3C_2}{{}_8C_2} = \frac{3}{28}$

Example

Liam randomly draws two marbles from a bag containing 12 green marbles and 16 red marbles. Determine the probability that the two marbles are green if the first marble is

a) replaced before the second marble is drawn

b) **not** replaced before the second marble is drawn

Solution

a) Since the first marble is replaced before the second marble is drawn, the two events of drawing a green marble are independent. Their individual probabilities are calculated and then multiplied, using the formula $P(\text{G}_1 \text{ and } G_2) = P(\text{G}_1) \times P(\text{G}_2)$.

$$\begin{aligned} P(\text{green and green}) &= \frac{12}{28} \times \frac{12}{28} \\ &= \frac{3}{7} \times \frac{3}{7} \\ &= \frac{9}{49} \end{aligned}$$

b) Since the first marble is not replaced, the two events of drawing a green marble are dependent. One approach to solve the problem is to use combinations.
The number of different selections of 2 marbles from 28 is ${}_{28}C_2$, and the number of different selections of 2 green marbles from 12 is ${}_{12}C_2$.

$$P(\text{both green}) = \frac{{}_{12}C_2}{{}_{28}C_2} = \frac{66}{378} = \frac{11}{63}$$

An alternative approach is to consider the successive draws and apply the formula for dependent events,
$P(\text{G}_1 \text{ and } G_2) = P(\text{G}_1) \times P(\text{G}_2|\text{G}_1)$.

$$P(\text{green and green})$$
$$= P(\text{first marble green}) \times$$
$$P\left(\begin{array}{l}\text{second marble green given first}\\ \text{marble green}\end{array}\right)$$
$$= \frac{12}{28} \times \frac{11}{27} = \frac{11}{63}$$

Related Questions: NR 6, 14

PRACTICE QUESTIONS—COUNTING AND PROBABILITY

Use the following information to answer the next question.

Gerry performed an experiment in which he flipped three coins and recorded the number coins that landed on heads in each trial. The results of his experiment are given in the table.

Number of Heads	0	1	2	3
Frequency	1	9	8	2

CHALLENGER QUESTION

1. Based on Gerry's results, what is the experimental probability that on his next trial, two of the three coins will land on heads?

A. $\frac{1}{10}$

B. $\frac{1}{4}$

C. $\frac{2}{5}$

D. $\frac{2}{3}$

2. A school district needs to choose one math teacher to send to a national conference. Each school in the district has 3 math teachers. The district must first choose whether the representative will come from school A, B, C, D, E, or F. The district must then choose which of the chosen school's math teachers to send. The size of the sample space that the district has to choose from is

A. 6

B. 9

C. 18

D. 36

Use the following information to answer the next two questions.

An experiment was conducted to determine the relative occurrence of the English Alphabet letters, in published material. One paragraph from a newspaper, one from a textbook, and one from a magazine were analyzed. In all, there was a total of 1 044 letters. The given table lists the number of occurrences of each letter of the alphabet.

Letter	Number of occurrences
A	78
B	22
C	33
D	33
E	140
F	24
G	22
H	63
I	60
J	2
K	9
L	35
M	30
N	74
O	74
P	27
Q	4
R	67
S	67
T	96
U	30
V	10
W	22
X	8
Y	13
Z	1

CHALLENGER QUESTION

3. If a letter is chosen at random from one of the three paragraphs analyzed, what is the probability that the letter is not a vowel (A, E, I, O, U)?

A. $\frac{5}{26}$ **B.** $\frac{47}{100}$

C. $\frac{331}{522}$ **D.** $\frac{21}{26}$

Numerical Response

1. If a letter is chosen at random from one of the three paragraphs analyzed, what is the probability, to the nearest thousandth, that it is the letter that occurs most often?

____

4. Andre chose, without looking, one marble from a bag containing 4 red marbles and 10 green marbles. What is the probability that he chose a purple marble?

A. 0

B. $\frac{2}{7}$

C. $\frac{5}{7}$

D. 1

5. Ivan wants to use a TI calculator to simulate the birth order by gender of 3 children born to the same parents. Assuming that it is equally likely that the parents will have a boy or a girl, which of the following randInt commands could Ivan run to generate a trial for this simulation?

A. randInt(1,3,2)

B. randInt(0,1,2)

C. randInt(0,2,3)

D. randInt(0,1,3)

Numerical Response

2. Marnie is taking a shot from the foul line in a game of basketball. The probability that she will make the basket is 0.73. What is the probability that Marnie will not make the basket? ***P*(not making the basket)** = _____

CHALLENGER QUESTION

6. Gill wrote the numbers 1 through 25 on separate chips and then placed them into a bag. He reached into the bag and drew one chip at random. If A represents the event of drawing an even number and B represents the event of drawing a perfect square, what is the probability of A or B?

A. $\frac{15}{17}$ **B.** $\frac{17}{25}$

C. $\frac{3}{5}$ **D.** $\frac{14}{25}$

CHALLENGER QUESTION

7. Shawna has two bags containing coloured marbles. Bag A contains 2 white and 2 green marbles. Bag B contains 3 white, 5 red, and 4 green marbles. If Shawna draws one marble at random from each bag, the probability of her drawing 1 white marble and 1 green marble is

A. $\frac{1}{6}$ **B.** $\frac{1}{8}$

C. $\frac{5}{24}$ **D.** $\frac{7}{24}$

Numerical Response

3. The probabilities that Xavier will pass Grade 12 math and Grade 12 physics this semester are 0.82 and 0.78, respectively. If these events are independent, then what is the probability, to the nearest hundredth, that he will pass math but not physics? __________

8. Ashley draws three cards successively without replacement, from a standard deck of 52 cards. The probability, to the nearest millionth, that all three cards are aces is

A. 0.000 171 **B.** 0.000 177

C. 0.000 181 **D.** 0.000 455

9. A teacher advisor must choose from 16 student council members to form an executive committee consisting of a president, vice president, treasurer, and secretary. How many different arrangements of student council members can he choose from to form the committee?

A. $\frac{16!}{4!}$

B. $\frac{16!}{4!2!}$

C. $\frac{16!}{12!}$

D. $\frac{16!}{12!4!}$

10. The names of 15 students are put into a hat. Of these, 4 students will be chosen for a school trip to Montreal. The number of different possible groups of 4 students that could be formed is

A. 4!

B. 15!

C. 1 365

D. 32 760

CHALLENGER QUESTION

11. In a 10-team baseball league, each team plays every other team twice. The number of games that the league must schedule is

A. 45

B. 90

C. 100

D. 180

Numerical Response

4. In a race with 12 runners, what is the number of orders in which the runners could finish first, second, and third? __________

12. The students in band class have practiced 6 marching songs and 5 traditional songs. For their march, they will choose a program in which they play 4 of the marching songs and 3 of the traditional songs. What is the number of different programs they can choose from, if the order of the songs does **not** matter?

A. 25

B. 35

C. 150

D. 330

Numerical Response

5. How many different numbers can be formed using the digits 4, 5, 6, and 9 if no digit can be repeated and at least one digit must be used?

____

Use the following picture to answer the next question.

CHALLENGER QUESTION

13. A pawn is placed on a game board as shown in the figure. The number of possible paths that the pawn can take to get to position C on the board is

A. 32 **B.** 34
C. 35 **D.** 42

CHALLENGER QUESTION

Numerical Response

6. In a box of 6 calculators, 2 calculators have dead batteries. If Jeannette randomly chooses 2 calculators from the box, what is the probability, to the nearest tenth, that they both have good batteries?

____

14. Diego draws two marbles, without replacement, from a bag containing 5 red marbles and 8 black marbles. The probability that he will draw one red marble and one black marble is

A. $\frac{20}{39}$ **B.** $\frac{14}{55}$

C. $\frac{5}{78}$ **D.** $\frac{40}{169}$

Open Response

OR1. The table given shows the results of a simulation experiment in which 3 coins were tossed simultaneously.

Trial	Coin 1	Coin 2	Coin 3
1	1	0	1
2	0	1	0
3	0	1	1
4	1	0	0
5	0	1	0
6	0	1	1
7	1	1	1
8	0	1	0
9	0	0	0
10	0	0	0
11	1	1	1
12	0	0	1
13	1	1	1
14	0	0	1
15	0	0	1
16	0	1	1
17	0	1	1
18	1	1	1

a) Explain how a collection of randomly generated ones and zeros can simulate the given experiment.

b) If the given table was generated by using the command randInt(_,_,_), then what are the values, in the correct order, that should be in the parentheses? ____________

c) Suppose that 1 represents heads and 0 represents tails. Based on the results of this simulation, what is the experimental probability, to the nearest hundredth of getting exactly 2 heads and 1 tail in one toss of the three coins? Explain your answer.

d) Explain how this experiment could also be used to simulate the birth order by gender of 3 children born to the same parents.

e) Describe an advantage of using a spreadsheet to simulate this experiment instead of repeatedly tossing the coins.

OR2. The school newspaper wants to send 4 student journalists to cover the provincial track-and-field meet.

There are 7 male and 5 female journalists available. Determine how many different groups of 4 journalists can be formed consisting of

a) 2 male and 2 female students

b) at most 2 female students

c) at least 1 male student

ANSWERS AND SOLUTIONS—PRACTICE QUESTIONS

1. C	**NR2. 0.27**	**10. C**	**NR6. 0.4**
2 C	**6. C**	**11. B**	**14. A**
3. C	**7. D**	**NR4. 1 320**	**OR1. See solution**
NR1. 0.134	**NR3. 0.18**	**12. C**	**OR2. See solution**
4. A	**8. C**	**NR5. 64**	
5. D	**9. C**	**13. B**	

1. C

The total number of trials is determined by adding the frequencies of each outcome.

$1+9+8+2=20$

Two of the three coins landed on heads 8 times out of the 20 trials. Therefore,

$P(\text{two coins landing on heads})=\frac{8}{20}=\frac{2}{5}$

2. C

To determine the size of the sample space, create a list of the outcomes and count them.

	1	**2**	**3**
A	A1	A2	A3
B	B1	B2	B3
C	C1	C2	C3
D	D1	D2	D3
E	E1	E2	E3
F	F1	F2	F3

There are 18, or 6×3, possible outcomes in the sample space.

3. C

To find the total number of favourable outcomes the occurrence of letters other than vowels add the frequencies of the vowels and subtract this sum from the total number of letters used in the sample.

Number of occurrences of consonants
$=1\ 044-(78+140+60+74+30)=662$

$P(\text{not a vowel})=\frac{662}{1044}=\frac{331}{522}$

NR1. 0.134

The letter that occurs most often is the letter E, and it occurs 140 times out of 1 044. The probability of choosing it is

$\frac{140}{1044}\approx 0.134$

4. A

There are no purple marbles in the bag; therefore, the probability of choosing a purple marble is 0. Probability values range from 0, the impossible event, to 1, the certain event. In this case, the certain event would be that the marble chosen is red or green.

5. D

The command radInt(0, 1, 3) generates a list of three numbers that can represent the genders of the 3 children. These numbers are either 0 or 1. Ivan can associate the number 0 with the parents having a boy and 1 with the parents having a girl.

NR2. **0.27**

The only alternative to Marnie making the basket is that she does not make it, therefore, the complement to making the basket is not making it. Since the events are complementary, the sum of their probabilities must be 1. The probability of Marnie not making the basket is determined by subtracting the probability of her making the basket from 1.

$$P(\text{not making the basket}) = 1 - P(\text{making the basket}) = 1 - 0.73 = 0.27$$

The probability that Marnie will **not** make the basket is 0.27.

6. **C**

There are 25 numbers in the sample space: 1 to 25, inclusive.
A is the set of even numbers:
{2, 4, 6, 8, 10, 12, 14, 16, 18, 20, 22, 24}
B is the set of perfect squares:
{1, 4, 9, 16, 25}
A and B are non-mutually exclusive events because they have the two outcomes 4 and 16 in common.
Therefore,

$$P(A \text{ or } B) = P(A) + P(B) - P(A \text{ and } B) = \frac{12}{25} + \frac{5}{25} - \frac{2}{25} = \frac{15}{25} = \frac{3}{5}$$

7. **D**

Shawna draws one marble from each bag, so

$P(1\text{ white and }1\text{ green}) =$

$P(1\text{ white from A and }1\text{ green from B}) +$

$(1\text{ white from B and }1\text{ green from A})$

$P(1\text{ white from A and }1\text{ green from B}) =$

$$\frac{2}{4} \times \frac{4}{12} = \frac{1}{6}$$

$P(1\text{ white from B and }1\text{ green from A}) =$

$$\frac{3}{12} \times \frac{2}{4} = \frac{1}{8}$$

Therefore,

$$P(1\text{ white and }1\text{ green}) = \frac{1}{6} + \frac{1}{8} = \frac{4}{24} + \frac{3}{24} = \frac{7}{24}$$

NR3. **0.18**

Not passing physics is the complement of passing physics).

$$P(\text{pass math and not pass physics}) = P(\text{pass math}) \times P(\text{not pass physics}) = 0.82 \times (1 - 0.78) = 0.82 \times 0.22 \approx 0.18$$

8. **C**

Since the cards are not replaced in the deck after being drawn, the events are dependent.

$$P(\text{drawing 3 aces}) = P(A_1) \times P(A_2/A_1) \times P[A_3/(A_1 \text{ and } A_2)] = \frac{4}{52} \times \frac{3}{51} \times \frac{2}{50} = \frac{1}{13} \times \frac{1}{17} \times \frac{1}{25} = \frac{1}{5525} \approx 0.000181$$

9. **C**

Since the students are given specific positions on the committee, permutations must be used to account for the different possible orders. Of the 16 student council members, 4 must be arranged.

$$_{16}P_4 = \frac{16!}{(16-4)!} = \frac{16!}{12!}$$

10. **C**

The number of different possible group of 4 students that can be chosen from 15 students is

$$_{15}C_4 = \frac{15!}{(15-4)!4!} = \frac{15!}{11!4!} = 1365$$

11. **B**

Every different selection of two teams from the ten teams represents a different game that must be played. . Order is not considered because team A playing team B is the same as team B playing team A. Therefore, the number of games required so that each team will play every other team once is $_{10}C_2 = 45$.

Since each team will play every other team twice, the number of games the league must schedule is

$2 \times 45 = 90$

NR4. **1320**

Since any 3 of the 12 runners could finish in the first 3 positions and the order of the 3 positions matters, this problem involves the permutation of 12 objects taken 3 at a time. $_{12}P_3 = 1\,320$ possible orders

12. **C**

Since order does not matter, this is a combinations problem. The students must choose 4 marching songs from the 6 they practiced and 3 traditional songs from the 5 they practiced. The number of different programs they can choose from is

$$_6C_4 \times {}_5C_3 = 15 \times 10$$
$$= 150$$

NR5. **64**

Since the order of the digits is important, this is a permutations problem. First, the number of 1-digit numbers, 2-digit numbers, 3-digit numbers, and 4-digit numbers that can be formed must be calculated. The sum of these numbers is the answer.

$$_4P_1 + {}_4P_2 + {}_4P_3 + {}_4P_4$$
$$= 4 + 12 + 24 + 24$$
$$= 64$$

13. **B**

One way to solve the problem is to indicate in each square the cumulative number of possible routes that lead to it. The numbers that result are values found in Pascal's triangle. The triangle is cut off by the edges of the board.

NR6. **0.4**

Using combinations, the number of different selections of 2 calculators from 6 is $_6C_2$, and the number of different selections of 2 calculators with good batteries from 4 with good batteries is $_4C_2$.

Thus,

$$P(2 \text{ with good batteries}) = \frac{_4C_2}{_6C_2}$$
$$= \frac{6}{15} = \frac{2}{5} = 0.4$$

An alternative approach is to consider the successive draws and apply the formula for dependent events,
$P(\mathrm{G}_1 \text{ and } G_2) = P(\mathrm{G}_1) \times P(\mathrm{G}_2|\mathrm{G}_1)$.

$P(2 \text{ with good batteries})$

$= P(\text{first good}) \times P\begin{pmatrix}\text{second good} \\ \text{given first good}\end{pmatrix}$

$= \frac{4}{6} \times \frac{3}{5} = \frac{2}{5} = 0.4$

14. A

The number of different selections of 2 marbles from 13 is ${}_{13}C_2$, and the number of different selections of 1 red marble from 5 and 1 black marble from 8 is ${}_5C_1 \times {}_8C_1$.
Thus,

$P(1 \text{ red and } 1 \text{ black}) = \frac{{}_5C_1 \times {}_8C_1}{{}_{13}C_2}$

$= \frac{40}{78} = \frac{20}{39}$

An alternative approach is to consider the successive draws in both possible orders and then use the additive counting principle.

$P(1 \text{ red and } 1 \text{ black})$

$= P(\text{red first and black second}) +$

$P(\text{black first and red second})$

$= \frac{5}{13} \times \frac{8}{12} + \frac{8}{13} \times \frac{5}{12}$

$= \frac{10}{39} + \frac{10}{39}$

$= \frac{20}{39}$

OR1.

a) Since there are only two possible outcomes when a coin is tossed, 0 could represent heads and 1 could represent tails.

b) **013**

This command generates 3 random numbers that are either 0 (representing heads) or 1 (representing tails).

c) **0.28**

In the given table, the trials with favourable outcomes (two 1s and one 0) are trials 1, 3, 6, 16, and 17. There are 5 favourable outcomes and 18 total trials for this simulation. Therefore,
P(getting exactly 2 heads and 1 tail)

$= \frac{5}{18} \approx 0.28$

d) A possible approach is to assign 0 to represent the birth of a boy and 1 to represent the birth of a girl. The 3 numbers generated randomly by tossing the coins would then represent the birth order by gender of the 3 children born to the family.

Therefore a spreadsheet could be used to quickly generate more trials, thus yielding more accurate results.

e) Tossing coins repeatedly is very time consuming. However, you know that the more trials conducted, the more likely the experimental probability will approach the theoretical probability.

OR2.

These are combinations problems because the order in which the group members are chosen is not important.

a) The 2 male students are chosen from 7, and the 2 female students are chosen from 5. The total number of groups that can be formed is therefore

${}_7C_2 \times {}_5C_2 = 21 \times 10$

$= 210$

b) A group with at most 2 female students is a group that consists of either 2 females and 2 males, 1 female and 3 males, or no females and 4 males. The total number of groups that can be formed is therefore

$_5C_2 \times {}_7C_2 + {}_5C_1 \times {}_7C_3 + {}_5C_0 \times {}_7C_4$

$= 10 \times 21 + 5 \times 35 + 1 \times 35$

$= 210 + 175 + 35 = 420$

c) The number of different groups with at least one male student is equal to the total number of possible groups minus the number of groups with no male students.

$_{12}C_4 - {}_7C_0 \times {}_5C_4$

$= 495 - 1 \times 5$

$= 495 - 5$

$= 490$

COUNTING AND PROBABILITY—UNIT TEST

1. The probability that a newly planted tree in Toronto will **not** survive its first winter is 0.05. If the city of Toronto planted 1 500 new trees in summer, then how many are expected to survive the winter?

   A. 75

   B. 143

   C. 750

   D. 1425

Use the following information to answer the next question.

Lori's math teacher gave her class a list of data sets and asked the students to classify each set as either a discrete or continuous sample space.

I All possible outcomes for drawing a card out of a standard deck of cards.

II All possible outcomes that represent the maximum distance the twenty students in a physical education class can throw a javelin.

III All possible outcomes that represent the amount of time it takes for ten runners to complete a 100-m race.

2. Which of the given data sets are examples of continuous sample spaces?

   A. **I** only

   B. **II** only

   C. **I** and **III**

   D. **II** and **III**

Use the following information to answer the next two questions.

A group of 100 students were asked to each chose a number from 1 to 5. The results are shown in the given table.

Number chosen	1	2	3	4	5
Number of students who choose the number	18	24	23	23	12

3. If a student is selected at random from the group of 100 students, what is the probability that this student chose a number **greater** than 3?

   A. $\frac{29}{50}$

   B. $\frac{21}{50}$

   C. $\frac{7}{20}$

   D. $\frac{23}{100}$

Numerical Response

1. If a student is selected at random from the group of 100 students, what is the probability to the nearest hundredth, that this student chose an even number? _________ .

Use the following information to answer the next question

Bindu is taking a true-false test consisting of 10 questions. She wants to estimate the probability that she would score 50% or better on the test if she answered each question strictly by guessing. Bindu uses 10 coins and designs a simulation model to make her prediction. She decides to let heads (H) represent the correct answer and tails (T) the wrong answer. She recorded her results in the given table.

Trial	Coin 1	Coin 2	Coin 3	Coin 4	Coin 5	Coin 6	Coin 7	Coin 8	Coin 9	Coin 10
1	H	T	T	H	T	T	H	T	H	H
2	H	T	T	H	T	T	T	H	H	H
3	T	T	H	T	T	H	H	H	T	T
4	H	T	T	H	H	H	T	T	H	H
5	T	T	H	T	H	T	H	T	H	T

CHALLENGER QUESTION

4. Based on the results in the table, what is the experimental probability of Bindu scoring 50% or better on the test if she answers each question strictly by guessing?

   A. 0.30 **B.** 0.40

   C. 0.50 **D.** 0.60

Use the following information to answer the next question.

Vance is designing a simulation that will allow him to estimate the probability that all 5 children born into a family are boys. He assumes that it is equally likely that the parents will have a boy or a girl. Vance decides to associate the number 0 with the birth of a boy and 1 with the birth of a girl, and then use the randInt command on his TI calculator.

Numerical Response

2. To generate a trial for this simulation, Vance uses the command randInt(*i*, *ii*, *iii*).

i = ____________

ii = ____________

iii = ____________

Use the following information to answer the next question.

Jack has invited many friends over for his birthday party. They all play a game in which Jack is blindfolded, gets spun around, and then has to reach out, grab a friend and guess the name of the friend.

3. If the probability that Jack grabs a girl is 0.69, then what is the probability that he grabs a boy?

P(Jack grabs a boy) = ____________

Use the following information to answer the next question.

Janelle's teacher gave her a set of shapes.

5. If Janelle chooses one of the shapes at random, what is the probability that she will choose either a circle or a black shape?

   A. $\frac{1}{9}$ **B.** $\frac{4}{9}$

   C. $\frac{7}{9}$ **D.** $\frac{7}{4}$

CHALLENGER QUESTION

6. Margaret writes the letters of the word TORONTO on separate slips of paper, folds them and places them in a hat. She mixes them and pulls two slips randomly, one after the other, without replacement from the hat. What is the conditional probability that the second letter she chose is an O, given that the first letter she chose was an O?

A. $\frac{1}{3}$ **B.** $\frac{2}{3}$

C. $\frac{1}{7}$ **D.** $\frac{3}{7}$

7. Bradley, Maureen, and Tim are the first 3 students standing in line for ice cream. If there are 7 students in line, the number of different orders in which the remainder of the students can line up behind the first 3 is

A. 24 **B.** 144

C. 840 **D.** 5040

8. Zach draws 20 points on the circumference of a circle. Using these points as vertices, how many different triangles can Zach draw?

A. ${}_{20}P_3$ **B.** ${}_{20}C_3$

C. 20! **D.** 17!

9. In the first term of Jon's college program, he must take an English course. He must also take any four of the following courses: Mathematics, Chemistry, Physics, Biology, Psychology, and French. In how many different ways can Jon select the 5 courses for his first term?

A. ${}_6C_4$ **B.** ${}_7P_5$

C. ${}_6P_4$ **D.** ${}_7P_5$

Numerical Response

4. In a contest printed on the back of a cereal box, 5 desirable kitchen features are listed, and contestants must arrange them in order of importance. Only one arrangement of the 5 features is considered to be correct, so the contestant who submits this arrangement wins the contest. How many different contest entries must be submitted to ensure that one is a winning entry? ____________

10. A ship has 6 different coloured flags on board. To send signals, the ship's crew arranges some or all of the flags vertically on a flagpole. How many different signals can be made if at **least** 4 flags must be used at a time?

A. 15 **B.** 360

C. 516 **D.** 1800

Numerical Response

5. At Aisha's favourite restaurant, the luncheon special consists of 1 salad, 2 sandwiches and 2 fruits. If the restaurant has prepared 3 different salads, 10 different sandwiches and 6 different fruits, how many different lunches could Aisha order? ____________

Use the following information to answer the next question.

Mary and Lisa live in different areas of Smithton. The given figure shows the roads that connect their houses.

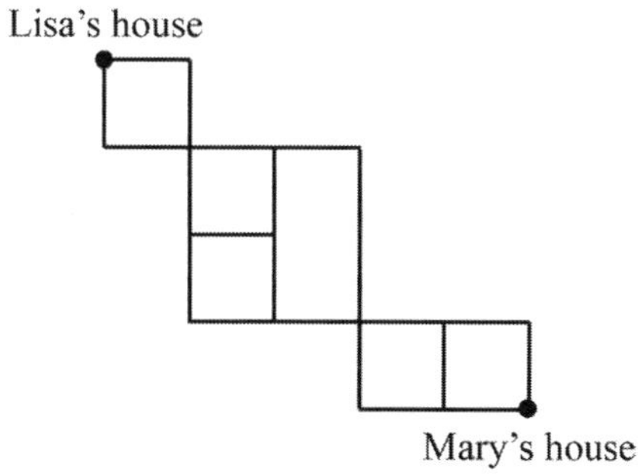

CHALLENGER QUESTION

11. Lisa decides to walk to Mary's house, travelling only west to east and north to south. How many different routes can she take to get to Mary's house?

A. 20 **B.** 24

C. 30 **D.** 34

12. Jack's mother randomly placed four blocks labelled J, A, C, and K on a shelf.
The probability that she placed them on the shelf so they spell JACK is

A. $\frac{1}{4}$ **B.** $\frac{1}{6}$

C. $\frac{1}{24}$ **D.** $\frac{1}{256}$

Numerical Response

6. How many different teams of 11 cricketers can be formed from a group of 16 cricketers?

____

CHALLENGER QUESTION

Numerical Response

7. Alice has 4 red balls, 2 green balls, 2 yellow balls, and 1 white ball. She is arranging them in a row. How many different arrangements can she make?

____

CHALLENGER QUESTION

Open Response

OR1. Brayden and Carter, two basketball players, each take a foul shot. Brayden has a $\frac{7}{10}$ chance of scoring a point, and Carter has a $\frac{3}{5}$ chance of scoring a point. Determine the following probabilities. Give the final probability as a fraction.

a) Both boys score a point

b) Neither boy scores a point

c) Only one of the boys scores a point

d) At least one of the boys scores a point

ANSWERS AND SOLUTIONS—UNIT TEST

1. D	**NR3. 0.31**	**NR4. 120**	**NR7. 3780**
2 D	**5. C**	**10. D**	**OR1. See solution**
3. C	**6. A**	**NR5. 2025**	
NR1. 0.47	**7. A**	**11. B**	
4. D	**8. B**	**12. C**	
NR2. 0, 1, 5	**9. A**	**NR6. 4368**	

1. **D**

To find the number of trees expected to survive, multiply the probability of a newly planted tree surviving the winter by the total number of trees planted. The probability that a tree will not survive is 0.05, so the probability that it will survive is 0.95.

Therefore, the number of trees expected to survive the winter is $0.95 \times 1\ 500 = 1425$

2. **D**

Data set I is a discrete sample space because each card in the deck represents an outcome. There are 52 possible outcomes.

Data set II is a continuous sample space because the outcomes must be measured. The twenty measured distances are the outcomes.

Data set III is also a continuous sample space because the outcomes are measured. The ten measured times are the outcomes.

3. **C**

The number of students who selected a number greater than 3 is $23 + 12 = 35$

$$P(\text{selected student chose a number} > 3) = \frac{35}{100}$$

$$= \frac{7}{20}$$

Recall that a number greater than 3 does not include 3.

NR1. **0.47**

The even number choices are 2 and 4. The total number of students who chose even numbers is $24 + 23 = 47$

$P(\text{selected student chose an even number})$

$$= \frac{47}{100} = 0.47$$

4. **D**

To score 50% or better on the test, Bindu would have to answer 5 or more questions correctly (a favourable outcome). There are 3 trials with favourable outcomes: trials 1, 2, and 4. Therefore,

$$P(\text{score} \geq 50\%) = \frac{3}{5} = 0.60$$

NR2. **0, 1, 5**

Vance uses the command radInt(0, 1, 5). The numbers would be entered as radInt(0, 1, 5). This associates 0 for the birth of a boy and 1 with the birth of a girl. The radInt command will generate 5 random integer values consisting of 0 and 1, inclusive. The outcome of 5 boys would be represented by 0 0 0 0 0.

NR3. **0.31**

Since Jack can grab only boys or girls, these events are complementary; therefore, the sum of the probabilities of these events is 1. To determine the probability that Jack grabs a boy, you subtract the probability of grabbing a girl from 1.

$P(\text{Jack grabs a boy}) = 1 - 0.69 = 0.31$

5. **C**

The events of a shape being black and a shape being a circle are non-mutually exclusive, so

$P(\text{circle or black}) = P(\text{circle}) + P(\text{black})$
$-P(\text{circle and black})$

$P(\text{circle or black}) = \frac{4}{9} + \frac{4}{9} - \frac{1}{9} = \frac{7}{9}$

6. **A**

$P(O_2|O_1)$

$= \frac{\text{Number of Os remaining after the first choice}}{\text{Total number of letters remaining after the first choice}}$

$= \frac{2}{6} = \frac{1}{3}$

7. **A**

This is a permutations problem because you are looking for the number of orders for the remaining 4 students in the line. The number of orders in which the 4 students can line up is $4! = 24$

8. **B**

Since the order in which the points are chosen for the vertices of the triangle is not important, this is a combinations problem.

Out of 20 points, the number of different choices of 3 points for vertices ${}^{15}_{20}C_3$.

9. **A**

Since Jan must take an English course, he must choose his remaining 4 courses from the 6 other courses listed. This is a combinations problem because the order of the selections is **not** important. The number of ways to select the 4 other courses is ${}_6C_4$.

NR4. **120**

Since order is important, this is a permutations problem. The number of permutations of 5 objects taken 5 at a time is

${}_5P_5 = 120$.

10. **D**

Since a different order of the flags on the pole would be a different signal, this is a permutations problem. Signals consist of 4, 5, or 6 flags; therefore, the number of different signals that can be made is

${}_6P_4 + {}_6P_5 + {}_6P_6$
$= 360 + 720 + 720$
$= 1800$

NR5. **2025**

The order in which Aisha chooses does **not** matter, so this is a combinations problem. To create her lunch, she must choose 1 salad from 3 salads, 2 sandwiches from 10 sandwiches, and 2 fruits from the 6 fruits. The number of different luncheon specials is therefore

${}_3C_1 \times {}_{10}C_2 \times {}_6C_2$
$= 3 \times 45 \times 15$
$= 2025$

11. **B**

In the given figure, each corner is numbered to show the number of routes Lisa can take to arrive at that particular corner.

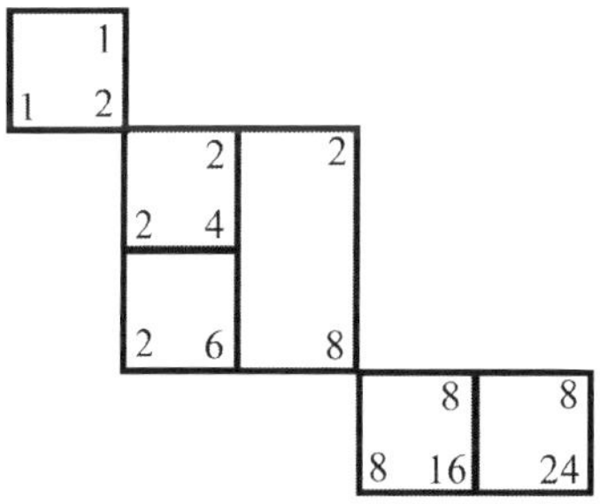

Lisa can take 24 different routes to get to Mary's house.

12. **C**

The total number of different arrangements of the 4 blocks on the shelf is $4! = 24$. Since only one of these arrangements spells JACK, the probability of this placement occurring is

$\frac{1}{4!} = \frac{1}{24}$

NR6. 4368

The number of possible groups of 11 cricketers that can be formed from a group of 16 cricketers is ${}_{16}C_{11}$.

$${}_{16}C_{11} = \frac{16!}{11!5!}$$
$$= 4368$$

The number of different teams of 11 that can be formed is 4368.

NR7. 3780

Number of arrangements: $\frac{9!}{4!2!2!1!}$

$$= 3780$$

Alice could make 3780 different arrangements of the balls in a row.

Open Response

OR1.

Let B be the event of Brayden scoring a point and C the event of Carter scoring a point.

a) $P(\text{B and C}) = P(\text{B}) \times P(\text{C})$

$$= \frac{7}{10} \times \frac{3}{5}$$
$$= \frac{21}{50}$$

b) $P(\overline{\text{B}} \text{ and } \overline{\text{C}}) = P(\overline{\text{B}}) \times P(\overline{\text{C}})$

$$= \frac{3}{10} \times \frac{2}{5}$$
$$= \frac{6}{50} = \frac{3}{25}$$

c) $P(\text{B and } \overline{\text{C}}) + P(\overline{\text{B}} \text{ and C})$

$$= P(\text{B}) \times P(\overline{\text{C}}) + P(\overline{\text{B}}) \times P(\text{C})$$
$$= \frac{7}{10} \times \frac{2}{5} + \frac{3}{10} \times \frac{3}{5}$$
$$= \frac{14}{50} + \frac{9}{50}$$
$$= \frac{23}{50}$$

d) $P(\text{at least one boy scores a point})$

$= P(\text{only one boy scores a point or both boys score a point})$

$= P(\text{only one boy scores a point}) + P(\text{both boys score a point})$

$$= \frac{23}{50} \text{ [see part c)]} + \frac{21}{50} \text{ [see part a)]}$$
$$= \frac{44}{50} = \frac{22}{25}$$

Or, using the concept of complementary events:

$P(\text{at least one boy scores a point})$

$= 1 - P(\text{neither boy scores a point})$

$$= 1 - \frac{3}{25} \text{[see part b)]}$$
$$= \frac{25}{25} - \frac{3}{25}$$
$$= \frac{22}{25}$$

Probability Distributions

PROBABILITY DISTRIBUTIONS

Table of Correlations			
	Specific Expectation	**Practice Questions**	**Unit Test Questions**
	By the end of the course, students will:		
PD1.1	recognize and identify a discrete random variable X (i.e., a variable that assumes a unique value for each outcome of a discrete sample space, such as the value x for the outcome of getting x heads in 10 tosses of a coin), generate a probability distribution [i.e., a function that maps each value x of a random variable X to a corresponding probability, $P(X = x)$] by calculating the probabilities associated with all values of a random variable, with and without technology, and represent a probability distribution numerically using a table	1, OR1	1
PD1.2	calculate the expected value for a given probability distribution [i.e., using $E(X) = \Sigma\, xP(X = x)$], interpret the expected value in applications, and make connections between the expected value and the weighted mean of the values of the discrete random variable	2, NR1	2, NR1
PD1.3	represent a probability distribution graphically using a probability histogram (i.e., a histogram on which each rectangle has a base of width 1, centred on the value of the discrete random variable, and a height equal to the probability associated with the value of the random variable), and make connections between the frequency histogram and the probability histogram	3, OR2	3, NR2
PD1.4	recognize conditions that give rise to a random variable that follows a binomial probability distribution, calculate the probability associated with each value of the random variable, represent the distribution numerically using a table and graphically using a probability histogram, and make connections to the algebraic representation $P(X = x) = \binom{n}{x} p^x (1-p)^{n-x}$	4, NR2	4, OR1
PD1.5	recognize conditions that give rise to a random variable that follows a hypergeometric probability distribution, calculate the probability associated with each value of the random variable, and represent the distribution numerically using a table and graphically using a probability histogram	5, NR3	5, NR3
PD1.6	compare, with technology and using numeric and graphical representations, the probability distributions of discrete random variables	6, NR4	6, NR4
PD1.7	solve problems involving probability distributions, including problems arising from real-world applications	7, OR3	7, NR5
PD2.1	recognize and identify a continuous random variable (i.e., a variable that assumes values from the infinite number of possible outcomes in a continuous sample space), and distinguish between situations that give rise to discrete frequency distributions and situations that give rise to continuous frequency distributions	8, NR5	8, NR6

PD2.2	recognize standard deviation as a measure of the spread of a distribution, and determine, with and without technology, the mean and standard deviation of a sample of values of a continuous random variable	9, 10	9, 10
PD2.3	describe challenges associated with determining a continuous frequency distribution, and recognize the need for mathematical models to represent continuous frequency distributions	11	11
PD2.4	represent, using intervals, a sample of values of a continuous random variable numerically using a frequency table and graphically using a frequency histogram and a frequency polygon, recognize that the frequency polygon approximates the frequency distribution, and determine, through investigation using technology, and compare the effectiveness of the frequency polygon as an approximation of the frequency distribution for different sizes of the intervals	12	12
PD2.5	recognize that theoretical probability for a continuous random variable is determined over a range of values, that the probability that a continuous random variable takes any single value is zero, and that the probabilities of ranges of values form the probability distribution associated with the random variable	13	13
PD2.6	recognize that the normal distribution is commonly used to model the frequency and probability distributions of continuous random variables, describe some properties of the normal distribution, and recognize and describe situations that can be modelled using the normal distribution	14, NR6	14, NR7
PD2.7	make connections, through investigation using dynamic statistical software, between the normal distribution and the binomial and hypergeometric distributions for increasing numbers of trials of the discrete distributions	15, 16, OR4	15, 16
PD2.8	recognize a z-score as the positive or negative number of standard deviations from the mean to a value of the continuous random variable, and solve probability problems involving normal distributions using a variety of tools and strategies, including problems arising from real-world applications	17, 18, NR7	17, OR2

PROBABILITY DISTRIBUTIONS

PD1.1 *recognize and identify a discrete random variable X [i.e., a variable that assumes a unique value for each outcome of a discrete sample space, such as the value x for the outcome of getting x heads in 10 tosses of a coin], generate a probability distribution [i.e., a function that maps each value x of a random variable X to a corresponding probability, P(X = x)], by calculating the probabilities associated with all values of a random variable, with and without technology, and represent a probability distribution numerically using a table*

PROBABILITY DISTRIBUTION

A discrete random variable, X, is a variable that assumes a countable number of distinct values that represent the unique outcome of a discrete random sample space.

A probability distribution presented in a table of values or by using a mathematical expression provides the probabilities of a discrete random variable for any of its possible values. For example, consider the theoretical probabilities for the sums resulting from the roll of two regular 6-sided number cubes. The sample space and distribution were shown in a previous outcome (1.1 of Counting and Probability). The sum of the two dice is a discrete random variable, X. The sum is the result of a random event and can be any whole number from 2 to 12. Thus, the probability of any sum can be denoted by $P(X = x)$, in which $2 \leq x \leq 12$. A sum of 4, for example, occurs 3 times in the sample space of 36 outcomes; therefore, $P(X = 4) = \frac{3}{36} = \frac{1}{12}$.

Example

Five balls numbered 1, 1, 2, 2, and 3 are placed in a box. Two balls are randomly and successively drawn from the box, with the first ball replaced after it is drawn, and the sum of their numbers recorded. Represent the probability distribution of the possible sums in a table.

Solution

The following chart illustrates the sample space showing all possible sums of the two balls drawn from the box.

		First Ball				
Second Ball		1	1	2	2	3
	1	2	2	3	3	4
	1	2	2	3	3	4
	2	3	3	4	4	5
	2	3	3	4	4	5
	3	4	4	5	5	6

Notice that there are 25 possible outcomes; however, some of these outcomes are the same sum.

Thus a table of probabilities for the distinct sums of the numbers on the two balls (the discrete random variable *X*) can be created from the sample space by listing the frequencies of each possible sum. This table is one method of representing the probability distribution of this discrete random variable.

Sum x	Frequency	Theoretical Probability $P(X = x)$
2	4	$\frac{4}{25}$
3	8	$\frac{8}{25}$
4	8	$\frac{8}{25}$
5	4	$\frac{4}{25}$
6	1	$\frac{1}{25}$
Total Probability		$\frac{25}{25}=1$

Related Questions: 1, OR1

PD1.2 *calculate the expected value for a given probability distribution [i.e., using $E(X)=\sum xP(X-x)$], interpret the expected value in applications, and make connections between the expected value and the weighted mean of the values of the discrete random variable*

Expected Value for a Probability Distribution

The expected value of a discrete random variable, *E(X)*, is the weighted mean of all possible outcomes of a probability experiment. The expectation is equal to the sum of the products of each outcome and its respective probability.

$$\begin{aligned} E(X) &= x_1P(x_1)+x_2P(x_2)+x_3P(x_3)+\ldots+x_nP(x_n) \\ &= \sum_{i=1}^{n} x_iP(x_i) \end{aligned}$$

Example

a) What is the expected number of points (expected value) for the game?

b) Is this game fair? Explain.

Solution

In this case, the discrete random variable is the **number of points** assigned to the roll. The points can be displayed in a table of values as follows.

Number	Point, x	$P(x)$	
1	3	$\frac{1}{6}$	Observe that the sum of the probabilities is again 1 and that in this case, the probabilities are all equal. This is called a **uniform distribution.**
2	–4	$\frac{1}{6}$	
3	9	$\frac{1}{6}$	
4	–8	$\frac{1}{6}$	
5	15	$\frac{1}{6}$	
6	–12	$\frac{1}{6}$	

a) The expected value rolled on the number cube is

$$\begin{aligned} E(X) &= 3\left(\frac{1}{6}\right)-4\left(\frac{1}{6}\right)+9\left(\frac{1}{6}\right)-8\left(\frac{1}{6}\right)+ \\ &\quad 15\left(\frac{1}{6}\right)-12\left(\frac{1}{6}\right) \\ &= \frac{3}{6}-\frac{4}{6}+\frac{9}{6}-\frac{8}{6}+\frac{15}{6}-\frac{12}{6} \\ &= \frac{3}{6} \\ &= \frac{1}{2} \end{aligned}$$

b) The game is not fair. For a game to be fair, the expected value must be 0, indicating that a **positive** or **negative** score on any given roll is equally likely. This game has a bias toward a positive number of points.

Related Questions: 2, NR1

PD1.3 represent a probability distribution graphically using a probability histogram [i.e., a histogram on which each rectangle has a base of width l, centred on the value of the discrete random variable, and a height equal to the probability associated with the value of the random variable], and make connections between the frequency histogram and the probability histogram (e.g., by comparing their shapes)

REPRESENTING A PROBABILITY DISTRIBUTION

A probability histogram is a graphical representation of a probability distribution. The heights of the rectangles represent the probability of each outcome. A frequency histogram is a graphical representation of the frequency at which each outcome occurs. The heights of the rectangles represent the frequency of each outcome.

Example

Sum (outcome)	Frequency of the sum	Probability
2	1	$\frac{1}{36} \approx 0.028$
3	2	$\frac{2}{36} \approx 0.056$
4	3	$\frac{3}{36} \approx 0.083$
5	4	$\frac{4}{36} \approx 0.111$
6	5	$\frac{5}{36} \approx 0.139$
7	6	$\frac{6}{36} \approx 0.167$
8	5	$\frac{5}{36} \approx 0.139$
9	4	$\frac{4}{36} \approx 0.111$
10	3	$\frac{3}{36} \approx 0.083$
11	2	$\frac{2}{36} \approx 0.056$
12	1	$\frac{1}{36} \approx 0.028$

a) Draw a frequency histogram to represent the information in the probability distribution.

b) Draw a probability histogram to represent the information in the probability distribution.

c) How do the two graphs compare?

Solution

a)

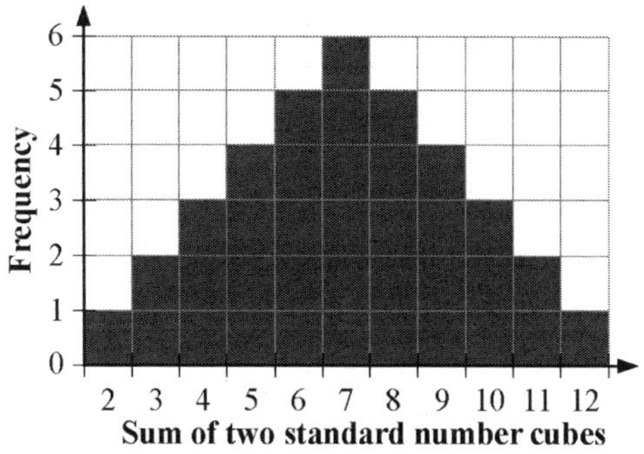

b)

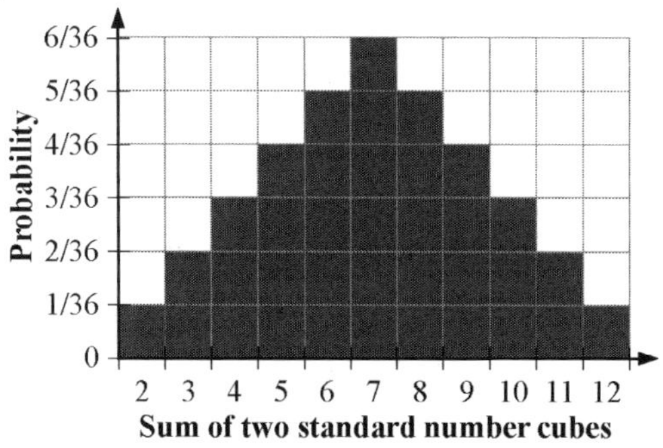

c) The two graphs are exactly the same shape with 100% of the data represented in both.

Related Questions: 3, OR2

PD1.4 *recognize conditions (e.g., independent trials) that give rise to a random variable that follows a binomial probability distribution, calculate the probability associated with each value of the random variable, represent the distribution numerically and graphically using a probability histogram, and make connections to the algebraic representation* $P(X=x)=\binom{n}{x}p^x(1-p)^{n-x}$

Binomial Probability Distribution

A binomial distribution has the following properties:

- The number of trials, n, is fixed.
- There are exactly 2 outcomes: success or failure.
- All trials are independent; that is, the outcome of one trial does not influence the result of another.
- The probability of success, p, is the same in every trial.
- The probability of failure in every trial is 1 – the probability of success.
- The distribution of the number of successes in the trials is a binomial distribution.
- The distribution of the probability of these successes is a binomial probability distribution.
- The probability of k successes in n trials is given by the formula $P(k) = {}_nC_k p^k(1-p)^{n-k}$, where p is the probability of success and $(1-p)$ is the probability of failure.

Example

CHALLENGER QUESTION

a) Write the binomial probability distribution function for the number of girls in a family of 5 children in the form $P(k) = {}_nC_k p^k(1-p)^{n-k}$.

b) Complete the table to show the probability distribution.

Number of Girls, *k*	**Probability, *P*(*k*)**
Total	

c) Draw the probability histogram to represent the results from part **b)**.

Solution

a) Since the probability of a child being born a girl is $\frac{1}{2}$, the formula that can be used to calculate the probability of k girls is

$$P(k) = {}_5C_k\left(\frac{1}{2}\right)^k\left(1-\frac{1}{2}\right)^{5-k}$$

$$= {}_5C_k\frac{1}{2}^k\left(\frac{1}{2}\right)^{5-k}$$

$$= C_k\frac{1}{2}^{k+5-k}$$

$$= {}_5C_k\left(\frac{1}{2}\right)^5$$

b)

Number of Girls, *k*	Probability, *P*(*k*)
0	$P(0) = {}_5C_0\left(\frac{1}{2}\right)^5 = \frac{1}{32}$
1	$P(1) = {}_5C_1\left(\frac{1}{2}\right)^5 = \frac{5}{32}$
2	$P(2) = {}_5C_2\left(\frac{1}{2}\right)^5 = \frac{10}{32} = \frac{5}{16}$
3	$P(3) = {}_5C_3\left(\frac{1}{2}\right)^5 = \frac{10}{32} = \frac{5}{16}$
4	$P(4) = {}_5C_4\left(\frac{1}{2}\right)^5 = \frac{5}{32}$
5	$P(5) = {}_5C_5\left(\frac{1}{2}\right)^5 = \frac{1}{32}$
Total	$\frac{32}{32} = 1$

c)

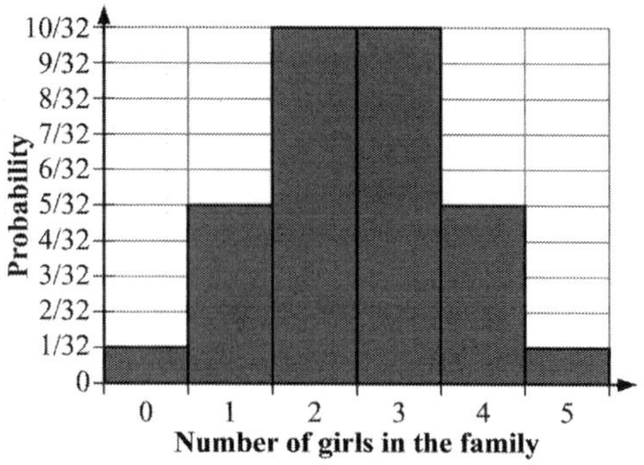

Related Questions: 4, NR2

PD1.5 *recognize conditions (e.g., dependent trials) that give rise to a random variable that follows a hypergeometric probability distribution, calculate the probability associated with each value of the random variable (e.g., by using a tree diagram; by using combinations), and represent the distribution numerically using a table and graphically using a probability histogram*

HYPERGEOMETRIC PROBABILITY DISTRIBUTION

A hypergeometric distribution has the following properties:

- There are exactly 2 outcomes: success or failure.
- All trials are dependent; that is, the outcome of one trial influences the result of another.
- The probability of success changes from one trial to the next.
- The distribution of the number of successes in the trials is a hypergeometric distribution.
- The distribution of the probability of these successes is a hypergeometric probability distribution.

The probability of x successes in r dependent trials is given by the formula

$P(x \text{ successes}) = \frac{{}_aC_x \times {}_{n-a}C_{r-x}}{{}_nC_r}$ where a is the number of successful outcomes among a total of n possible outcomes.

Example

a) Complete the table to determine the probability distribution for the number of women on a six-member committee. Round the probabilities to the nearest hundred-thousandth.

Number of Women, x	Probability, $P(x)$
0	
1	
2	
3	
4	
5	
6	
Total	

b) Draw the probability histogram to show the results in **a)**. Use decimals on the vertical axis.

Solution

a) The selection process involves dependent trials since each person who is already chosen for the committee cannot be selected again. The total number of ways the 6 members can be selected from the pool of 18 is $_{18}C_6 = 18\ 564$. There can be from 0 to 6 women on the committee. The number of ways in which x women can be selected is $_{10}C_x$. The men can fill the remaining $6-x$ positions on the committee in $_8C_{6-x}$ ways.

Thus, the number of committees with x women is $_{10}C_x \times {_8C_{6-x}}$, and the probability of a committee with x women is $P(x) = \dfrac{_{10}C_x \times {_8C_{6-x}}}{_{18}C_6}$.

Number of Women, x	Probability, $P(x)$
0	$P(0) = \dfrac{_{10}C_0 \times {_8C_6}}{_{18}C_6} \approx 0.0015\ 1$
1	$P(1) = \dfrac{_{10}C_1 \times {_8C_5}}{_{18}C_6} \approx 0.0301\ 7$
2	$P(2) = \dfrac{_{10}C_2 \times {_8C_4}}{_{18}C_6} \approx 0.1696\ 8$
3	$P(3) = \dfrac{_{10}C_3 \times {_8C_3}}{_{18}C_6} \approx 0.3619\ 9$
4	$P(4) = \dfrac{_{10}C_4 \times {_8C_2}}{_{18}C_6} \approx 0.3167\ 4$
5	$P(5) = \dfrac{_{10}C_5 \times {_8C_1}}{_{18}C_6} \approx 0.1086\ 0$
6	$P(6) = \dfrac{_{10}C_6 \times {_8C_0}}{_{18}C_6} \approx 0.0113\ 1$
Total	1

b)

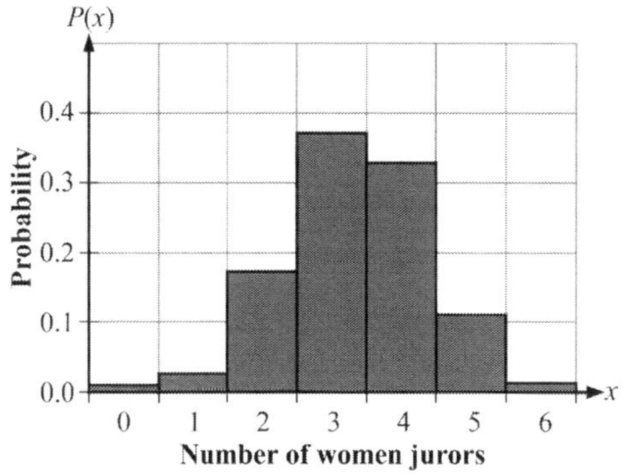

Related Questions: 5, NR3

PD1.6 compare, with technology and using numeric and graphical representations, the probability distributions of discrete random variables (e.g., compare binomial distributions with the same probability of success for increasing numbers of trials; compare the shapes of a hypergeometric distribution and a binomial distribution)

Probability Distribution of Discrete Random Variables

The main difference between binomial and hypergeometric probability distributions is that the binomial probability distributions involve replacement, whereas the hypergeometric distributions do not involve replacement. The trials are independent in the binomial probability distributions, whereas the trials in the hypergeometric probability distributions are dependent.

If the number of trials is very large, the graph of the binomial distribution will be very close to the graph of the hypergeometric distribution because non-replacement will not change the ratio of successes to the population a significantly.

Example

a) Complete the following table to construct probability distributions with replacement of the card and without replacement of the card.

With Replacement		**Without Replacement**	
Number of Face Cards (x)	$P(x) = {}_nC_x p^x (1-p)^{n-x}$	Number of Face Cards (x)	$P(x) = \frac{{}_aC_x \times {}_{n-a}C_{r-x}}{{}_nC_r}$
0		0	
1		1	
2		2	
3		3	

b) Draw the probability distributions histograms for the tables in part **a)**.

c) Compare the shapes of the two distributions.

Solution

a)

With Replacement	
Number of Face Cards (x)	$P(x) = {}_nC_x p^x (1-p)^{n-x}$
0	$P(0) = {}_3C_0 \left(\frac{12}{52}\right)^0 \left(\frac{40}{52}\right)^3$ ≈ 0.45517
1	$P(1) = {}_3C_1 \left(\frac{12}{52}\right)^1 \left(\frac{40}{52}\right)^2$ ≈ 0.40965
2	$P(2) = {}_3C_2 \left(\frac{12}{52}\right)^2 \left(\frac{40}{52}\right)^1$ ≈ 0.12289
3	$P(3) = {}_3C_3 \left(\frac{12}{52}\right)^3 \left(\frac{40}{52}\right)^0$ ≈ 0.01229

Without Replacement	
Number of Face Cards (x)	$P(x) = \frac{{}_aC_x \times {}_{n-a}C_{r-x}}{{}_nC_r}$
0	$P(0) = \frac{{}_{12}C_0 \times {}_{40}C_3}{{}_{52}C_3}$ ≈ 0.44706
1	$P(1) = \frac{{}_{12}C_1 \times {}_{40}C_2}{{}_{52}C_3}$ ≈ 0.42353
2	$P(2) = \frac{{}_{12}C_2 \times {}_{40}C_1}{{}_{52}C_3}$ ≈ 0.11964
3	$P(3) = \frac{{}_{12}C_3 \times {}_{40}C_0}{{}_{52}C_3}$ ≈ 0.00995

Note that these distributions can be done quickly by using a graphing calculator.

Enter the possible values for x in L_1, then enter the formula for $P(x)$, using actual numbers for x, in L_2. The resulting histograms can also be drawn on the graphing calculator.

These calculations can also be done using a spreadsheet.

b)

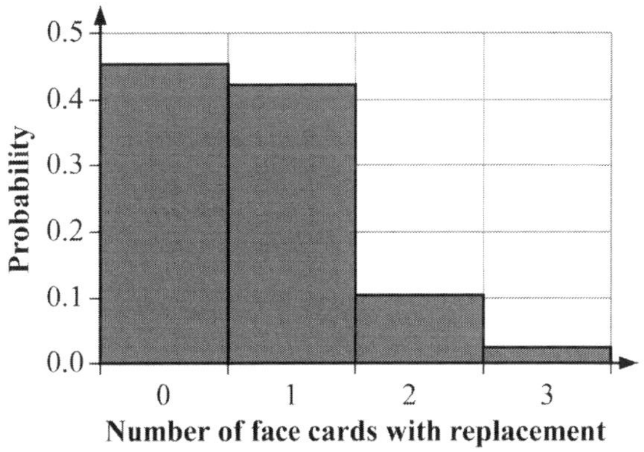

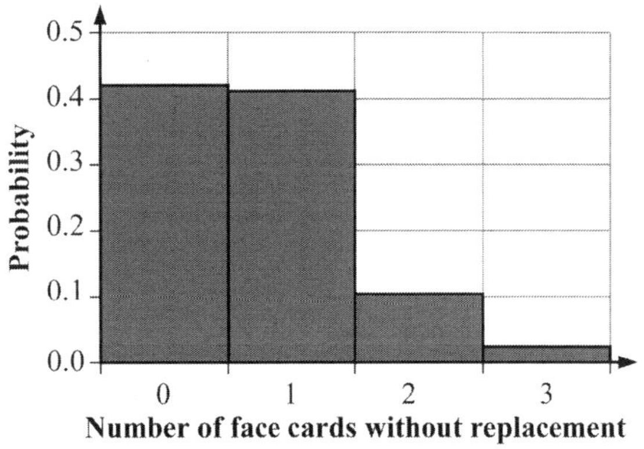

c) The probability distribution with replacement is a binomial probability distribution because the probability of getting a face card stays the same for each trial. The probability distribution without replacement is a hypergeometric probability distribution because the probability of getting a face card changes for each trial. The graph of the hypergeometric distribution will approach the shape of the graph of the binomial distribution as the number of trials increases.

In this case, the graphs are certainly quite similar in shape, but if the number of trials, n, were very large, the graph of the binomial distribution would be even more similar in shape to the graph of the hypergeometric distribution. This is because non-replacement of successes will not significantly change the ratio of successes to failure in a large sample.

Example

Consider two different scenarios:

Scenario 1: A bag contains four red marbles and five green marbles.

Scenario 2: A bag contains 400 red marbles and 500 green marbles.

Solution

In Scenario 1, non-replacement has a great effect on the probability of drawing two red marbles because the bag only contains nine marbles to begin with, and is diminished to eight after the first marble is drawn.

However, in Scenario 2, non-replacement has little effect on the probability of drawing two red marbles because the bag contains 900 marbles to begin with, and still 899 after the first marble is drawn.

Related Questions: 6, NR4

PD1.7 *solve problems involving probability distributions (e.g., uniform, binomial, hypergeometric), including problems arising from real-world applications.*

SOLVE PROBLEMS INVOLVING PROBABILITY DISTRIBUTION

The following are the types of probability distributions:

A uniform distribution is one in which each outcome has an equal probability. In the probability histogram, the height of each rectangle is the same.

A binomial distribution is one in which there is a certain number of independent trials and two possible outcomes for each trial, with the probabilities of these outcomes being constant in each trial. The number of successes creates the distribution.

A hypergeometric distribution is one in which there is a certain number of dependent trials, each having two possible outcomes. The probability of success changes for each trial. The number of successes creates the distribution.

Example

1. When rolling a fair six-sided number cube, each of the outcomes of the six faces has an equal chance of facing upward.
2. Counting the number of 3s that show up in rolling a fair six-sided number cube 10 times.
3. Counting the number of hearts dealt in a hand of 5 cards from a standard deck of 52 cards.

Solution

1. This is a uniform distribution because each outcome has $\frac{1}{6}$ chance of happening.
2. This is a binomial distribution. The trials are independent and there are only 2 outcomes: getting a 3 or not getting a 3.

3. This is a hypergeometric distribution because the trials are dependent. The cards are dealt without replacement.

Related Questions: 7, OR3

PD2.1 recognize and identify a continuous random variable [i.e., a variable that assumes values from the infinite number of possible outcomes in a continuous sample space] and distinguish between situations that give rise to discrete frequency distributions and situations that give rise to continuous frequency distributions (e.g., counting the number of outcomes for drawing a card or tossing three coins) and situations that give rise to continuous frequency distributions ((e.g., measuring the time taken to complete a task or the maximum distance a ball can be thrown)

Continuous Random Variable

A continuous random variable assumes values from the infinite number of possible outcomes in a continuous sample space. Examples of continuous sample spaces are

- Measuring the time it takes to complete a task
- Measuring the maximum distance a ball can be thrown

Continuous distributions have graphs that are smooth curves, with no breaks or interruptions, because the random variable can take on any of the real number values in the sample space.

Related Questions: 8, NR5

PD2.2 recognize standard deviation as a measure of the spread of a distribution, and determine, with and without technology, the mean and standard deviation of a sample of values of a continuous random variable.

Random Deviation

A population is any collection of items, events, or people to be studied. A sample is a portion of the population from which inferences can be made regarding the entire population.

The mean (average), a measure of the central tendency of the data, and the standard deviation, a measure of dispersion (spread of data), are often used in analysing samples.

Mean Of A Sample Of Values

The mean of a set of data values is found by dividing the sum of all data values by the number of data values. Two symbols are used to represent the mean. The symbol $\overline{x}$ represents the mean of a sample, and μ represents the mean of an entire population. The formula used to determine the mean for both a sample or an entire population is

$$\mu \text{ or } \overline{x} = \frac{\sum_{i=1}^{n} x_i}{n}.$$

$$\text{or } \frac{\Sigma x}{n}$$

Σ (sigma) indicates that all the individual values of x_i, from $i = 1$ to n, are added together. The sum is then divided by the number of values in the set, n.

Standard Deviation

The standard deviation is essentially the average distance that all the data values are away from the mean. The symbol σ represents the standard deviation of a population. The formula is given as $\sigma = \sqrt{\frac{\Sigma(x_i - x\mu)^2}{n}}$. However, your calculator can be used to determine this value.

Example

Eagles		Hawks	
Player	Height (cm)	Player	Height (cm)
Linda	183	Sara	167
James	162	Millie	163
Marda	143	Charles	168
Jackson	179	Tessa	161
Brayden	173	Carter	165
Andrew	150	Austin	166

Solution

Since you are considering the teams as two separate populations, calculate the mean and standard deviation for each population, using technology or manually using the formulas. If using a TI-83 calculator press STAT ENTER then input the heights of the Eagle players into L1 and the heights of the Hawks players into L2. Then, press STAT, scroll right to CALC, and press ENTER so the display shows 1-Var Stats. Then press 2nd 1 to calculate using the data from L1 (Eagles). Press ENTER. The value of $\overline{x}$ represents the mean and the σx value represents the standard deviation.

The mean height of the Eagles team is 165 cm and the standard deviation is 14.7 cm. Repeat the steps above but enter 2nd 2 for the last step to calculate using the data from L2 (Hawks). Press ENTER. The Hawks team also has a mean height of 165 cm but their standard deviation is only 2.4 cm.

The Eagles have a much wider spread in height than the Hawks as indicated by the larger standard deviation. Since the two teams have the same mean height, the difference in the standard deviations indicates that some Eagle players are much taller and much shorter than any of the Hawks. The heights of the players on the Hawks team are clustered close to the mean height of 165 cm, since the standard deviation is small.

Related Questions: 9, 10

PD2.3 *describe challenges associated with determining a continuous frequency distribution (e.g., the inability to capture all values of the variable, resulting in a need to sample; uncertainties in measured values of the variable), and recognize the need for mathematical models to represent continuous frequency distributions*

CONTINUOUS FREQUENCY DISTRIBUTIONS

In continuous frequency distributions, the random variable has an infinite number of values. Therefore, it is impossible to list all values of the variable. Consequently, the best chance we have of determining continuous frequency distribution is to analyse a sample of the population. From a representative sample, predictions about the population can be made. It is important that the sampling process is representative of the population and that the sample is sufficiently large to decrease the likelihood that the sample data differ significantly from the corresponding population data.

For example, to determine the expected lifetime of a particular brand of light bulb, the experiment must run until the light bulb fails to produce light. Performing the experiment on the entire supply of the light bulbs would serve no purpose because there would be no light bulbs to sell to customers. In this situation, a random sample must be used to make predictions about the corresponding population. However, too small a sample (such as 3 light bulbs) would likely have a mean lifetime and a standard deviation that is significantly different from the population of all light bulbs produced. To address this potential problem of inaccurate findings, manufacturers test a small, yet representative percentage of every batch produced.

Another challenge in measured values of the variable is the uncertainty involved with measurement. Depending on the tool used for measuring, the measurement may or may not be sufficiently accurate or consistent.

There is a need for mathematical models to represent continuous frequency distributions.

A **mathematical model** is a model that describes the behaviour of the population in a quantitative fashion.

Related Question: 11

PD2.4 *represent, using intervals, a sample of values of a continuous random variable numerically, using a frequency table and graphically using a frequency histogram and a frequency polygon, recognize that the frequency polygon approximates the frequency distribution, and determine, through investigation using technology (e.g., dynamic statistical software, graphing calculator), and compare the effectiveness of the frequency polygon as an approximation of the frequency distribution for different sizes of the intervals*

SAMPLE OF VALUES OF A CONTINUOUS FREQUENCY TABLE

For a sample of values of a continuous random variable, the data are often grouped into intervals, which make it easier to construct and interpret both tables and graphs. The intervals, of which there must be at least 5, must be of equal width and cover the entire range from the **smallest** to the **largest** value of the variable. Different interval widths will produce different results.

Frequency tables or frequency distributions, frequency histograms, and frequency polygons can then be constructed to give a convenient overview of the distribution of values of the variable.

Example

5.0	5.0	6.4	5.0	6.0	5.6	6.5	5.0	5.5
6.0	5.7	5.0	6.5	5.0	5.7	6.0	5.6	6.2
5.8	5.4	6.0	7.2	6.3	5.0	7.0	5.5	5.2
5.0	5.0	5.0	5.0	5.7	5.6	5.7	5.0	7.2
6.5	5.6	4.6	6.4					

a) Determine appropriate intervals that will include all the lifetimes of the batteries in the sample.

b) Construct a frequency distribution using these intervals.

c) Draw the frequency histogram that represents the frequency distribution.

d) Draw the frequency polygon that represents the frequency distribution.

e) Use a graphing calculator to investigate the resulting frequency histogram and frequency polygon.

f) Keep the data from (e) in your calculator and investigate the different frequency histograms that result when you change the width of the intervals.

g) Describe the resulting histogram when you make the width of the interval narrower. To do this, change the window settings Xscl = 0.1.

h) Describe the resulting histogram when you make the interval wider with Xscl = 1.

Solution

a) To determine intervals that will provide a display that accurately summarizes the distribution of the data, find the **smallest** and **largest** lifetimes in the table and calculate the range of the data.
Then, choose a number of intervals of equal width that divides the range evenly.

The range is **largest** lifetime – **smallest** lifetime = 7.2 – 4.6 = 2.6, which could be rounded up to 3. Using 6 intervals, an interval width of 0.5 can be used.

The interval width

$$= \frac{\text{range}}{\text{number of intervals}}$$
$$= \frac{3.0}{6}$$
$$= 0.5$$

To ensure no piece of data lies on the borderline between the two intervals, make the intervals 4.35 – 4.85, 4.85 – 5.35, 5.35 – 5.85, 5.85 – 6.35, 6.35 – 6.85, and 6.85 – 7.35.

Note that to account for the added 0.4 in the actual range, the smallest value in the lowest interval is smaller than the smallest data value and the highest value in the highest interval is larger than the largest data value.

b) Create a frequency distribution in which you record the number of batteries that fall into each of the intervals.

Interval	Midpoint	Tally	Frequency
4.35 – 4.85	4.6	|	1
4.85 – 5.35	5.1	𝍸 𝍸 |||	13
5.35 – 5.85	5.6	𝍸 𝍸 ||	12
5.85 – 6.35	6.1	𝍸 |	6
6.35 – 6.85	6.6	𝍸	5
6.85 – 7.35	7.1	|||	3

c) Use the frequency distribution to draw the resulting frequency histogram.

Lifetime of Brand ⊠ Batteries

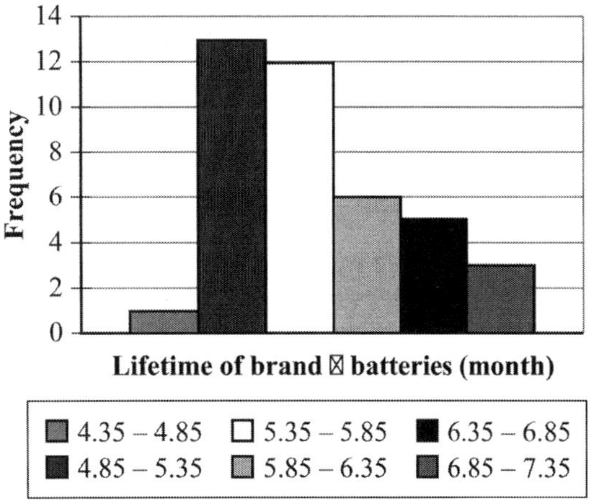

d) To draw the frequency polygon, determine the midpoint of each interval and plot the frequencies versus the midpoint value. Then, join the points with straight lines.

Frequency Polygon

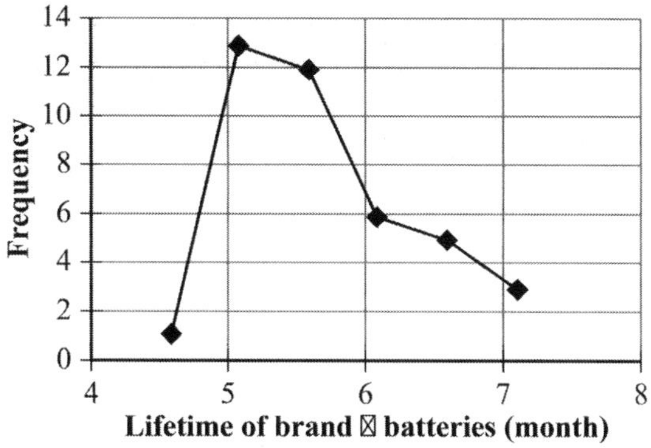

The frequency polygon approximates the frequency distribution.

e) To use a TI-83 Plus graphing calculator, press STAT ENTER and input the 40 data values into L1.
Press 2nd Y= to use the STAT PLOT feature on your calculator. Press 1. Turn Plot 1 on by highlighting on and pressing ENTER. Choose the histogram and set the following:

Xlist:L1
Freq:1

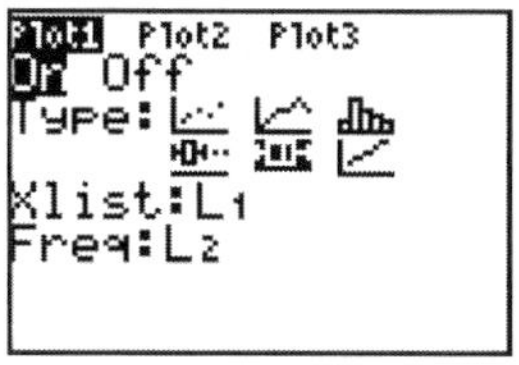

Press ZOOM and choose 9:ZoomStat. The calculator determines an appropriate interval width and organizes the data into these intervals. The TRACE button will allow you to check the intervals and frequencies from the data using the arrow keys. Note that the graphing calculator displays a histogram different from the one created in **c)**.

By adjusting the window settings to Xmin = 4.35, Xmax = 7.35, Xscl = 0.5, Ymin = , Ymax = 14 and Yscl = 2, then pressing GRAPH, the calculator displays a histogram similar to the histogram in (c).

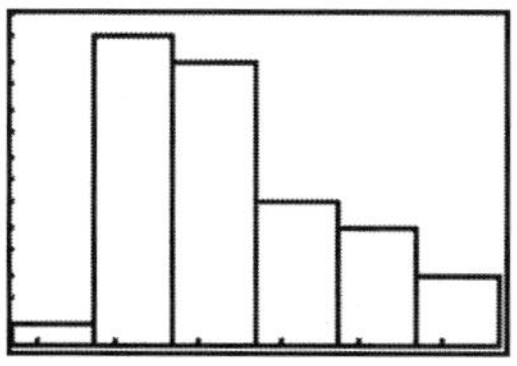

To draw the frequency polygon, enter the midpoint of each interval into L_2, and the frequency of the interval into L_3. Use the STAT PLOT 2 feature to draw the frequency polygon by setting Xlist:L_2 and Ylist:L_3. Turn STAT PLOT 1 off to avoid seeing the histogram as well as the frequency polygram.

f/g) When the interval width is 0.1 (narrower), there are spaces in the histogram because some of the frequencies of the intervals are 0. There are too many bars as well. This histogram does not effectively represent the data and neither will the resulting frequency polygon.

h) When the interval width is increased to 1, only 3 bars appear. There should be at least 5 intervals in the data so that a representative display is achieved. The resulting frequency polygon will not be appropriate for the data.

Related Question: 12

PD2.5 *recognize that theoretical probability for a continuous random variable is determined over a range of values, (e.g., the probability that the life of a light bulb is between 90 hours and 115 hours), that the probability that a continuous random variable takes any single value is zero, and that the probabilities of ranges of values form the probability distribution associated with the random variable*

THEORETICAL PROBABILITY FOR A CONTINUOUS RANDOM VARIABLE

Often, you want to find the probability that a continuous random variable falls in a particular range of values. This kind of probability can be determined from the area under the distribution histogram within the appropriate interval.

The probability that a continuous random variable takes on any single value is 0.

Example

		$\frac{1}{44} \approx 2.27\%$
		$\frac{6}{44} \approx 13.64\%$
		$\frac{15}{44} \approx 34.09\%$
		$\frac{15}{44} \approx 34.09\%$
		$\frac{6}{44} \approx 13.64\%$
		$\frac{1}{44} \approx 2.27\%$

a) less than 850 h

b) between 800h and 850 h

c) between 850 h and 1000 h

d) exactly 900 h

Solution

a) The percentage of bulbs that lasted less than 850 h is 13.64 + 2.27 = 15.91%. Based on these results, the probability that a randomly chosen bulb will last less than 850 h is 0.1591.

b) Since approximately 13.64% of the bulbs sampled lasted between 800 and 850 h, the probability that a randomly chosen bulb will last within this interval is 0.1364.

c) Thirty-six of the 44 bulbs lasted between 850 and 1 000 h. Based on these results, the probability that a randomly selected bulb lasts between 850 and 1000 h is 0.8182.

d) The number of bulbs that lasted exactly 900 h cannot be determined from the grouped data because individual data values are lost with grouping. However, this probability must be zero, since the probability that a continuous random variable takes a single value is zero.

Related Question: 13

PD2.6 *recognize that the normal distribution is commonly used to model the frequency and probability distributions of continuous random variables, describe some properties of the normal distribution (e.g., the curve has a central peak; the curve is symmetric about the mean; the mean and median are equal; approximately 68% of the data values are within one standard deviation of the mean and approximately 95% of the data values are within two standard deviations of the mean), and recognize and describe situations that can be modelled using the normal distribution (e.g., birth weights of males or of females, household incomes in a neighbourhood, base ball batting averages)*

NORMAL DISTRIBUTION

A probability distribution is a list of all the possible outcomes of an experiment with their associated probabilities. One way that this can be done is by using a histogram. As the total number of data values increases, the bars of the distribution become more defined. There are many kinds of probability distributions, each with a different shape, but the most common one is the Normal Distribution, which is a Bell-Shaped Curve.

A normal distribution has the following properties:

- The total area under the curve is 1 with 50% of the data below the mean and 50% of the data above the mean.
- It is symmetrical; the mean, median, and mode are all the same value and fall on the line of symmetry.
- Approximately 68% of the data is within one standard deviation of the mean.
- Approximately 95% of the data is within two standard deviations of the mean.
- Approximately 99.5% of the data is within three standard deviations of the mean.

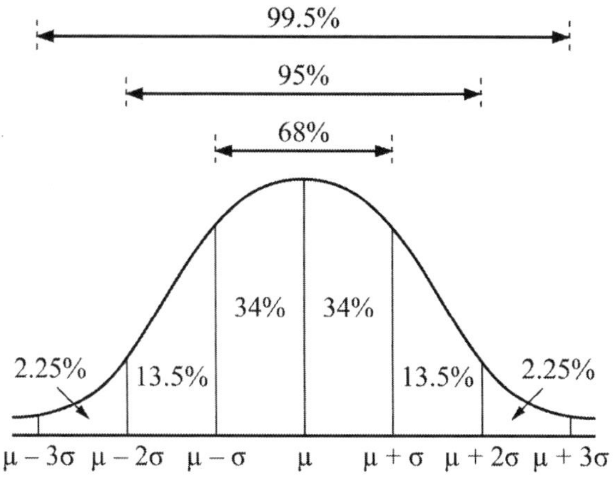

In every normal distribution, regardless of the population under analysis, the standard deviation always divides the population into the same regions, representing the same percentages.

The area under the normal distribution curve, between any two data values, represents the probability that a data value picked at random is between the two given values.

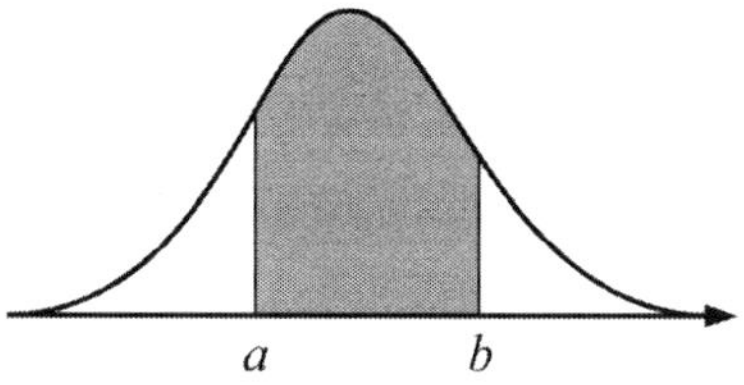

$P(a \leq x \leq b) =$ area under the curve between a and b.

Example

The fuel economy of today's vehicles tends to be normally distributed. The data below shows the approximate city fuel economy (FE) of 50 new vehicles.

City FE (L/100 km)	Frequency
18	2
22	8
26	14
30	16
34	9
38	1

a) Sketch and label a normal curve that could be used to represent this data. Round the mean to the nearest whole number and round the standard deviation to the nearest tenth.

b) What is the probability that a randomly selected new vehicle will have a city FE of 23.5 L/100 km or better?

Solution

a) Use your calculator to determine the mean and the standard deviation for grouped data. Enter the data into L1 and L2 and then use 1-Var Stats L1, L2 as shown.

The mean is 28 L/100 km and the standard deviation = 4.5 L/100 km.
The data is distributed as shown in the diagram.

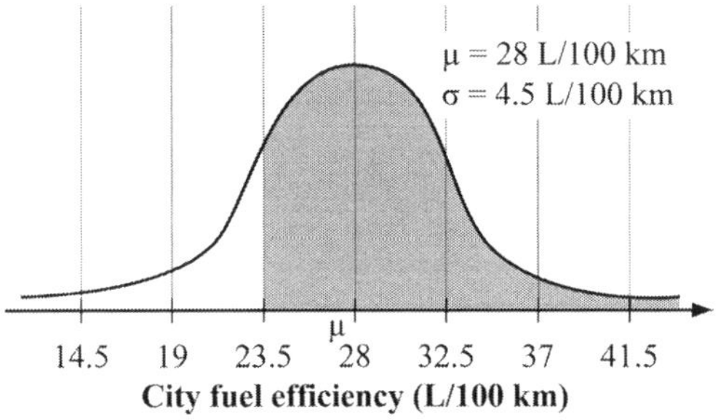

b) The shaded region shows the percentage of vehicles that use more than 23.5 L/100 km. Add these probabilities from each shaded region (0.34 + 0.50) to determine the probability that a vehicle will have a fuel efficiency rating better than 23.5 L/100 km.

The probability that a randomly selected vehicle will have a city FE of 23.5 L/100 km or better is 0.84.

Related Questions:14, NR6

PD2.7 make connections, through investigation using dynamic statistical software, between the normal distribution and the binomial and hypergeometric distributions for increasing numbers of trials of the discrete distributions

Connecting Normal Distributions to Binomial and Hypergeometric Distributions

The binomial distribution has a different structure than the normal distribution, but if the sample space is large enough, the normal distribution may be used to approximate binomial probabilities as long as the following two conditions are satisfied:

1. The situation involves a binomial distribution; i.e., there are only **two** possible outcomes: *success* and *failure*.
2. The number of trials, or the sample space, is considered large enough to justify using a normal distribution as an approximation of the actual distribution. The sample space is considered large enough when $np > 5$ and when $n(1-p) > 5$, where n is the total number of trials in the experiment, p is the probability of the success, and $1-p$ is the probability of failure.

When the normal approximation is determined to be appropriate, find the mean and standard deviation for the experiment. This is done with the following formulas:

$\mu = np$ and $\sigma = \sqrt{np(1-p)}$

It has been previously demonstrated that with increasingly large samples, the binomial and hypergeometric distributions become more aligned.

Once the mean and standard deviation are determined, estimates of the probability of a range of scores of values can be determined using the techniques illustrated in the previous outcome.

Example

After 178 times at bat, a baseball player calculated his batting average to be 0.309 (which means he got a hit 30.9% of the times he went to bat). What is the probability that the player will get more than 60 times in his next 178 times at bat?

Solution

To use the normal distribution to approximate this probability, the following two conditions **must** first be met:

1. It is a binomial distribution since there are two possible outcomes: *success* when he gets a hit and *failure* when he does not get a hit and the rest of the criteria for a binomial distribution are met (as listed in *PD1.4*).
2. That the sample space is large enough to use the normal approximation.

To do this, you must check that $np > 5$ and $n(1-p) > 5$.

First, identify the variables: $n = 178$, $p = 0.309$, $1 - p = 1 - 0.309 = 0.691$.

$np > 5$

$np = (178)(0.309) = 55.002$

and

$n(1-p) > 5$

$n(1-p) = 178(0.691) = 122.998$

Since both are greater than 5, a normal approximation is appropriate in this instance.

Now, find the mean and standard deviation for this situation based on 178 times at bat, to the nearest whole number.

$$\begin{aligned}\mu &= np \\ &= (178)(0.309) \\ &\approx 55\end{aligned}$$

and

$$\begin{aligned}\sigma &= \sqrt{np(1-p)} \\ &= \sqrt{(178)(0.309)(0.691)} \\ &\approx 6.16\end{aligned}$$

This means that for every 178 times the player goes to bat, the expected (mean) number of hits is 55 with a standard deviation of 6 hits.

Sketch a normal curve to help predict this player's future performance and to determine the probability that this player will get more than 61 hits in his next 178 times at bat. Shade the region that you are interested in.

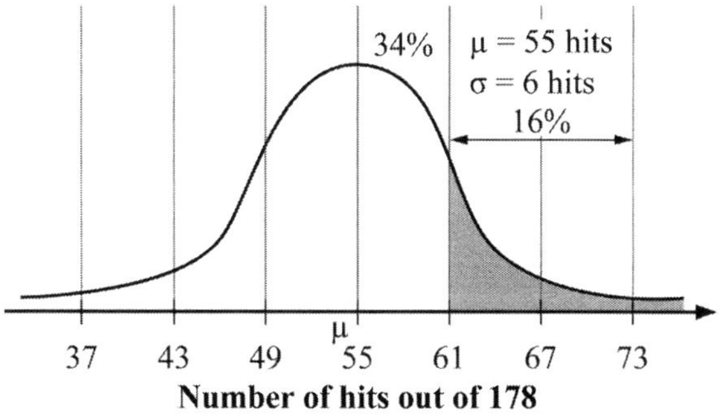

Use the percentages from the normal distribution. The probability that this player will get more than 61 hits in his next 178 times at bat is approximately 0.50 – 0.34 = 0.16.

Related Questions: 15, 16, 17, OR4

PD2.8 recognize a z-score as the positive or negative number of standard deviations from the mean to a value of the continuous random variable, and solve probability problems involving normal distributions using a variety of tools and strategies (e.g., calculating a z-score and reading a probability from a table; using technology to determine a probability), including problems arising from real-world applications

SOLVING PROBABILITY PROBLEMS

Z-Scores

A z-score measures how many standard deviations a data value is away from the mean, and it is calculated by the following formula:

$$z = \frac{x - \mu}{\sigma}$$

Where z is the z-score, x is the data value, μ is the mean, and σ is the standard deviation.

Example

A group of 400 students wrote an exam. The marks were normally distributed with a mean of $\mu = 65$ and a standard deviation of $\sigma = 8$. Determine the z-scores of the marks 77 and 57.

Solution

The z-score for $x = 77$,

$$z = \frac{x - \mu}{\sigma} = \frac{77 - 65}{8} = \frac{12}{8} = 1.5$$

For $x = 57$,

$$z = \frac{57 - 65}{8}$$
$$= \frac{-8}{8}$$
$$= -1$$

The calculations from the z-scores indicate that a mark of 77 lies 1.5 standard deviations **above** the mean, and a mark of 57 lies 1 standard deviation **below** the mean.

To summarize, z-scores are positive for data values greater than the mean, and negative for data values less than the mean.

- The primary application of z-scores is to find areas under the standard normal distribution curve. The **standard** normal distribution has a mean of $\mu = 0$ and a standard deviation of $\sigma = 1$. Remember that the area of any interval under the standard normal distribution is equal to the percent of the population that lies in that interval.

A graph of the standard normal curve is shown below:

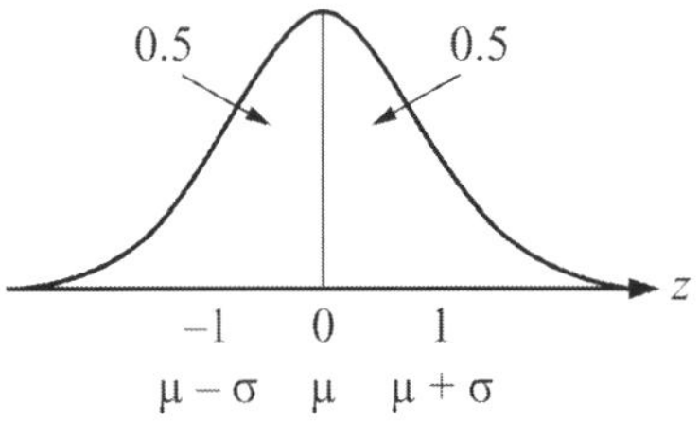

Following are some points to note about the graph:

- The total area under the curve is 1.0
- The area to the right of $z = 0$ is 0.5
- The area to the left of $z = 0$ is 0.5

The z-score tables (see Data Booklet) give, for any z-score, the area under the standard normal curve to the **left** of the z-score.

Example

For the exam described in the first example, determine the percentage of students who received a mark less than 77 and the percentage of students who received a mark greater than 57.

Solution

For a mark of 77, the z-score is 1.5 (see previous example). According to the table for z-scores in the Data Booklet, the area to the left of $z = 1.5$ is 0.9332, correct to 4 decimal places.

This means that approximately $0.9332 = 93.32\%$ of the students obtained marks less than 77.

Since the total area below the standard normal curve is 1, the percentage of students who received a mark greater than 77 is $1.0 - 0.9332 = 0.0668$. Thus, 6.68% of the students received a mark greater than 77.

These areas are shown in the following graph:

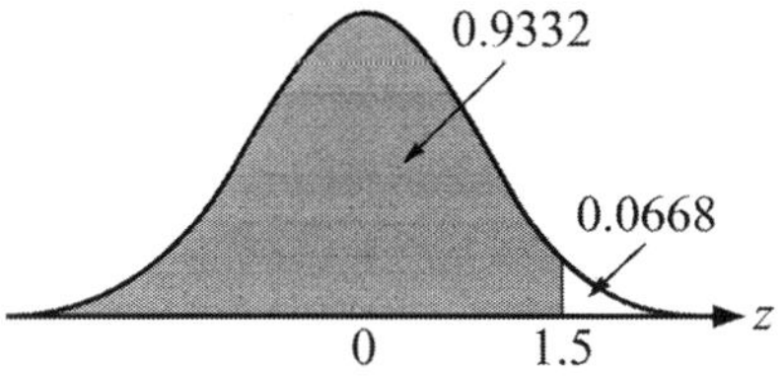

For a mark of 57, the z-score is -1. According to the table for z-scores in the Data Booklet, the area to the left of $z = 1.5$ is 0.1587.

That is, approximately $0.1587 = 15.87\%$ of the students obtained marks of less than 57, and approximately $1.0 - 0.1587 = 0.8413 = 84.13\%$ obtained marks greater than 57.

These areas are shown in the following graph:

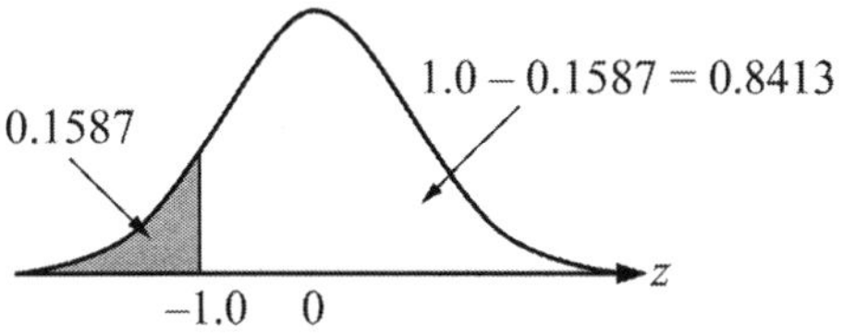

As an aside, since 400 students wrote the test, there were $0.8413 \times 400 \approx 337$ students who received a mark greater than 57.

PROBABILITY AND THE TI GRAPHING CALCULATOR FEATURES

Z-scores can also be used to answer questions about probabilities. The area under the normal curve for a particular interval is equal to the probability that a data value will be in that interval.

A graphing calculator can also be used to determine the probability or area under the normal curve. There may be discrepancies between answers arrived at using a calculator and the z-score tables because the tables are limited to z-scores rounded to the nearest hundredth.

On a TI-83 graphing calculator, the normalcdf command will return the proportion of data that lies on a normal distribution between two given z-scores. It must be entered as follows:

normalcdf(low score, high score, mean, standard deviation).

To access normalcdf, input [2nd] [VARS] [2]. If the scores are z-scores, then the mean and standard deviation do not need to be entered. The calculator assumes the mean to be 0 and the standard deviation to be 1 (of course, if you wish, you may enter these numbers for the mean, σ, and standard deviation, 1, when dealing with z-scores.)

On a TI graphing calculator, the command invNorm, accessed by inputting [2nd] [VARS] [3], returns the score of the normally distributed data that has the given percentage of data less than the score. It must be entered as follows:

invNorm(area, mean, standard deviation)

If the mean and standard deviation are not entered, the calculator assumes the mean to be 0 and the standard deviation to be 1 (a standard normal distribution), and the returned value will be a z-score.

On the TI graphing calculator, the command

ShadeNorm(low score, high score, mean, standard deviation)

will draw a graph and give the area under the curve between your boundaries. To access ShadeNorm, input [2nd] [VARS], scroll right to DRAW [1]. Appropriate window settings must be entered in order to display the graph of the normal distribution.

USING THE TI GRAPHING CALCULATOR FEATURES

Example

A factory produces 8000 containers of ice cream a day. The mean mass of the container of ice cream is 2 kg with a standard deviation of 0.2 kg.

a) What is the probability, to the nearest ten thousandth, that a container of ice cream chosen at random will have a mass less than 1.7 kg?

Solution

a) To answer this question, it is helpful to sketch the normal curve as shown.

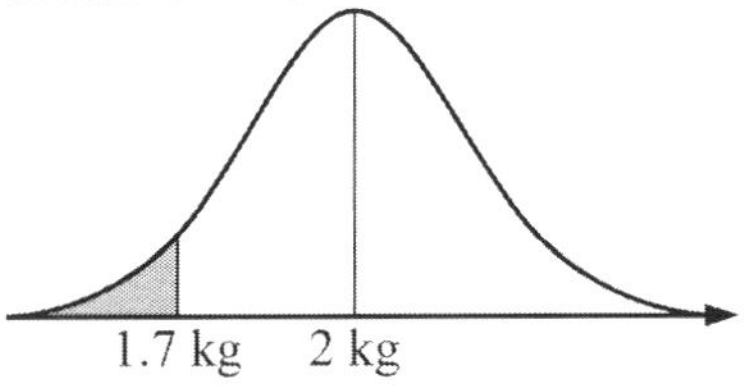

$P(\text{mass} < 1.7) = \text{normalcdf}(0, 1.7, 2, 0.2)$
≈ 0.0668

Note that the low score used was 0 because the mass cannot be lower than this (any value that is 10 standard deviations or more below the mean may be used).

b) What is the probability, to the nearest ten thousandth, that a container will have a mass greater than 2.5 kg?

Solution

Again, it is helpful to sketch the normal curve to answer the question.

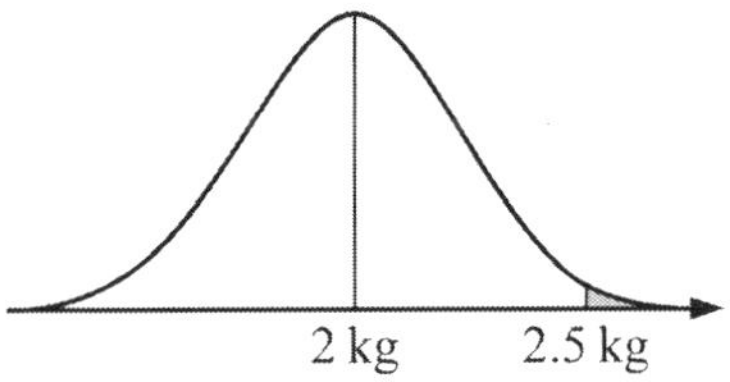

$P(\text{mass} > 2.5) = \text{normalcdf}(2.5, 100, 2, 0.2)$
≈ 0.0062

Note that the high score can be any number as long as it is 10 or more standard deviations above the mean.

c) How many containers can be expected to have a mass between 1.8 kg and 2.3 kg?

Solution

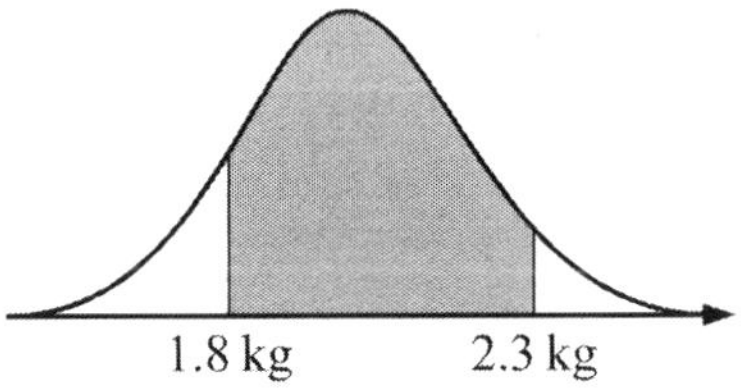

The percentage of containers between 1.8 kg and 2.3 kg:

$P(1.8 < \text{mass} < 2.3) = \text{normalcdf}(1.8, 2.3, 2, 0.2)$
≈ 0.7745

Therefore, the number of containers that have a mass between 1.8 kg and 2.3 kg is

$\approx 0.7745 \times 8000 \approx 6196$. The number of containers must be a whole number.

d) What is the smallest mass a container can have so that its mass is in the top 25% of production? Answer to the nearest tenth.

Solution

In this case, a probability or area under the curve is given, and you need to find the appropriate data value.

The smallest mass the container can have so that its mass is in the top 25% is

$\approx \text{invNorm}(1 - 0.25, 2, 0.2) \approx 2.1$ kg. The area that was entered is 1 – 0.25 = 0.75 because the area to the left of data value must be entered, and the 25% corresponds to the area on the right of the data value.

e) Use the ShadeNorm feature on your calculator to graph and determine the probability that a container will have a mass between 2.1 kg and 2.6 kg. Answer to the nearest ten thousandth.

Solution

Appropriate window settings need to be entered. These can vary.

Suggested window settings: Xmin = 0, Xmax = 3, Xscl = .2, Ymin = –0.15, Ymax = 2, Yscl = .1.

The probability that a container will have a mass between 2.1 kg and 2.6 kg is approximately

$\text{ShadeNorm}(2.1, 2.6, 2, 0.2) \approx 0.3072$.

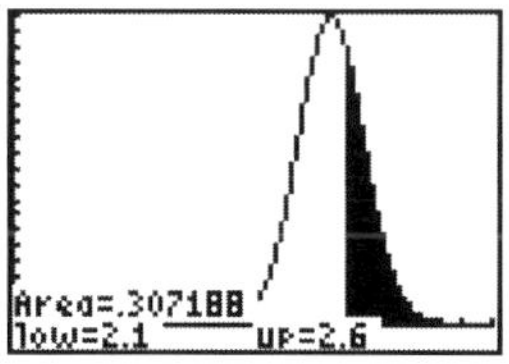

Related Questions: 17, 18, NR8

PRACTICE QUESTIONS

1. Which of the following variables can be classified as discrete random variables?

1. The number of applications received by a business for a particular job.
2. The time it takes a student to complete math homework.
3. The life span of a light bulb.
4. The number of defective parts in a sample taken from a factory.

A. 1 only

B. 2 only

C. 1 and 4 only

D. 2 and 3 only

Use the following information to answer the next question.

A circular spinner has four congruent sectors as shown.

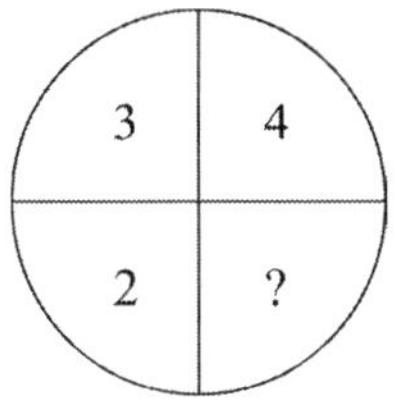

2. If the expected value of the spinner is 4, how many points are in the fourth sector of the spinner?

A. 1

B. 5

C. 7

D. 10

Numerical Response

Use the following information to answer the next question.

x	$P(x)$
1	$\frac{1}{6}$
2	$\frac{1}{5}$
3	$\frac{1}{4}$
4	$\frac{1}{3}$
5	$\frac{1}{20}$

1. Given the probability distribution that is shown, the expected value to the nearest tenth is ____________.

3. Which of the following graphs is a probability histogram?

A.

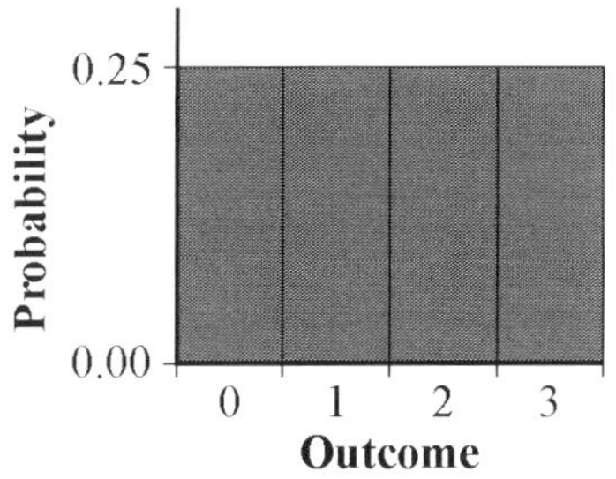

B.

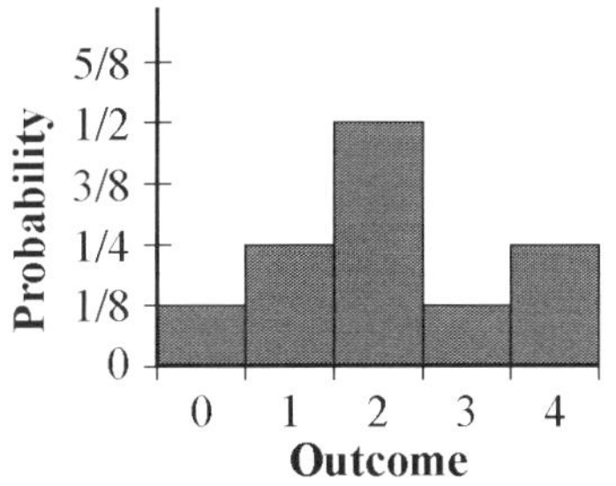

C.

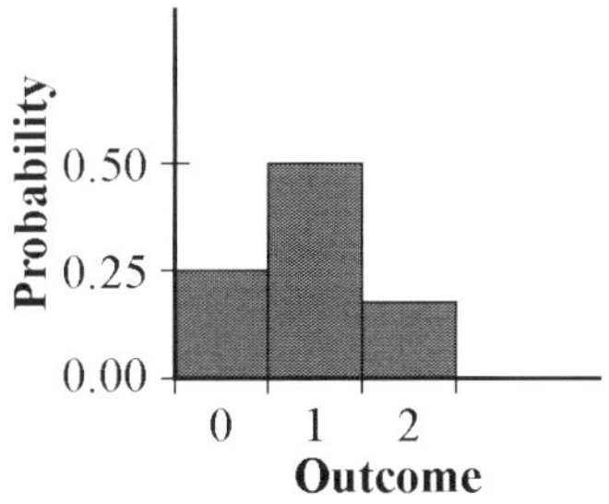

D.

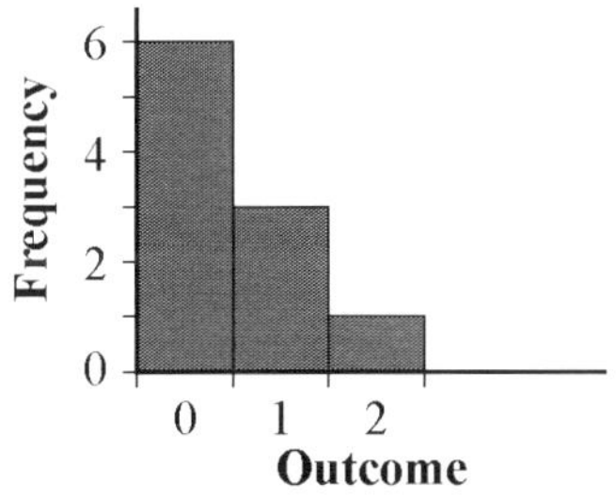

4. When taking a certain drug, 20% of patients suffer from side effects. If the drug is given to 8 patients, then the probability that exactly 2 will suffer from side effects, to the nearest thousandth, is

A. 0.706

B. 0.294

C. 0.002

D. 0.001

Numerical Response

2. Eighty-three percent of the residents of a large city who are of voting age are registered to vote. In a sample of 20 residents, the probability, to the nearest hundredth, that at **least** 18 are registered to vote is _______________.

5. Which of the following random variables has a hypergeometric distribution?

A. The number of dogs chosen at random from a pet shop that has 5 cats and 7 dogs.

B. The number of 2's produced by a random number generator.

C. The number of defective screws in a random sample of 20 taken from a production line that has a 2% defective rate.

D. The number of boys in a family of 5 children.

Numerical Response

3. A twelve-member jury will be selected from a pool of 14 men and 11 women. The probability that the jury will have 6 men and 6 women on the jury, rounded to the nearest hundredth, is _________________.

6. Which of the following statements is incorrect?

A. As the number of trials increases, the binomial distribution and hypergeometric distribution will be very close in shape.

B. Hypergeometric and binomial distributions are similar in that there are 2 outcomes: success or failure.

C. In hypergeometric distributions, the trials are independent, whereas in the binomial distribution, the trials are dependent.

D. In hypergeometric distributions, the probability of success changes from trial to trail, whereas in the binomial distribution, the probability of success does not change from trial to trial.

CHALLENGER QUESTION

Numerical Response

4. Two candies are drawn from a bag containing 2 green, 3 red, and 2 yellow candies. The probability of getting exactly 1 red candy is determined with replacement and then without replacement. The difference in these probabilities, to the nearest hundredth, is ________.

CHALLENGER QUESTION

7. How many of the following random variables have a hypergeometric probability distribution?

   1. The number of diamonds dealt from a deck of 52 cards.
   2. The number of 4's produced by a random number generator.
   3. The number of male names on a page selected at random from a telephone book.
   4. The number of left-handed people in a group selected from the general population.

   A. 1 **B.** 2
   C. 3 **D.** 4

8. Which of the following situations does **not** give rise to a continuous random variable?

   A. Measuring the time it takes to complete a task

   B. Measuring the heights of the students in your class

   C. Measuring the maximum distance that a javelin can be thrown

   D. Counting the number of heads that occur when three coins are tossed

Numerical Response

5. How many of the following four statements are correct? _____

   1. A binomial probability distribution and a hypergeometric distribution both deal with discrete data.
   2. In continuous distributions, the random variable may have fractional or decimal values.
   3. Continuous probability distributions have graphs that are smooth curves.
   4. Continuous random variables can be determined using counting principles.

9. A litter of puppies is born, and the veterinarian records the weights of the 10 puppies. In ounces, the puppies weigh 16.9, 16.9, 17.3, 16.8, 17.2, 16.9, 17.5, 16.8, 17.1, and 17.3. Expressed to the nearest tenth, the mean and the standard deviation of these weights are, respectively,

   A. 16.9 oz and 0.2 oz

   B. 16.9 oz and 0.7 oz

   C. 17.1 oz and 0.2 oz

   D. 17.1 oz and 0.7 oz

Use the following information to answer the next question.

> Terrance played golf on the same course during each of two seasons. In the first season, his mean score was 72 with a standard deviation of 3.8. In the second season, his mean score was 76 with a standard deviation of 2.3.

10. The standard deviation of Terrance's scores for the two seasons indicates that his

   A. average score was better in the first season

   B. average score was better in the second season

   C. scores were more consistent in the first season

   D. scores were more consistent in the second season

11. Terrence wants to create a continuous frequency distribution of wind speeds by measuring (with an anemometer) and then recording wind speeds every 15 minutes over an eight-hour period. Terrence will have difficulty creating the continuous frequency distribution because

A. the wind speed might be zero at some time periods.

B. the wind can change direction.

C. the sampling technique will not capture a significant portion of the variable.

D. wind speed is not a continuous variable.

12. Which of the following interval widths would be most appropriate to form five uniform intervals for the following data?
0.59, 0.46, 0.48, 0.52, 0.15, 0.60, 0.86, 0.55, 0.97, 0.35, 0.60, 0.94, 0.65, 0.34, 0.60, 0.70, 0.37, 0.86

A. 0.1

B. 0.2

C. 0.3

D. 0.8

Use the following information to answer the next question.

A sample of car drivers in a particular city was surveyed to determine the length of time people spend in their cars getting to work in the morning. The data was collected, and the probabilities for certain time intervals were displayed in a probability distribution as shown.

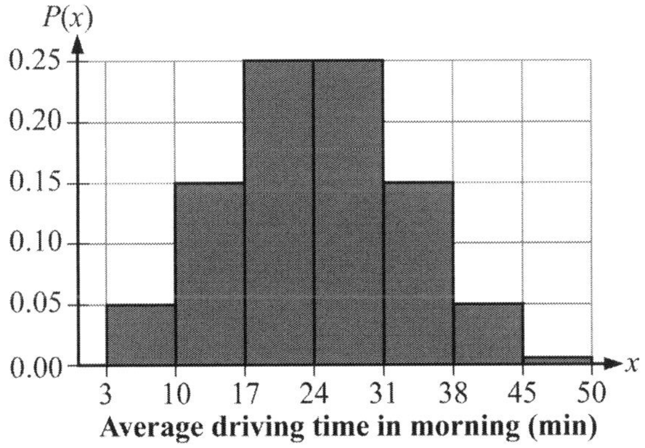

13. Of the following probabilities, the one that **cannot** be determined using the probability distribution shown is the probability that a driver chosen at random takes

A. between 10 and 31 minutes to get to work in the morning

B. between 17 and 24 minutes to get to work in the morning

C. more than 26 minutes to get to work in the morning

D. more than 31 minutes to get to work in the morning

14. The heights of the males taking a first-year math class at university are normally distributed with a mean of 174 cm and a standard deviation of 5.4 cm. The heights of the females taking the same class are also normally distributed with a mean of 162 cm and a standard deviation of 5.4 cm.
If the two probability distributions are graphed on the same axis, then the bell curve representing the males compared with the bell curve for the females would be

A. shorter and wider

B. taller and narrower

C. congruent and shifted to the left

D. congruent, and shifted to the right

Numerical Response

6. Statistics taken on a random sample of ticket buyers for a concert revealed that the amount of time they waited in line to purchase their tickets was normally distributed with a mean of 160 minutes and a standard deviation of 10 minutes. What percentage of the people stood in line between 150 and 180 minutes?
Leave your answer to the nearest tenth of a percent. _____

15. Which of the following binomial situations can be reasonably approximated by a normal distribution?

A. 10 trials, probability of success on each trial is 0.4

B. 50 trials, probability of failure on each trial is 0.06

C. 1000 trials probability of success on each trial is 0.05

D. 1000 trials, probability of success on each trial is 0.001

16. Of the items produced in a factory, statistics show that 10% are defective. In a sample of 400 items, the mean and standard deviation for the number of defective items are, respectively,

A. 40 , 6

B. 40, 36

C. 360, 6

D. 360, 36

Numerical Response

7. A recent survey of 415 Grade 12 students revealed that 170 have jobs. If you were to survey another group of 415 students based on the recent survey, what is the probability, to the nearest thousandth, that between 150 and 180 students out of 415 would have a job? _______

17. In one year, the mean number of movies attended per person was 19 with a standard deviation of 3.3. If the data forms a normal distribution, then the percentage of the population, to the nearest tenth, that went to less than 15 movies was

A. 11.3%

B. 38.7%

C. 61.3%

D. 88.7%

Use the following information to answer the next question.

Pat's unit test marks are shown below with the class mean and standard deviation for each unit test.

Subject	Pat's Mark	Mean Mark	Standard Deviation	z-score
Statistics	82	73	12	
Biology	81	71	13	
Chemistry	74	64	16	
Calculus	79	68	13	

18. By calculating z-scores, determine the test on which Pat performed the best, when compared with the population writing the test.

A. Statistics

B. Biology

C. Chemistry

D. Calculus

Numerical Response

8. The life of a certain brand of tire is normally distributed with a mean of 90 000 km and a standard deviation of 8000 km.
What percent of the population, expressed to the nearest tenth, will last longer than 105 000 km? _______%

Open Response

OR1. For what reason is the sum of all probabilities in a probability distribution for a discrete random variable equal to 1?

OR2. Twenty-two students in a class were surveyed about their shoe sizes. The results are tabulated in the table below.

Shoe size (Outcome)	Number of students (Frequency of each outcome)	Probability of each shoe size
6	3	$\frac{3}{22} \approx 0.136$
7	5	
8	8	
9	4	
10	2	

a) Complete the table above, giving the probabilities to the nearest thousandth.

b) Draw a frequency histogram that represents the data in the table.

c) Draw a probability histogram that represents the data in the table.

d) Compare the two histograms.

OR3. Kathy's Coffee House prints prize coupons under the rims of 20% of its paper cups. When you purchase 10 cups of coffee, the probability of getting a prize coupon is determined.

a) What type of distribution is this? Explain.

b) What is the probability, to the nearest hundredth, that you would win at most 2 prize coupons?

OR4. What are the conditions that **must** be satisfied in order for a normal distribution to be used to approximate a binomial distribution?

ANSWERS AND SOLUTIONS—PRACTICE QUESTIONS

1. C	**4. B**	**7. C**	**11. C**	**16. A**
OR1. See solution	**NR2. 0.31**	**OR3. See solution**	**12. B**	**NR7. 0.815**
2. C	**5. A**	**8. D**	**13. C**	**OR4. See solution**
NR1. 2.9	**NR3. 0.27**	**NR5. 3**	**14. D**	**17. A**
3. A	**6. C**	**9. C**	**NR6. 81.5**	**18. D**
OR2. See solution	**NR4. 0.08**	**10. D**	**15. C**	**NR8. 3.0**

1. C

A discrete random variable must assume a distinct value for each outcome. Variables 2 and 3 have continuous sample spaces; therefore, they are not discrete variables.

2. C.

Since the spinner is divided into 4 equal sectors, the probability of each outcome is $\frac{1}{4}$. This is a uniform distribution. The expected value of the spinner is 4 so, if n represents the number of points in the fourth sector,

$$E(X)=\begin{pmatrix} 2\left(\frac{1}{4}\right)+3\left(\frac{1}{4}\right) \\ +4\left(\frac{1}{4}\right)+n\left(\frac{1}{4}\right) \end{pmatrix}$$
$$=4$$

$$\frac{2}{4}+\frac{3}{4}+\frac{4}{4}+\frac{n}{4}=4$$
$$\frac{9+n}{4}=4$$
$$9+n=16$$
$$n=7$$

The missing number is 7.

NR1 **2.9**

$$E(X)=\begin{pmatrix} 1\left(\frac{1}{6}\right)+2\left(\frac{1}{5}\right)+3\left(\frac{1}{4}\right) \\ +4\left(\frac{1}{3}\right)+5\left(\frac{1}{20}\right) \end{pmatrix}$$
$$=2.9$$

3. A

Because a probability histogram represents a probability distribution, the sum of the probabilities given in the histogram must be 1. This is only the case for the probability histogram in choice **A** $(0.25 + 0.25 + 0.25 + 0.25 = 1)$.
Since the probability of each outcome is the same, this is a uniform distribution.
Choice **B** is not a probability histogram because the sum of the probabilities of the outcomes is more than 1.
Choice **C** is not a probability histogram because the sum of the probabilities of the outcomes is less than 1.
Choice **D** is not a probability histogram because the vertical axis represents the frequency of each outcome, not the probability of each outcome.

4. B

$n = 8,\ k = 2, p = 0.20$

$$P(2) = {}_8C_2\left(0.20\right)^2\left(1-0.20\right)^{8-2} \approx 0.294$$

NR2. **0.31**

At least 18 means that 18, 19, or 20 residents are registered.

$$P(\text{at least } 18) = P(18) + P(19) + P(20)$$
$$=\begin{pmatrix} {}_{20}C_{18}(0.83)^{18}(0.17)^2 \\ +{}_{20}C_{19}(0.83)^{19}(0.17)^1 \\ +{}_{20}C_{20}(0.83)^{20}(0.17)^0 \end{pmatrix}$$
$$\approx 0.19189 + 0.09862 + 0.02407$$
$$\approx 0.31$$

5. **A**

The selection process in choice **A** involves dependent trials because each dog that is chosen cannot be selected again.
Choice **B** is a binomial distribution.
The probability of getting a 2 remains the same from trail to trial.
Choice **C** is a binomial distribution. The probability of getting a defective screw remains the same from trial to trial.
D. The probability of having a boy remains the same from child to child.

NR3. **0.27**

Using the formula,

$$P(x \text{ successes}) = \frac{{}_aC_x \times {}_{n-a}C_{r-x}}{{}_nC_r}.$$

$$P(6 \text{ men and } 6 \text{ women}) = \frac{{}_{14}C_6 \times {}_{11}C_6}{{}_{25}C_{12}} \approx 0.27$$

6. **C**

In hypergeometric distributions, the probability of success changes for each trial. Therefore, the trials are dependent. In binomial distributions, the probability of success remains the same for each trial. Therefore, the trials are independent.

NR4. **0.08**

With replacement, the probability is

$${}_2C_1\left(\frac{3}{7}\right)^1\left(\frac{4}{7}\right)^1 \approx 0.489\,79$$

Without replacement, the probability is

$$\frac{{}_3C_1 \times {}_4C_1}{{}_7C_2} \approx 0.5714\,28$$

The difference is 0.5714 28 – 0.489 79 = 0.08 (to the nearest hundredth).

7. **C**

Random variables 1, 3, and 4 are hypergeometric distributions because the probability changes with each trial. The trials are dependent.

Random variable 2 is a binomial distribution because the number 4 has the same probability of occurring for each trial. The trials are independent.

8. **D**

Continuous random variables arise from situations that involve measurement, rather than counting. The number of heads that occur when three coins are tossed is a discrete random variable because the possible values of the random variable are 0, 1, 2, or 3 **only**.

NR5. **3**

There are 3 correct statements. Statements 1, 2, and 3 are correct. Statement 4 is not correct. Only discrete random variables are determined using counting principles.

9. **C**

The mean and the standard deviation of this data can be determined using your calculator. Enter the information in L1 and then calculate 1 – variable statistics on that list. You will see that $x = 17.07 \approx 17.1$ and $\sigma x \approx 0.233 \approx 0.2$.

10. **D**

Standard deviation is a measure of how tightly the data is clustered around the average. A low standard deviation indicates that all data values are close to the mean. Terrance's scores for the second season have a smaller standard deviation, therefore his scores were more consistent in that season.

11. **C**

Recording the wind speed every 15 minutes will give very few values of the variable and, because wind often gusts, may not represent the distribution of values. Choices A and B are not difficulties, and choice D is incorrect, because wind speed is a continuous variable.

12. **B**

$$\text{Interval Width} = \frac{\text{Max Value} - \text{Min Value}}{\text{Number of Intervals}}$$
$$= \frac{0.97 - 0.15}{5}$$
$$= \frac{0.82}{5} \approx 0.164 \approx 0.2$$

13. **C**

The probability cannot be determined for more than 26 minutes because 26 minutes falls within an interval in the probability distribution.

14. **D**

If the two graphs are drawn on the same axis, because the standard deviation for both distributions is 5.4 cm and the total area below each curve equals 1, the graph corresponding to the males is congruent to the graph for the females. The graph of male heights would be shifted to the right, however, because the mean is greater for the males.

NR6. **81.5**

Begin by drawing the normal distribution and shade the area in which you are interested. Add these percentages together to find the percentage of people who waited between 150 and 180 minutes.

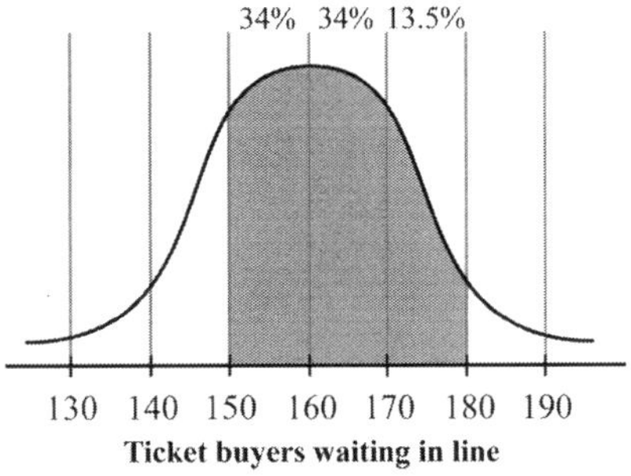

$34 + 34 + 13.5 = 81.5\ \%$

15. **C**

To use a normal distribution to approximate a binomial probability, there must be a sufficient number of trials, such that the following two conditions are met.

$np > 5$

$np = (1000)(0.05) = 50$

and

$n(1 - p) > 5$

$n(1 - p) = 1000(0.95) = 950$

Choice **C** is the only choice that satisfies these two conditions.

16. **A**

First, check that the binomial approximation is appropriate:

$$np = (400)(0.10) = 40 > 5$$
$$n(1 - p) = (400)(0.90) = 360 > 5$$

Based on the sample of 400 items, the mean number of defective items in the sample is $\mu = np$

$$= (400)(.10)$$
$$= 40$$

and the standard deviation is

$$\sigma = \sqrt{np(1 - p)}$$
$$= \sqrt{(400)(0.10)(1 - 0.10)}$$
$$= \sqrt{36}$$
$$= 6$$

NR7. **0.815**

First, check that the binomial approximation is appropriate:

$$np = (415)\left(\frac{170}{415}\right) = 170 > 5$$
$$n(1 - p) = (415)\left(\frac{415 - 170}{415}\right) = 245 > 5$$

Next, find the mean and standard deviation of a binomial distribution based on the data. Round each value to the nearest whole number:

$$\mu = np$$
$$= (415)\left(\frac{170}{415}\right)$$
$$= 170$$

and

$\sigma = \sqrt{np(1-p)}$

$= \sqrt{(415)\left(\frac{170}{415}\right)\left(1-\frac{170}{415}\right)} \approx 10$

This means that for every 415 Grade 12 students, the expected (mean) number of students who have jobs is 170 with a standard deviation of 10 students.

Once the mean and standard deviation are determined, a normal curve can be drawn and used to estimate the probability that between 150 and 180 students from a group of 415 will have jobs. Shade the region that you are interested in.

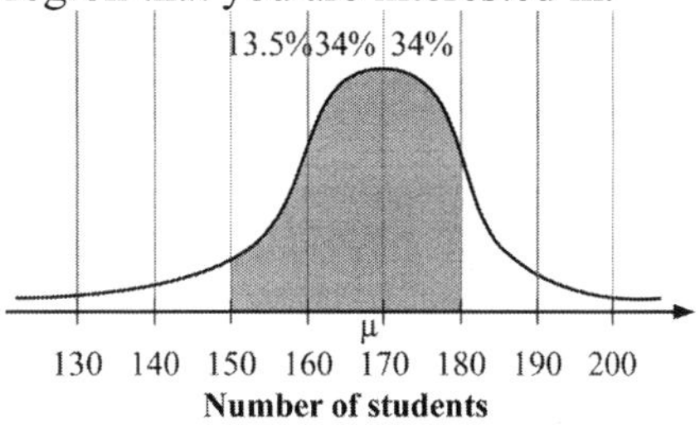

Change each of the percentages in the shaded region to probabilities and add them together.

The probability that between 150 and 180 students in a group of 415 students have jobs is 0.135 + 0.34 + 0.34 = 0.815.

17. **A**

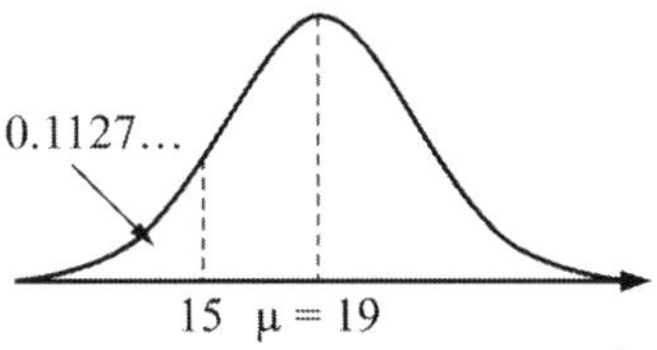

Since you cannot attend less than 0 movies, use the lower score to be 0. To be less than 15 movies, use the highest score to be 15. The mean is 19 and the standard deviation is 3.3. Using the TI graphing calculator:

normalcdf$(0,15,19,3.3) \approx 0.112\,733\,051$

To the nearest tenth of a percentage, the number of people who went to less than 15 movies was 11.3%.

18. **D**

For Statistics:

$z = \frac{x-\mu}{\sigma} = \frac{82-73}{12} = \frac{9}{12} = 0.75$

For Biology:

$z = \frac{x-\mu}{\sigma} = \frac{81-71}{13} = \frac{10}{13} \approx 0.77$

For Chemistry:

$z = \frac{x-\mu}{\sigma} = \frac{74-64}{16} = \frac{10}{16} \approx 0.63$

For Calculus:

$z = \frac{x-\mu}{\sigma} = \frac{79-68}{13} = \frac{11}{13} \approx 0.85$

In comparing results on the tests, it appears that Pat did best in Statistics because her mark was the highest in Statistics. However, these tests have different means and standard deviations, so you must look at standardizing the scores to compare them. The *z*-score shows where she ranked with respect to the other students who wrote each test. Since her *z*-score in Calculus is the highest, she performed best in Calculus relative to her peers.

NR8. **3.0**

Using a TI-83 calculator, the instruction normalcdf(105 000, 170 000, 90 000, 8 000) gives a result of .030396, so to the nearest tenth of a percentage, the value is 3.0%.

(**Note** that the upper bound 170 000 is ten standard deviations above the mean, but any number larger than this value could be used.)

OR1.

A probability distribution gives the probabilities of every possible outcome; if the probabilities of all outcomes are added, the sum must be 1.

OR2. a)

Shoe size (Outcome)	Number of students (Frequency of each outcome)	Probability of each shoe size
6	3	$\frac{3}{22} \approx 0.136$
7	5	$\frac{5}{22} \approx 0.227$
8	8	$\frac{8}{22} \approx 0.364$
9	4	$\frac{4}{22} \approx 0.182$
10	2	$\frac{2}{22} \approx 0.091$

b)

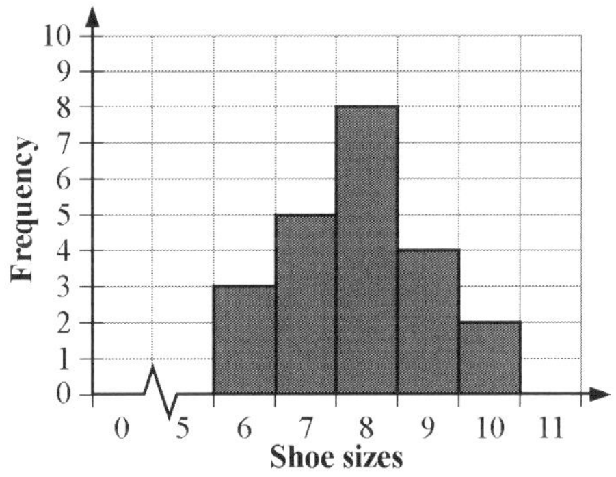

c)

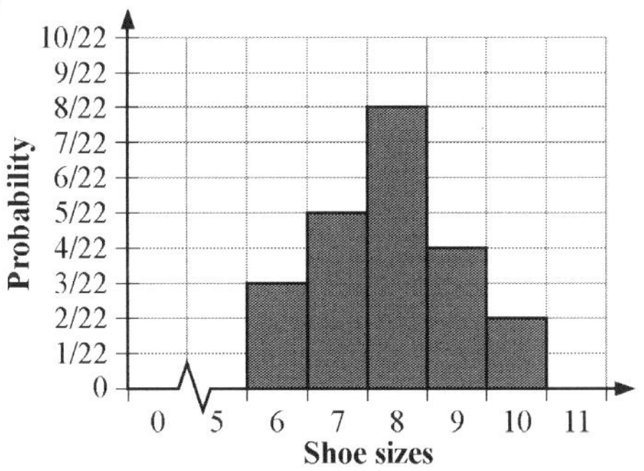

d) The histograms have the same shape. The only difference is the numbers on the vertical axis. For the frequency histogram, the vertical axis represents the frequency of each shoe size. In the probability histogram, the vertical axis represents the probability of each shoe size. One hundred percent of the data is represented in both histograms. Identify the variables and substitute them into the probability distribution formula.

OR3.

a) This is a binomial distribution because each of the 10 cups has a 20% chance of having a winning coupon. The trials are independent, with 2 outcomes, there is either a winning cup or not a winning cup.

b) The probability that you would win at most 2 coupons means you would win none, 1, or 2 coupons.

$$\begin{aligned} P(\text{at most } 2) &= P(0) + P(1) + P(2) \\ &= {}_{10}C_0 (0.2)^0 (0.8)^{10} + \\ &\quad {}_{10}C_1 (0.2)^1 (0.8)^9 + {}_{10}C_2 (0.2)^2 (0.8)^8 \\ &\approx 0.68 \end{aligned}$$

OR4.

The normal distribution can be used to approximate a binomial distribution if the number of trials, or the sample space, n, is large enough. The sample space is considered large enough when $np > 5$ and $n(1-p) > 5$, where n is the total number of trials in the experiment, p is the probability of the success, and $1-p$ is the probability of failure.

PROBABILITY DISTRIBUTIONS—UNIT TEST

1. Which of the following distributions is a valid probability distribution of a random variable?

A.

x	$P(x)$
0	0.5
1	0.25
2	0.25

B.

x	$P(x)$
0	0.3
1	0.2
2	0.2
3	0.2

C.

x	$P(x)$
0.1	0.15
0.2	0.55
0.3	0.6

D. Each of the distributions shown in **A**, **B**, and **C** is a valid probability distribution.

Use the following information to answer the next question.

An insurance company has analyzed its claims per policy on the loss of household contents. Each policy is based on no deductible; that is, when the claim is made, the policyholder does not have to pay any amount.

Annual Claim Amount ($)	**Probability**
0 (no claim)	0.95
1000	0.04
5000	0.002
10 000	0.007
25 000	0.001

2. What annual premium should the insurance company charge per policy if the company adds a 33% mark-up to the expected amount?

A. $47.85

B. $145.00

C. $192.85

D. $386.00

Numerical Response

1. On a particular hole in a golf tournament, seven golfers score 4, ten golfers score 5, four golfers score 6, and four golfers score 7. The average (weighted mean) score on this hole, correct to the nearest tenth, is ____________.

3. Which of the following statements is **not** correct?

A. In a probability histogram, the sum of the probabilities is 1.

B. In a probability histogram, the probability is represented by the height of each rectangle.

C. For a set of data, the frequency histogram and the probability histogram have the same shape.

D. In both a frequency histogram and a probability histogram, the outcomes are on the vertical axis.

Use the following information to answer the next question.

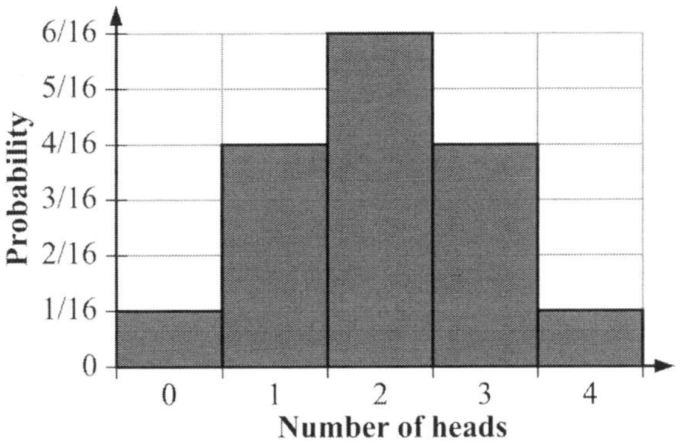

Numerical Response

2. The probability histogram that is shown represents the probability of the number of heads obtained when a single coin is flipped four times. From this histogram, the probability of flipping at most three heads when a coin is flipped four times, to the nearest hundredth, is ___________.

4. A certain soccer player has scored on 82% of his penalty kicks throughout his career. Based on this information, the probability that he will score on exactly 4 of his next 5 penalty kicks, correct to the nearest hundredth, is

A. 0.80

B. 0.66

C. 0.41

D. 0.08

5. Three toys are selected at random from a box of 9 toys, 3 of which are defective.
The probability, to the nearest hundredth, that of the 3 toys selected at least 2 are defective is

A. 0.08

B. 0.21

C. 0.23

D. 0.77

Numerical Response

3. A bag contains 2 red, 5 black, and 4 green marbles. Four marbles are drawn at random without replacement. The probability, to the nearest hundredth, that exactly 2 are green and none are red, is ___________.

6. Which of the following statements describes the difference between a hypergeometric distribution and a binomial distribution?

A. The probability of success changes for a binomial distribution whereas the probability of success remains constant from trial to trial for a hypergeometric distribution.

B. A binomial distribution has 2 possible outcomes for each trial whereas a hypergeometric distribution has more than 2 outcomes for each trial.

C. A binomial distribution involves independent trials and a hypergeometric distribution involves dependent trials.

D. The probabilities are greater for a hypergeometric distribution than for a binomial distribution.

Numerical Response

4. A round spinner is divided into five equally-sized sectors numbered 1 to 5. If the spinner is spun 10 times, the probability that it lands on the number 3 exactly 5 times, to the nearest hundredth, is ______________.

7. Patrick buys two of a total of 30 raffle tickets. There are 2 winning numbers. The probability that Patrick wins exactly one prize is

A. $\frac{56}{435}$ **B.** $\frac{28}{435}$

C. $\frac{2}{435}$ **D.** $\frac{1}{435}$

Numerical Response

5. The names of 15 students, 6 girls and 9 boys, are put in a bag. Four names are chosen at random to receive a free movie pass. The probability that at least one girl's name is chosen, to the nearest hundredth is __________.

8. Which of the following tables of values represents a probability distribution with a continuous random variable?

A.

Heights of police officers (cm)	Frequency
175–180	10
180–185	20
185–190	16

B.

Number of Heads	Frequency
0	2
1	3
2	5
3	2

C.

Age	Number of Accidents
20–25	700
25–30	600
30–35	630
35–40	425

D.

Prize Amount	Number of Prizes
1 000 000	1
50 000	5
1000	10
50	50

Numerical Response

6. How many of the following characteristics apply to a continuous random variable? ___

- A continuous random variable has a smooth curve for its graph.
- Continuous random variables arise from counting principles.
- Continuous random variables arise from the measurement of a quantity.
- Continuous random variables can take real number values.

9. Coins are minted and put into circulation. Over time, the wear and tear on the coins causes them to lose mass and become thinner. After the coins have been in circulation for many years, the standard deviation of the mass of these coins

A. will increase

B. will decrease

C. will remain the same

D. cannot be determined

An airline gives out small bags of peanuts to its travellers. The bags do **not** always contain the same number of peanuts. The following table represents a sample of 31 bags showing the number of peanuts per bag.

Number of Peanuts	28	29	30	31	32	33
Frequency	2	5	10	9	4	1

10. Expressed to the nearest tenth, the mean number of peanuts and the standard deviation for this sample, respectively, are

A. 30.5 and 1.85

B. 30.5 and 1.71

C. 30.4 and 1.20

D. 30.4 and 1.18

11. Which of the following challenges is associated with determining a continuous frequency distribution?

A. The uncertainties in measured values of the variable.

B. The frequencies of a discrete-valued variable.

C. Determining the range of the values of the variable to a certain accuracy.

D. A continuous frequency distribution cannot be represented by a mathematical model

12. How can the width of the interval used in a histogram be used to misrepresent the data?

A. If the interval is too narrow, the histogram may have too many bars and therefore will not effectively summarize the distribution.

B. If the intervals are not of equal width or do not include all values of the data to be summarized, the data will be misrepresented.

C. If an interval width has a frequency of 0, no bar will appear and it will not look like a histogram.

D. All of the above.

Use the following information to answer the next question.

The members of a particular fitness club were surveyed, and the number of minutes they spent at the gym on a particular day was recorded. The histogram below shows the probability that a particular member chosen would exercise for certain specified amounts of time.

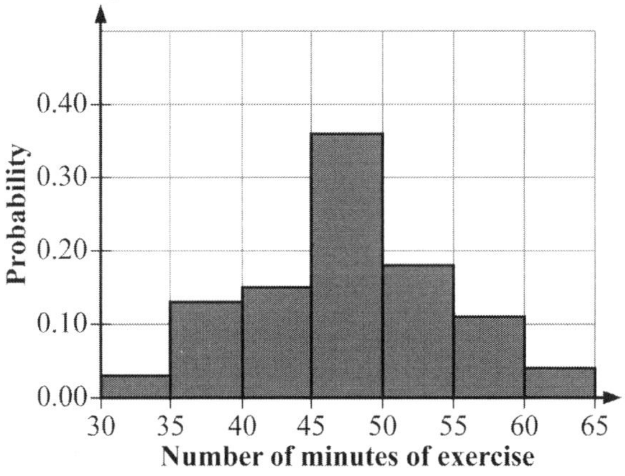

13. The probability that a member chosen at random on any given day would exercise between 45 minutes and 55 minutes is

A. 0.36

B. 0.18

C. 0.54

D. The probability cannot be determined from the given distribution

14. The manufacturers of "Dryclean" clothes dryers gathered information on how soon after purchase the dryers require their first repair. The data is normally distributed with a mean of 7.5 years and a standard deviation of 1.5 years. If 35 000 "Dryclean" dryers were sold in one year, then the number of those "Dryclean" dryers expected to require repairs in the first 6 years would be

A. 5600

B. 11 900

C. 17 500

D. 29 400

Numerical Response

7. The masses of apples grown on a farm in the Okanagan Valley are normally distributed with a mean of 170 g and a standard deviation of 4.0 g. Determine, to the nearest whole number, the upper bound of the interval symmetrical about the mean that would contain the masses of 95% of the apples. ______

15. Statistics show that 8% of the apples in a store are damaged. The apples are packed in boxes of 150 and priced for sale. The mean and the standard deviation of the number of apples per box that are not damaged are, respectively,

A. 12, 3.32

B. 12, 11.04

C. 138, 3.32

D. 138, 11.04

16. A school has enrolled the same number of boys and girls. Two hundred students are selected at random to participate in a survey. Using a normal approximation to the binomial distribution, the probability that at least 93 girls are selected is

A. 0.16

B. 0.34

C. 0.50

D. 0.84

17. On the standard normal distribution, the probability that a z-score lies between 0.3 and 1.2 is about

A. 0.1151

B. 0.2670

C. 0.3821

D. 0.4713

Open Response

OR1. The probability that a college student will graduate is 0.45. You and four of your friends are college students.

a) Complete the probability distribution table below, with probabilities to the nearest thousandth.

Number who graduate	Probability this number graduate
0	
1	
2	
3	
4	
5	

b) Use the completed table to determine the probability, to the nearest thousandth, that 2 or more of you will graduate.

c) Use the completed table to determine the probability, to the nearest thousandth, that all of you or none of you will graduate.

Open Response

OR2. A lawnmower manufacturer gathers information on how soon after purchase the mowers required their first repair. The data is normally distributed with a mean of 7.5 years and a standard deviation of 2 years. If 35 000 of his mowers are sold in one year, and 3703 of the mowers required repairs under warranty, determine the length of the warranty, to the nearest year.

ANSWERS AND SOLUTIONS—UNIT TEST

1. A	OR1. See solution	NR5. 0.91	12. D	17. B
2. C	5. C	8. A	13. C	OR2. See solution
NR1. 5.2	NR3. 0.18	NR6. 3	14. A	
3. D	6. C	9. A	NR7. 178	
NR2. 0.94	NR4. 0.03	10. D	15. C	
4. C	7. A	11. A	16. D	

1. **A**

In a probability distribution of a random variable, the sum of the probabilities must have a sum of 1. This is only true for the distribution shown in A.

2. **C**

The expected claim, E, for this policy is the sum of the products of the claim amount and probability for all possible claims.

$$\begin{aligned} E &= 0\times 0.95 + 1000\times 0.04 + 5000\times 0.002 + \\ &\quad 10\ 000\times 0.007 + 25\ 000\times 0.001 \\ &= 0+40+10+70+25 \\ &= 145 \end{aligned}$$

The company expects to pay out $145. The premium, with a 33% mark-up added to the expected amount, is

$$\begin{aligned} E+(0.33)E &= 145+(0.33)145 \\ &= 192.85 \end{aligned}$$

The company should charge an annual premium of $192.85 per policy.

NR1. **5.2**

Score, x	Probability, $P(x)$
4	$\frac{7}{25}$
5	$\frac{10}{25}$
6	$\frac{4}{25}$
7	$\frac{4}{25}$

Observe that the sum of the probabilities is equal to 1, but that the probabilities are not equal.

This distribution is not uniform.

$$\begin{aligned} E(X) &= 4\left(\frac{7}{25}\right)+5\left(\frac{10}{25}\right)+6\left(\frac{4}{25}\right)+7\left(\frac{4}{25}\right) \\ &= 5.2 \end{aligned}$$

Thus, the average score on the hole is 5.2.

3. **D**

In both a frequency histogram and a probability histogram, the outcomes are listed on the horizontal axis.

NR2 **0.94**

There are two possible approaches:

Add the probabilities of 0, 1, 2, or 3 heads.

$$\frac{1}{16}+\frac{4}{16}+\frac{6}{16}+\frac{4}{16}=\frac{15}{16}\approx 0.94$$

Or, use complementary events.

$$\begin{aligned} P(\text{at least 3 heads}) &= 1-P(\text{no heads}) \\ &= 1-\frac{1}{16}=\frac{15}{16}\approx 0.94 \end{aligned}$$

4. **C**

$$\begin{aligned} P(4) &= {}_5C_4(0.82)^4(0.18)^1 \\ &\approx 0.4069 \\ &\approx 0.41 \end{aligned}$$

5. **C**

At least 2 are defective means that 2 are defective and 1 is not defective or all 3 are defective.

P(2 are defective and 1 is not defective)

$$=\frac{{}_3C_2 \times {}_6C_1}{{}_9C_3}$$

P(3 are defective)

$$=\frac{{}_3C_3 \times {}_6C_0}{{}_9C_3}$$

Thus, the probability that at least 2 are defective is

$$\frac{{}_3C_2 \times {}_6C_1}{{}_9C_3}+\frac{{}_3C_3 \times {}_6C_0}{{}_9C_3} \approx 0.23$$

NR3. **0.18**

$$P(\text{2 are green and none are red}) = \frac{{}_4C_2 \times {}_5C_2}{{}_{11}C_4}$$

$$\approx 0.1818 \approx 0.18$$

6. **C**

In a binomial distribution, the probability of success stays constant from trial to trial and therefore the trials are independent. In a hypergeometric distribution, the probability of success changes from trial to trial and therefore the trials are dependent. The statements in the other choices are not true.

NR4 **0.03**

Note that a decision must be made as to which type of distribution is used.

A binomial distribution is required here because the trials are independent.

P(landing on 3 exactly 5 times)

$$= {}_{10}C_5(0.2)^5(0.8)^5$$

$$\approx 0.03$$

7. **A**

This problem involves hypergeometric probability because the result from drawing the first ticket affects the probability for the second ticket.

Probability of exactly one prize =

$$\frac{{}_2C_1 \times {}_{28}C_1}{{}_{30}C_2} = \frac{2 \times 28}{435} = \frac{56}{435}$$

NR5. **0.91**

The probability that at least one girl's name is drawn is equal to 1 – (Probability that no girl's name is drawn).

$P(\text{at least one girl}) = 1 - P(\text{no girls})$

$$= 1 - \frac{{}_6C_0 \times {}_9C_4}{{}_{15}C_4}$$

$$\approx 0.91$$

8. **A**

A continuous random variable results from the measurement of a quantity. And, of the given tables, the heights of police officers represent the only measured data.

NR6. **3**

Since continuous random variables may have any real number value arising from measurement, they appear graphically as a smooth curve. Discrete random variable arise from counting principles.

9. **A**

When the coins are new, the mass of the coins will be closely clustered around the mean mass. As time passes, some coins will lose more mass than others because they are handled more. The mass of the coins becomes more dispersed causing the standard deviation to increase.

10. **D**

Calculating the mean and the standard deviation for grouped data is done on a TI-83 calculator as follows:
Enter the number of peanuts in L_1 and the frequency in L_2. Input 1-Var Stats L_1, L_2. The calculator will show statistical information that includes the mean and standard deviation. For this course, use the standard deviation for population data. So, the mean is 30.354 8…, or approximately 30.4, and the standard deviation for a population, σx, is 1.179 07…, or approximately 1.18.

11. A

Because the variable is continuous, it is always necessary to round the values to a certain degree of accuracy. This can influence the distribution and affect the mathematical model that is used to represent it. Choice **B** is incorrect because the variable is not discrete-valued (it is continuous). Choice **C** is generally not a problem, because a maximum and minimum value are recorded. Choice **D** is incorrect because continuous frequency distributions are often represented by mathematical models.

12. **D**

Each of the given statements must be considered when determining the appropriate width for the intervals used for a histogram.

13. C

The probability for a particular time interval is equal to the sum of the heights of the bars in this interval. The probability that the chosen person exercises between 45 and 55 minutes is 0.36 + 0.18 = 0.54.

14. **A**

Begin by drawing a normal distribution showing the mean and spread about the mean as shown.

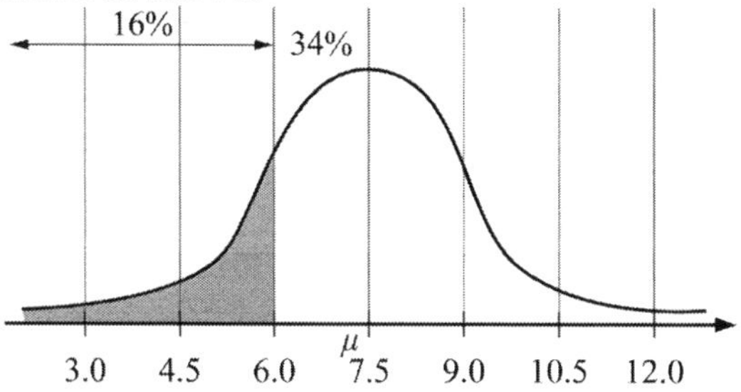

You are interested in the percentage of the dryers sold that need repair within the first 6 years. Since 50% of the data is below the mean and 34% of the data are between 6.0 years and the mean,
50% – 34% = 16% of the dryers need repair within the first 6 years.

Since 35 000 dryers are sold, 16% of 35 000 = 0.16 × 35 000 = 5600 dryers will need repair within the first 6 years.

NR7. **178**

One of the characteristics of a normal distribution is that 95% of the data falls within 2 standard deviations of the mean. To determine the upper bound of this interval, add the mean and 2 standard deviations (170 + 2 × 4.0 = 178 g).

15. **C**

First check that the binomial approximation is appropriate:

$np = (150)(0.08) = 12 > 5$

$n(1-p) = (150)(0.92) = 138 > 5$

Since 8% of the apples are damaged, 92% of the apples are not damaged.
The mean and standard deviation of the number of apples that are not damaged can be calculated using $n = 150$ and $p = 0.92$:

$$\begin{aligned}\mu &= np\\ &= (150)(0.92)\\ &= 138\end{aligned}$$

and

$$\begin{aligned}\sigma &= \sqrt{np(1-p)}\\ &= \sqrt{(150)(0.92)(1-0.92)}\\ &\approx 3.32\end{aligned}$$

16. **D**

Determine the mean and standard deviation for the data and the normal distribution curve to estimate the probability that at least 93 girls are selected where $n = 200$ and $p = 0.5$:

$$\begin{aligned}\mu &= np\\ &= (200)(0.5)\\ &= 100\end{aligned}$$

and

$$\begin{aligned}\sigma &= \sqrt{np(1-p)}\\ &= \sqrt{(200)(0.5)(1-0.5)}\\ &\approx 7\end{aligned}$$

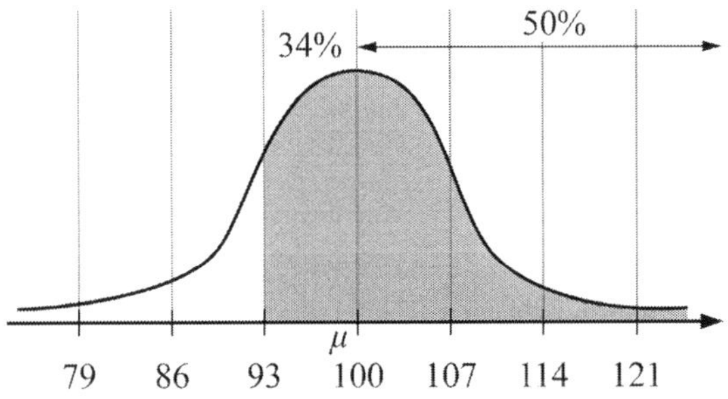

Since at least 93 girls would be selected 84% of the time, the probability that at least 93 girls are selected for the survey is 0.84.

17. **B**

Input normalcdf(0.3,1.2) on a TI-83 calculator. This will give a value of $0.267\,0189\,104 \approx 0.2670$.

Open Response

OR1. **a)**

Number who graduate	Probability this number graduate
0	$P(0) = {}_5C_0(0.45)^0(0.55)^5 \approx 0.050$
1	$P(1) = {}_5C_1(0.45)^1(0.55)^4 \approx 0.206$
2	$P(2) = {}_5C_2(0.45)^2(0.55)^3 \approx 0.337$
3	$P(3) = {}_5C_3(0.45)^3(0.55)^2 \approx 0.276$
4	$P(4) = {}_5C_4(0.45)^4(0.55)^1 \approx 0.113$
5	$P(5) = {}_5C_5(0.45)^5(0.55)^0 \approx 0.018$

b) $$\begin{aligned}P(2\text{ or more}) &= P(2)+P(3)+P(4)+P(5)\\ &\approx 0.337+0.276+0.113+0.018\\ &\approx 0.744\end{aligned}$$

c) $$\begin{aligned}P(\text{all or none}) &= P(5)+P(0)\\ &\approx 0.018+0.050\\ &\approx 0.068\end{aligned}$$

OR2.

Calculate the percentage of the mowers that required repairs:

$$\frac{3703}{35\ 000} \times 100 = 0.1058$$

Use this percentage to find the z-score corresponding to an area of 0.1058 in the tables.
The corresponding z-score is -1.25.
Use the z-score formula to solve for the warranty.

$$z = \frac{x - \mu}{\sigma}$$

$$-1.25 = \frac{x - 7.5}{2}$$

$$-1.25(2) = x - 7.5$$

$$-2.5 = x - 7.5$$

$$x = 7.5 - 2.5 = 5.0$$

The warranty on the lawnmowers was for 5 years.

Organization of Data for Analysis

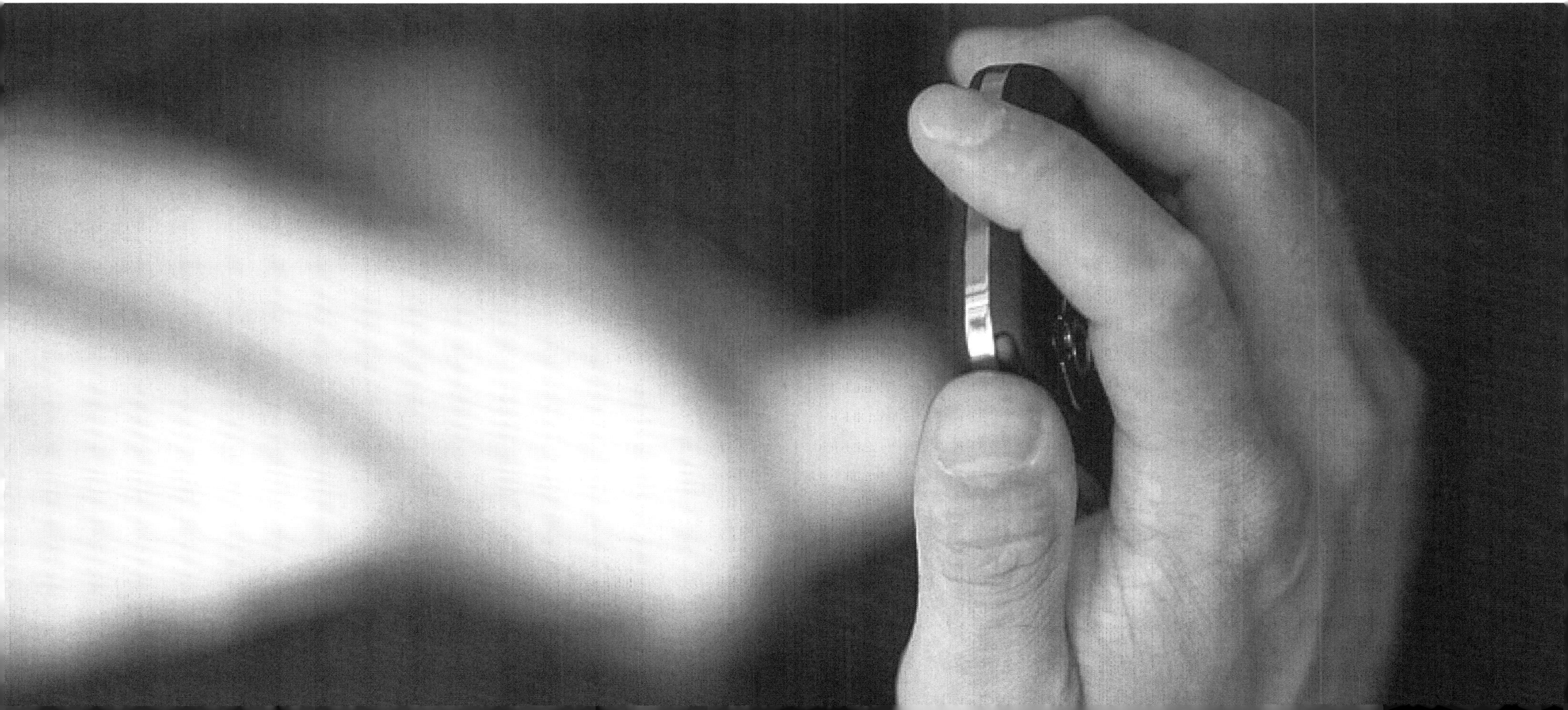

ORGANIZATION OF DATA FOR ANALYSIS

Table of Correlations		
Specific Expectation	**Practice Questions**	**Unit Test Questions**
By the end of this course, students will:		
DA1.1 recognize and describe the role of data in statistical studies, describe examples of applications of statistical studies, and recognize that conclusions drawn from statistical studies of the same relationship may differ	1, OR1	1, 2
DA1.2 recognize and explain reasons why variability is inherent in data, and distinguish between situations that involve one variable and situations that involve more than one variable	2, 3, 4, OR2	3
DA1.3 distinguish different types of statistical data (i.e., discrete from continuous, qualitative from quantitative, categorical from numerical, nominal from ordinal, primary from secondary, experimental from observational, microdata from aggregate data) and give examples	5, OR3	OR1
DA2.1 determine and describe principles of primary data collection and criteria that should be considered in order to collect reliable primary data	6, OR4, OR5	4, OR2
DA2.2 explain the distinction between the terms population and sample, describe the characteristics of a good sample, explain why sampling is necessary, and describe and compare some sampling techniques	7, 8, OR6	5, OR3
DA2.3 describe how the use of random samples with a bias or the use of non-random samples can affect the results of a study	9, 10, OR7	6
DA2.4 describe characteristics of an effective survey, and design questionnaires or experiments for gathering data	11, 12	7, OR4
DA2.5 collect data from primary sources, through experimentation, or from secondary sources, and organize data with one or more attributes to answer a question or solve a problem	13, 14, OR8	8, OR5

ORGANIZATION OF DATA FOR ANALYSIS

DA1.1 recognize and describe the role of data in statistical studies, describe examples of applications of statistical studies, and recognize that conclusions drawn from statistical studies of the same relationship may differ

STATISTICAL STUDIES

Statistics affect almost every aspect of our lives. From choosing a car to family planning, they enter virtually every field of study and occupation. People in areas like business administration, economics, medicine, psychology, public health, and sports all use statistics to make decisions.

Normally statistics are classified as descriptive or inferential. Descriptive statistics uses graphs, tables, charts, and averages, to help display large amounts of data in compact, understandable forms. Inferential statistics use the information that is gathered from a sample to make statements concerning the population from which the sample was selected. Organizations usually use inferential statistics when they are conducting what is known as a statistical study.

Repeated experiments and recorded experiences yield varying results. Although there is a large amount of variation in the data, once statistical data is organized, a recognizable pattern often emerges. The interpretations of the pattern however, may still have a great variance.

Related Questions: 1, OR1

DA1.2 recognize and explain reasons why variability is inherent in data, and distinguish between situations that involve one variable and situations that involve more than one variable

VARIABILITY, ONE-VARIABLE AND TWO-VARIABLE SITUATIONS

Variability in data may arise from:

- limited accuracy in measurement
- variations in the conditions of an experiment
- differences in samples in a survey

One-variable statistics are applied when the distribution of a single factor is needed.

Some examples of situations that involve one variable are:

- a set of class marks
- the life spans of mass-produced items, such as batteries or light bulbs
- the heights of players on a basketball team
- the sum that results each time two standard number cubes are rolled
- the daily temperatures in July for a city in Ontario

Two-variable statistics involve two variables and are applied when one wants to determine the relationship or the correlation between the variables.

In situations that involve more than one variable, relationships between variables can be determined, and predictions can be developed. Some examples of situations that involve more than one variable are:

- the number of hours students study and their marks on a subsequent exam
- the speed by which drivers exceed the speed limit and the amount they are charged on the resulting traffic fines
- income and level of education
- the growth of a bacterial culture over time
- the number of scholarships a student receives and the number of job offers a student receives upon graduation

Related Questions: 2, 3, 4, OR2

DA1.3 distinguish between different types of statistical data and give examples.

TYPES OF STATISTICAL DATA

A summary of the different types of data and corresponding examples are listed below. Statistical data may be described using more than one of the following classifications.

Discrete Data	Continuous Data
Discrete data is data derived from an enumeration or count. It is data that can be described using whole numbers.	Continuous data is data resulting from the measurement of a quantity. It is data that is measurable with real numbers.
Examples: the number of people attending a movie, the number of vehicles that go through an intersection, the number of crimes reported to the police	**Examples:** the mass, age, cholesterol level, or height of students in your class; the time it takes to complete a task; the distance that a football can be kicked

Qualitative Data	Quantitative Data
Qualitative data is data that cannot be measured numerically. It is often descriptive or narrative data. It is usually collected through focus groups or questionnaires with open-ended questions.	Quantitative data is data that can be measured numerically.
Examples: eye colour, hair colour, gender, opinions, feelings	**Examples:** height, weight, distance, number of words on a page
Categorical Data	**Numerical Data**
Categorical data is data that can be sorted or divided by type rather than by numerical values.	Numerical data is data that can be represented by numbers.
Examples: hair colour (red, blond, brown, black); smoking status (non-smoker or smoker); marital status (single, married, divorced, widowed).	**Examples:** number of students late for class, time to complete a homework assignment, ages of students.
Nominal Data	**Ordinal Data**
Nominal data is categorical data, however, the categories are assigned labels such as numbers. The order of the categories is arbitrary.	Ordinal data is categorical data, however the categories are assigned a number are there is a logical ordering to the categories.
Examples: Martial status, 1 = single, 2 = married, 3 = divorced, 4 = widowed, 5 = other, The order of the categories does not affect the recorded data	**Examples:** On many surveys, a scale is used for your responses, 1 = Strongly agree, 2 = Agree, 3 = Neutral, 4 = Disagree, 5 = Strongly disagree

Primary Data	Secondary Data
Primary data is data collected by the researcher. The data that you collect is firsthand information.	Secondary data is data collected from other sources.
Examples: A survey of the number of students in your class, a tally of the number of cows in a corral.	**Examples:** Using the school database or databases that are available on the internet.
Experimental Data	**Observational Data**
Experimental data is data produced by an experimental design. It could be quantitative or qualitative data, depending on the different investigations.	Observational data is data resulting from noting or reporting something about the population being studied. The observed characteristic could be qualitative or quantitative. It is often subjective.
Examples: clinical research, testing of new automobile fuels.	**Examples:** drawing inferences about the effect of a treatment on subjects, recording behaviour of animals at various times of the year.

Micro Data	Aggregate Data
Micro data sets include data of all sorts on individual objects. When individual people are surveyed, codes, which are usually numbers, are used to represent the responses to every question the person is asked. Each of these records has an identifier that allows a researcher to retrieve a particular record or set of records which may contain tens of thousands of records.	Aggregate data is summary-level data. It is the result of applying statistical analyses to micro-level data sets. Aggregate data is often used to reveal trends over specific time periods or information about selected characteristics of the entire population surveyed.
Examples: Canadian Census, individual health records.	**Examples:** The number of Canadian males in the age group from 25 – 30 can be determined by using the information collected in the Canadian Census. The number of occurrences of a particular disease can be found by examining health records.

Related Questions: 5, OR3

DA2.1 determine and describe principles of primary data collection and criteria that should be considered in order to collect reliable primary data

PRIMARY DATA

Data collection is termed primary when the researcher (the person doing the study) collects the data directly. The researcher has control of how the data is collected. Experimental studies must include the principles of randomization, replication, and control. Sample surveys must be administered randomly within the population they represent.

Randomization of the data involves collection techniques that ensure all members of the population are equally likely to be selected for the sample. Such techniques reduce the likelihood that the results will be inappropriately weighted in favour of one particular group within the population.

Sample statistics from a single sample may differ radically from that of the population. Statisticians try to address this problem by repeated sampling.

In order to reduce the effect of extraneous or external variables, researchers will often compare an experimental group with a control group. These two groups should be as similar as possible so that the extraneous variables will have approximately the same affect on both groups. The researcher will then vary the independent variable, or what they are testing, for the experimental group but not for the control group. Any difference in the dependent variables for the two groups can then be attributed to the changes in the independent variable.

There are a number of factors that affect the reliability of primary data, including: appropriateness of survey questions, potential sources of bias, and sample size.

Related Questions: 6, OR4, OR5

DA2.2 explain the distinction between the terms population and sample, describe the characteristics of a good sample, explain why sampling is necessary, and describe and compare some sampling techniques

POPULATION VS. SAMPLE

Often a company, organization, or political party wants to find out how the entire population feels about a particular idea. It is important to note that a population does not necessarily refer to a group of people but is only the subject of investigation. Often, collecting information from the entire population is impossible, so a sample, or portion of the population, is chosen to represent the population. The information gathered from the sample is utilized to make conclusions about the population from which the sample was selected.

Sampling is necessary for the following reasons:

- Sometimes the population is so large that it is difficult or impossible to collect data on every member of the population.
- It is usually less expensive to collect data from a sample rather than the entire population.
- To collect data from the entire population would take a lengthy period of time.
- In experiments to determine expected lifetimes of products, the experiment must run until the product fails. To perform this experiment on the entire population would obliterate the supply.

The sample that is to represent the population must be chosen carefully.

- It must truly be representative of the population from which it was drawn.
- The sampling process must be purely random in that all members of the population share an equal chance of being selected.
- The sample must be large enough to ensure that the sample data does not differ significantly from the corresponding population data.

When selecting a sample from the population you must take great care that your sample is valid and reliable. Reliability refers to consistency, which means obtaining the same results under the same conditions. Validity tells you whether the question really measures what it is supposed to measure.

Various sampling techniques may be used:

1. Simple Random Sampling – this method requires that each member of the population has an equally likely chance of being represented.
2. Systematic Sampling – this method is used when testing a fixed percentage of the population. The members of a population are placed in a list and every n^{th} member is included in the sample.
3. Stratified Random Sampling – the population is divided into groups called strata (e.g., Age groups, gender, grade, etc). A simple random sample is then selected from each stratum. The size of the sample for each stratum is proportional to the stratum's size.
4. Convenience Sampling – A sample is selected simply because it is easily accessible. This technique is not as random as the other techniques but can still generate helpful information.
5. Voluntary Response Sampling – any member of the population is invited to participate in a survey.

Example

Identify the sampling method for each situation.

a) Every 10th person on a list of the population is part of the sample.

b) 50 randomly selected students from each grade in your school are part of the sample.

c) A survey is sent in the mail in your city and participants mail in their opinions.

d) All the guests at a party are surveyed.

Solution

a) This is a systematic method of sampling. The population has been put on a list then the sample is chosen in a systematic way, i.e., every 10th person on the list.

b) This is a stratified method of sampling. The population has been put into strata, in this case grades, and a simple random sample of each stratum is chosen.

c) This is a voluntary sample. The sample will consist of the people who chose to respond to the survey.

d) This is a convenience sample. The information gathered about the population is based on the results of the people at the party.

Related Questions: 7, 8, OR6

DA2.3 describe how the use of random samples with a bias or the use of non-random samples can affect the results of a study

SAMPLING BIAS

The results of a study can be accurate only if the method used for choosing the sample and collecting the data is free from bias. Statistical bias is any factor that favours a certain outcome or response and therefore skews the results of the study.

Sampling bias occurs when the sample does **not** reflect the characteristics of the population.

Example

Identify the bias in the given survey and suggest how it could be avoided.

Traffic volume will be estimated by counting the number of cars travelling through an intersection during the researcher's lunch hour.

Solution

Since the volume of traffic at lunch hour is usually higher than at other times of the day, it is not representative of the volume of traffic over the whole day. A poor choice of sampling technique makes the results of the survey invalid. To avoid the sampling bias, the volume of traffic through the intersection should be checked at various times during the day.

Non-response bias occurs when particular groups are under-represented in a survey because they choose not to participate. Non-response bias is a form of sampling bias.

Example

Identify the bias in the given survey and suggest how it could be avoided.

Tony hands out survey forms to his classmates to be returned to him next week.

Solution

The method by which the survey forms are collected could lead to non-response bias. It is highly likely that some classmates would not return the forms. This non-response would mean that the sample may not be representative of the entire class. To avoid non-response bias, you must ensure that the sampling process is truly random. Rather than having the class return the survey forms next week, James could give more time to ensure he gets them all.

Measurement bias occurs when a data collection process affects the variable it is measuring.

Example

Identify the bias in the given survey and suggest how it could be avoided.

A highway engineer suggests that an economical way to survey traffic speeds on a particular stretch of highway would be to have the police officers who patrol that area record the speed of the traffic around them every half hour.

Solution

Most drivers who are speeding tend to slow down when they see police car. A survey by police officers would underestimate the average speed. In this case, the data collection method would decrease the values of the variable being measured, so there is measurement bias. A survey using unmarked cars or hidden speed sensors would give a more accurate result.

Response bias occurs when there are factors in the sampling method that influence the results.

Example

Identify the bias in the given survey and suggest how it could be avoided.

You ask people about their recycling habits on behalf of the Green Team.

Solution

Identifying the person or company for whom the survey is being conducted may lead to biased responses. To obtain honest responses, it is usually not a good idea to identify the researcher or researching organization.

Related Questions: 9, 10, OR7

DA2.4 describe characteristics of an effective survey and design questionnaires or experiments for gathering data

SURVEYS AND QUESTIONNAIRES

Any conclusion based on data should be made from the analysis of the results of a survey. A survey must be carefully planned and designed. A well-designed survey involves these steps:

- Identify the population
- Select an unbiased sample
- Prepare the survey question or item
- Collect the data
- Calculate the results
- Make an inference about the population

Two factors are paramount for an effective survey. The first is the selection of the sample; the second is the wording of the question.

When selecting a sample, you must consider

- ethics
- privacy
- honest responses
- possible sources of bias, including cultural bias

Good questions are

- simple
- relevant
- specific
- readable

Good questions avoid

- jargon
- abbreviations
- leading respondents
- insensitivity

Related Questions: 11, 12

DA2.5 collect data from primary sources, through experimentation, or from secondary sources, and organize data with one or more attributes to answer a question or solve a problem

Collecting and Organizing Data

Data can be collected from primary sources, and experimentation. Data from secondary sources can be collected by using:

- the Internet to access reliable data from a well-organized database such as E-STAT or
- print sources such as newspapers and magazines.

Data then needs to be organized with one or more attributes. This can be done using tables and/or graph using statistical software or spreadsheets.

After analyzing the organized data, you should be able to make predictions or inferences about the population.

Related Questions: 13, 14, OR8

PRACTICE QUESTIONS—ORGANIZATION OF DATA FOR ANALYSIS

1. Which of the following groups of data would **best** be interpreted by descriptive statistics, as opposed to inferential statistics?
   A. The number of goals each NHL team scored last season.
   B. An insurance company's record of the number of auto accidents involving their drivers over the age of 70 for the previous 5 years.
   C. Data collected from a sample by a food manufacturer on the average shelf life of one of their products.
   D. Data collected from a sample by a drug company on the side effects of one of their cold remedies.

2. Which of the following situations involves more than one variable?
   A. The life span of a rare breed of cat
   B. The number of houses sold per month by a real-estate agent
   C. The ages of the players on the Calgary Flames hockey team
   D. The amount of alcohol consumption and the incidence of automobile accidents

3. Which of the following factors does **not** cause variability in data?
   A. Sample size
   B. Population size
   C. Varying conditions
   D. Accuracy of measurement

4. To determine the average height of students attending a high school, five random samples of equal size were selected from the students. The mean and median height of the students in each of the five samples was calculated. Which of the following statements **most** likely describes the results?
   A. The mean and median vary from sample to sample.
   B. The mean and median are the same for each sample.
   C. The mean for all the samples may vary, but the median is the same.
   D. The mean and median are the same as those of the entire population.

5. Data was collected on the seating capacity of different makes of vehicles. The data collected can be identified as
   A. Qualitative and continuous
   B. Qualitative and discrete
   C. Quantitative and continuous
   D. Quantitative and discrete

6. Which of the following characteristics is **not** a consideration of primary data collection for experimental studies?
   A. Randomization
   B. Central tendency
   C. Replication
   D. Control

7. A survey is conducted among high school basketball players in the city. The basketball players at Survey High are asked to fill out a questionnaire. The population and sample, respectively, are

A. all high school students in the city, all students at Survey High

B. all high school students in the city, basketball players at Survey High

C. all high school basketball players in the city, basketball players at Survey High

D. all students at Survey High, all basketball players at Survey High

8. You need a sample of 20 students, so you go to the school cafeteria and ask every 5th person in line. What kind of sampling is this?

A. Simple random sampling

B. Stratified random sampling

C. Systematic sampling

D. Convenience sampling

9. When a phone questionnaire is conducted, most people with call display will **not** answer their phone. What kind of bias does this represent?

A. sample bias

B. non-response bias

C. response bias

D. measurement bias

10. In collecting data for a project by using a survey, truth is your goal. To avoid response bias

A. your sample must reflect the characteristics of the population

B. your sampling technique must ensure that all people in the population have an equal chance of being selected

C. your survey question must be worded carefully so as not to influence the response

D. you must ensure that particular groups are not under-represented in a survey because they chose not to participate.

11. Which of the following examples, meets the requirements of a good survey question?

A. Do you think that the large amounts of homework given by instructors should be reduced?

B. Given the number of injuries in a professional hockey league because of the brutal nature of some of its players, do you think that players should be fined for fighting?

C. Do you agree that all corporations should pay higher taxes?

D. What are reasons that forestry companies should not clear cut?

Use the following information to answer the next question.

Brianna and Lee are doing a survey to find the top five favourite television programs among Manitoba teenagers. To start, they compile a list of the most popular TV programs. Next, they plan to survey everyone in the lunch room of their junior high school during the noon hour. They will ask each student to select their five favourite television programs from the given list. They will repeat their survey every day for a week to make sure they include the students that have lunch hour commitments.

12. The reason their survey will **not** be effective is that

A. the population was not identified

B. surveying students at one school may not reflect the opinion of the population

C. the survey question is not simple or relevant

D. they may not nave included an equal number of boys and girls

Use the following information to answer the next question.

A library catalogue is a database. In the past, library databases were accessed through a card catalogue. Most libraries are now computerized, with books listed by title, author, publisher, subject, a Dewey Decimal or Library of Congress catalogue number, and an international standard book number (ISBN). Records can be sorted and searched using the information from any of the fields.

13. Which of the following statements about library catalogues is **not** correct?

A. These catalogues are examples of well-organized databases because they are easy to access using keywords and searches in multiple fields, many of which are cross referenced

B. School libraries are often linked to other libraries.

C. A database of books, newspapers, magazines, and television and radio transcripts can be accessed online through the database Electric Library Canada.

D. All of the given statements are correct.

Use the following information to answer the next question.

The table below shows the average hourly earning ($/hour) for employees in 11 countries.

Country	2003	2004	2005	2005	2007
A	11.03	11.52	11.90	12.34	12.92
B	10.00	10.72	11.32	11.90	12.62
C	7.56	8.33	8.92	8.92	9.62
D	9.51	10.11	10.59	10.88	11.40
E	9.63	10.02	10.49	10.97	11.41
F	10.00	10.57	10.97	11.26	11.87
G	11.94	12.53	12.56	12.84	13.28
H	9.26	9.96	10.43	10.80	11.33
I	9.55	10.16	10.82	11.41	12.11
J	11.63	12.28	13.11	13.98	14.90
K	11.09	11.52	11.80	12.46	13.02

14. Which of the following conclusions is **not** correct based on this table?

A. The hourly earnings have increased in all countries from 2003 to 2007.

B. Country G's average hourly earnings were consistently above Country A's average hourly rate.

C. The average hourly rate Country J was the highest in each year from 2003 to 2007.

D. Country C had the lowest hourly rate from 2003 through 2007 when compared to the other countries.

Open Response

OR1. List 3 disciplines that use statistical studies extensively in decision-making.

-
-
-

OR2. Give two reasons that variability in data occurs.

OR3. Describe the difference between nominal and ordinal data. Your description should include an example of each type of data.

OR4. State three criteria that should be considered in order to collect reliable primary data.

OR5. Why is it important to have randomization when selecting a sample?

OR6. State three characteristics of a good sample.

-
-
-

OR7. A poll by a TV network included the given question:

"Do you think that fighting should be eliminated from professional hockey so that skilled players can restore the high standards of the game?"

Identify the type of bias in the question and suggest how it could be avoided.

OR8. A music store keeps its inventory records on a computerized database. The record for each different CD could have many categories for information. The computer can search databases for matches in any of the data categories.

a) List some of the categories that the music store would use.

b) What categories would the staff of the music store want to check regularly?

ANSWERS AND SOLUTIONS—PRACTICE QUESTIONS

1. A	**9. B**	**OR3 See solution**
2. D	**10. C**	**OR4 See solution**
3. B	**11. C**	**OR5 See solution**
4. A	**12. B**	**OR6. See solution**
5. D	**13. D**	**OR7. See solution**
6. B	**14. C**	**OR8. See Solution**
7. C	**OR1. See solution**	
8. D	**OR2. See solution**	

1. **A**
The purpose of descriptive statistics is to summarize and display (i.e., in a chart or graph) what actually happened without inferences being made about a larger population. The other choices would all likely involve making an inference about a population from the sample given.

2. **D**
The amount of alcohol consumption and the incidence of automobile accidents is a situation involving two variables.

3. **B**
Population size does not cause variability in data.

4. **A**
If the mean height and median height of all the students in the five samples were calculated, they would be more representative of the entire population. From sample to sample, however, the mean and median usually vary.

5. **D**
Since the data collected will be numerical using only whole numbers, the data will be quantitative and discrete.

6. **B**
The data collection needs to be random, repeated, and a controlled. This will ensure the reliability of the data. Choice B, central tendency, may or may not be important, depending on the purpose of the experimental study.

7. **C**
The survey is conducted among high school basketball players in the city (population). Basketball players at Survey High are asked to fill out the questionnaire (sample).

8. **D**
The reason this is convenience sampling is that students are gathered in the cafeteria. From this group, you are choosing the sample randomly.

9. **B**
Many people will ignore the call and not respond to the questionnaire and thus influencing the results of the survey. To minimize this type of bias, the company may attempt to have its name blocked from the call display.

10. **C**
All of the choices are essential to avoid bias in the survey but response bias occurs when participants in a survey are influenced by the wording of the question.

11. **C**

Good questions must be simple and avoid bias by leading the respondent or using language that may bias the response.

12. **B**

The population was defined as teenagers in Manitoba. By surveying only their school, the sample may not reflect the opinions of the population.

13. **D**

All of the given statements are correct. Information regarding databases can be found in your school or public library.

14. **C**

Country J did have the highest hourly rate in 2005 to 2007. However, in 2003 and 2004, Country G had higher hourly rates.

OR1.

Answers may include business, economics, psychology, medicine, education, politics, agriculture, engineering, etc.

OR2.

Variability in data occurs because of:

- differences in the samples
- limited accuracy in measurement
- variations in the conditions of the experiment

OR3.

Nominal data is a type of categorical data in which objects fall into unordered categories. The ordering of the categories is arbitrary. For example, data collected from surveying people about which colours they prefer: red, blue, green, yellow, or orange. There is no logical order to the categories.

Ordinal data is a type of categorical data in which there is a logical ordering to the categories. For example, data collected when students are asked to respond to a change in school start time; the students can choose: angry, neutral, or happy.

OR4.

1. Sample size
2. Appropriateness of the survey question
3. Potential sources of bias

OR5.

Every member of the population must be equally likely to be selected. If one group of the population is not represented in the sample, there would be potential for bias. The sample must reflect the characteristics of the population.

OR6.

1. The sample must be random
2. The sample must represent the population
3. The sample must be large enough so the data is close to that of the population

OR7.

Measurement bias. This question contains wording or information intended to influence the respondents' answers. A question with straightforward, neutral language will produce more accurate data. For example, the question could simply be, "Should fighting be eliminated from professional hockey?"

OR8.

a) Categories that the music store might use are title, artist, publisher, music type, price, number in stock, product code (bar code), date of recording, and best sellers

b) Number of units in stock, the price, other CDs in stock by the same artist.

ORGANIZATION OF DATA FOR ANALYSIS—UNIT TEST

Use the following information to answer the next question.

Consider the following organizations:
Universities
Baseball teams
Insurance companies

1. How many of the listed organizations are likely to use statistical studies as part of their decision-making processes?

   A. None

   B. One

   C. Two

   D. Three

2. When data is collected from more than one sample of the population

   A. the results are the same

   B. the results may vary from sample to sample

   C. no conclusion can be made

   D. repeated samples are not helpful in making predictions

3. Which of the following situations involves one variable?

   A. The air temperature at given altitudes

   B. The annual income of 100 surveyed families

   C. The height of a ball at given times after it is thrown straight up into the air

   D. The distance travelled by cars driven at varying speeds in the same time frame

4. The reason that researchers often use repeated samples when collecting data is **most** likely that

   A. repeated sampling verifies that the data collected does not differ significantly from the population

   B. individual samples are too small

   C. the experiment must be replicable

   D. samples of different sizes must be used

5. Ben is working on a class project for which he must interview ten of his classmates. He places the names in a hat and selects 10 names. This type of sampling is

   A. systematic sampling

   B. simple random sampling

   C. stratified random sampling

   D. convenience sampling

6. A TV talk show host whose program airs in the afternoon asked her viewers to go to her website and respond to the question, "Would you marry your wife or husband if you had it to do all over again?" What type of bias does this represent?

   A. response bias

   B. measurement bias

   C. non-response bias

   D. sampling bias

Use the following information to answer the next question.

> A jury is a panel of randomly selected citizens of legal age and reasonable intelligence who weigh the evidence presented in a legal proceeding. Jurors are summoned by the clerk of the court to appear before the attorneys in the case. Either one or both attorneys may challenge the suitability of prospective jurors, and eliminate them from the proceedings.

7. When examining a juror, an attorney may find which of the following characteristics to be the **least** likely potential source of bias?

A. Race

B. Sex

C. Height

D. Religion

Open Response

OR1. Data that is collected and then sorted by type rather than numerical values is called __________________ data.

OR2. Explain why sample size is a consideration for reliable data.

OR3. There are 300 grade 10 students and 200 grade 12 students. You randomly select 12 grade 10 students and 8 grade 12 students to obtain a sample size of 20. The type of sampling used is __________________.

Use the following information to answer the next question.

> "Given the large amount of pollutants that are spewed out of smelters, should mining companies be forced to clean up their act? "

OR4. Assess the given survey question based on the criteria listed in the chart. Rewrite the survey question to meet the listed criteria.

Criterion	Criterion Met Y/N
Simple	
Specific	
Readable	
Avoids jargon	
Avoids abbreviations	
Avoids negatives	
Avoids being leading	
Avoids insensitivity	

OR5. The importance of having a computer is given by age in the table below.

The Importance of Having a Computer by Age			
Age (years)	**Girls**	**Boys**	**All students**
		average score on 1000	
8	427	492	460
9	444	500	473
10	424	480	453
11	442	529	485
12	508	545	526
13	566	591	578
14	607	620	616
15	653	653	533
16	640	655	648
17	658	648	653
18	653	660	657
19	611	678	650

a) Using the data given, predict a trend in the importance of having a computer.

b) Using the given data state a reason why a computer is not as important at age 19.

c) According to the statistics, at what age do the girls find a computer more important than boys?

ANSWERS AND SOLUTIONS—UNIT TEST

1. D	**OR2. See solution**	**OR4, See solution**
2. B	**5. B**	**OR5. See solution**
3. B	**OR3. See solution**	
OR1. See solution	**6. D**	
4. A	**7. C**	

1. **D**

All of these groups make decisions using statistics collected over time.

2. **B**

Repeated sampling should show a recognizable pattern if there is any relationship

3. **B**

The annual income of 100 surveyed families is a situation that involves only one variable.

4. **A**

The purpose of repeated sampling is to verify that the data collected does not differ significantly from the population. Choices B and C refer to the size of samples, which is not necessarily part of repeated sampling. Considering choice C: repeated sampling may help ensure that an experimental study is replicable, however, there are many additional factors.

5. **B**

Since the names of all students in the class have an equally likely chance of being drawn, this is a simple random sampling technique. This type of sampling may not be representative of the population.

6. **D**

The people who respond to her survey will not be representative of the population. Since the program airs in the afternoon, only people who are home during this time, tuned into the program, and with computer access, would respond.

7. **C**

Sex, race, and religion can all be sources of bias that influence a juror's opinion, since each can shape and mold a person's ideologies and judgments. This is especially true when the particular court case contains evidence and events that are personal to a juror's sex, race, or religion. For example, all of the following are sources of bias:
Sex—a female juror may be more sympathetic to a female assault victim than a male. Race—if the defendant is the same race as a juror, the juror may feel more compelled to side with the defendant despite the evidence. Religion—a juror, because of his religion, may be opposed to the death penalty and therefore find the defendant innocent to save him from the death penalty. Of the factors listed, height would be least likely to shape or mold our belief systems in a way that would predictably bias our opinions and judgments.

OR1. **CATEGORICAL**

Categorical data is data that is collected and sorted by type, rather than by numerical value; for example: hair colour, race.

OR2.

Sample size is important for reliable data because you want the sample to be representative of the population being studied. Too small of a sample may not reflect the opinions or characteristics of the population.

OR3. STRATIFIED RANDOM SAMPLING

The population has been divided into 2 groups or strata. A sample is selected from each stratum in proportion to the strata size.

OR4.

Criterion	Criterion Met Y/N	Rationale
Simple	N	Too much information
Specific	Y	
Readable	Y	
Avoids jargon	N	"Clean up their act"
Avoids abbreviations	Y	
Avoids negatives	Y	
Avoids being leading	N	"Given the large amounts … "
Avoids insensitivity	N	The wording of the question evokes anger in the responder.

The question could be reworded as follows: "Should mining companies be forced to decrease the amount of pollutants being emitted by smelters? "

OR5.

a) It appears that the level of importance connected a computer increases from age 8 to age 18.

b) Students are out of school so may not need a computer for school work.

c) At age 17 more girls than boys found that having a computer is important.

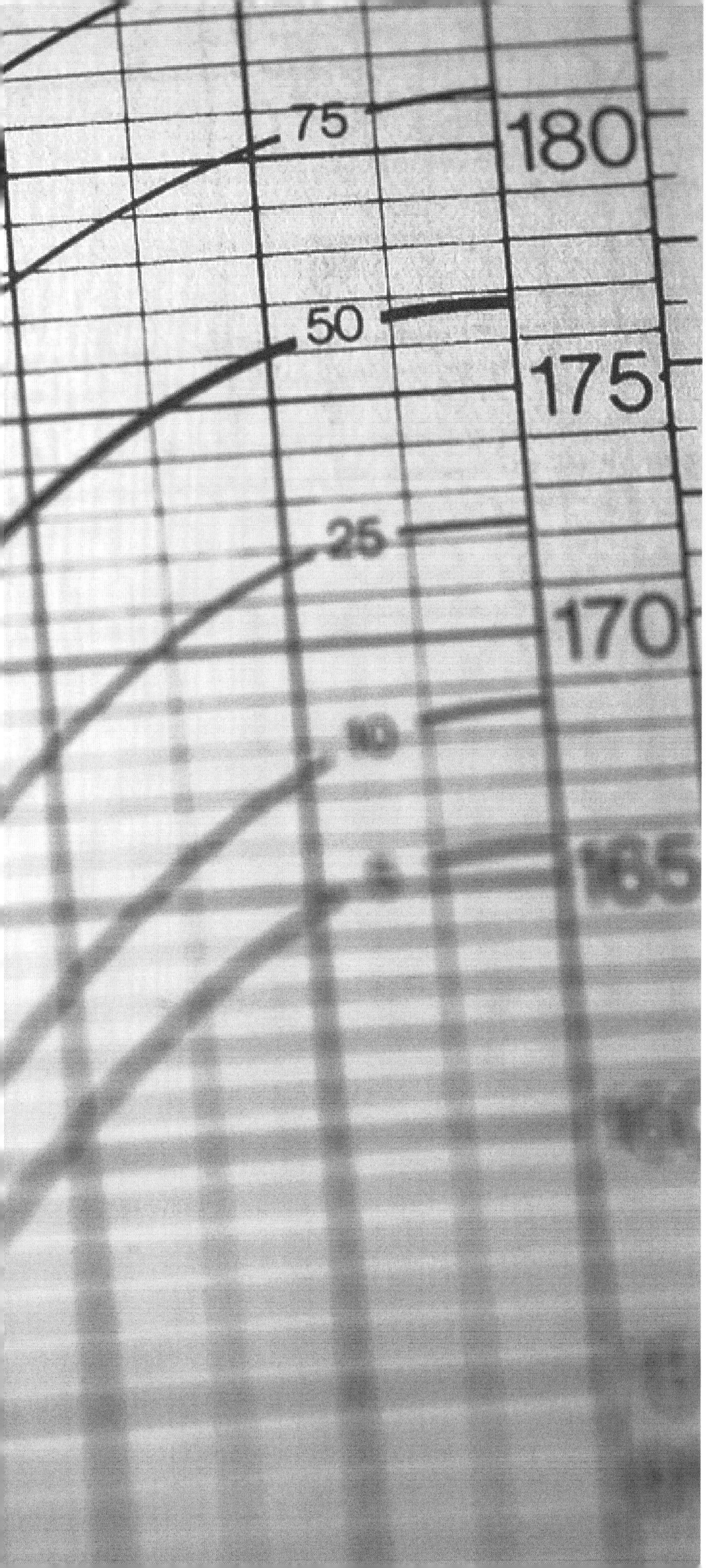

Statistical Analysis

STATISTICAL ANALYSIS

Table of Correlations

Specific Expectation	Practice Questions	Unit Test Questions
By the end of the course, students will:		
SA1.1 recognize that the analysis of one-variable data involves the frequencies associated with one attribute, and determine, using technology, the relevant numerical summaries (i.e., mean, median, mode, range, interquartile range, variance, and standard deviation)	1, NR1	1, NR1
SA1.2 determine the positions of individual data points within a one-variable data set using quartiles, percentiles, and z-scores, use the normal distribution to model suitable one-variable data sets, and recognize these processes as strategies for one-variable data analysis	2, NR2	2, NR2
SA1.3 generate, using technology, the relevant graphical summaries of one-variable data based on the type of data provided	3, 4	3, 4
SA1.4 interpret, for a normally distributed population, the meaning of a statistic qualified by a statement describing the margin of error and the confidence level, and make connections, through investigation using technology, between the sample size, the margin of error, and the confidence level	5, 6	5, OR1
SA1.5 interpret statistical summaries to describe the characteristics of a one-variable data set and to compare two related one-variable data sets; describe how statistical summaries can be used to misrepresent one-variable data; and make inferences, and make and justify conclusions, from statistical summaries of one-variable data orally and in writing, using convincing arguments	7, 8, OR1	6
SA2.1 recognize that the analysis of two-variable data involves the relationship between two attributes, recognize the correlation coefficient as a measure of the fit of the data to a linear model, and determine, using technology, the relevant numerical summaries	9, 10, OR2	7
SA2.2 recognize and distinguish different types of relationships between two variables that have a mathematical correlation	11	8
SA2.3 generate, using technology, the relevant graphical summaries of two-variable data based on the type of data provided	12, 13	9, 10
SA2.4 determine, by performing a linear regression using technology, the equation of a line that models a suitable two-variable data set, determine the fit of an individual data point to the linear model, and recognize these processes as strategies for two-variable data analysis	14, 15, OR3	11, OR2
SA2.5 interpret statistical summaries to describe the characteristics of a two-variable data set and to compare two related two-variable data sets: describe how statistical summaries can be used to misrepresent two-variable data; and make inferences, and make and justify conclusions, from statistical summaries of two-variable data orally and in writing, using convincing arguments	16, 17	12, OR3
SA3.1 interpret statistics presented in the media, and explain how the media, the advertising industry, and others use and misuse statistics to promote a certain point of view	18, 19	13, 14
SA3.2 assess the validity of conclusions presented in the media by examining sources of data, including Internet sources (i.e., to determine whether they are authoritative, reliable, unbiased, and current), methods of data collection, and possible sources of bias, and by questioning the analysis of the data and conclusions drawn from the data	20, OR4	15, OR4

STATISTICAL ANALYSIS

SA1.1 recognize that the analysis of one-variable data involves the frequencies associated with one attribute, and determine, using technology, the relevant numerical summaries (i.e., mean, median, mode, range, interquartile range, variance, and standard deviation)

ANALYSING ONE-VARIABLE DATA

Data that is not associated with another data set is called one-variable data. Some examples of one-variable data include the weights of all the students in your class, their ages, their math marks, or the distance they travel to get to school. Several different numerical summaries can be applied to one-variable data.

MEASURES OF CENTRAL TENDENCY

MEAN

The mean of a data set is the sum of all of the values divided by the number of values in the set. In other words, if the data set is $\{x_1, x_2, x_3, \dots x_{n-1}, x_n\}$, then the mean is

$$\mu = \frac{x_1 + x_2 \dots x_n}{n}.$$

MEDIAN

For a data set with an odd number of values, the median is the middle value of the set when the data is listed in ascending order. For a data set with an even number of values, the median is the mean of the two middle values of the set when the data is listed in ascending order.

MODE

The mode is the value or values that occur most frequently within a data set.

MEASURES OF DISPERSION

RANGE

The range of a data set is the difference between the maximum data value and the minimum data value.

INTERQUARTILE RANGE

The interquartile range is the difference between the third quartile (Q_3) and the first quartile (Q_1) of the data set $Q_3 - Q_1$.

VARIANCE

The variance (v) is calculated as

$$v = \frac{(x_1 - \mu)^2 + (x_2 - \mu)^2 + \dots + (x_n - \mu)^2}{n},$$ where

μ represents the mean.

STANDARD DEVIATION

The standard deviation (σ) is the square root of the variance,

$$\sigma = \sqrt{\frac{(x_1 - \mu)^2 + (x_2 - \mu)^2 + \dots + (x_n - \mu)^2}{n}}.$$

USING TECHNOLOGY TO DETERMINE NUMERICAL SUMMARIES

A TI-83 graphing calculator is programmed to calculate the mean, median, range, variance, standard deviation, and interquartile range for a data set.

Example

Find the mean, median, range, standard deviation, variance, and the interquartile range for the data set $\{3, 12, 6, 8, 7, 2, 9, 5\}$, using a T1-83 graphing calculator.
Round the approximate measures to the nearest hundredth.

Solution

Follow the steps using a TI-83 graphing calculator:

Press [2nd] [+] [4:ClrAllLists] [ENTER]

Press [STAT] [1:Edit] and enter the data in L1

Press [STAT] ▷ to highlight "CALC", then [1:1-Var SA], [ENTER]

You should see the following screen:

```
1-Var Stats
 x̄=6.5
 Σx=52
 Σx²=412
 Sx=3.251373336
 σx=3.041381265
↓n=8
```

Press the down arrow several times to view the following additional information.

```
1-Var Stats
↑n=8
 minX=2
 Q1=4
 Med=6.5
 Q3=8.5
 maxX=12
```

From the screen display you can see that, to the nearest hundredth, the measures are:

Mean = 6.6
Median = 6.5
Range = Xmax – Xmin = 12 – 2 = 10
Standard deviation ≈ 3.04

Variance = $\sigma^2 \approx 3.041^2 \approx 9.24$
Interquartile range $= Q_3 - Q_1 = 8.5 - 4 = 4.5$

Related Questions: 1, NR1

SA1.2 *determine the positions of individual data points within a one-variable data set using quartiles, percentiles and z-scores, use the normal distribution to model suitable one-variable data sets, and recognize these processes as strategies for one-variable analysis*

ANALYSING ONE-VARIABLE DATA

When a data set contains a large number of values and the values are in numerical order, the distribution of the data values approaches a normal distribution. A normal distribution on a graph has the shape of a bell-shaped curve with the mean, median, and mode all in the centre of the curve. The position of an individual data value in the distribution can be described by using percentiles or z-scores.

PERCENTILES

The percentile, or percentile rank, for any data value indicates that a certain percent of values fall beneath that data value. The percentile for a data value, x, is given by the formula:

$$\text{Percentile for } x = \frac{B + \frac{1}{2}E}{n} \times 100$$

where: B = number of data values below x
E = number of values equal to x
n = total number of values in the data set

Percentiles are usually truncated to the nearest whole number.

The 25th percentile is equal to the first quartile, Q_1.

The is 50th percentile is equal to the second quartile, Q_2.

The 75th percentile is equal to the third quartile, Q_3.

Example

In a set of 414 mathematics scores, 164 are below a score of 50% and 8 are equal to 50%. What is the percentile rank of a score of 50%?

Solution

Percentile for a score of 50%

$$= \frac{164 + \frac{1}{2}(8)}{414} \times 100$$

$$= \frac{168}{414} \times 100$$

$$= 40.6$$

Therefore, a score of 50% is in the 40th percentile in this distribution.

Z-SCORES

The z-score for a data value of x is the number of standard deviations of the value from the mean of the data set. For example, a z-score of 1.6 means the data value is 1.6 standard deviations above the mean, whereas a z-score of –2.1 means the data value is 2.1 standard deviations below the mean. The z-score for a data value x is given by the following formula:

$$z = \frac{x - \mu}{\sigma}$$

where:
σ = standard deviation
μ = mean of the set of data

Example

In Kelly's English class, the marks for the 39 students have a normal distribution, with a mean of 67% and a standard deviation of 11.5. Kelly has a mark of 71%.
What is Kelly's z-score, rounded to the nearest hundredth?

Solution

Kelly's z-score is determined using the formula $z = \frac{x - \mu}{\sigma}$, where $x = 71$, $\mu = 67$, and $\sigma = 11.5$.

$$z = \frac{71 - 67}{11.5}$$

$$= \frac{4}{11.5} = 0.35$$

Related Questions: 2, NR2

SA1.3 generate, using technology, the relevant graphical summaries of one-variable data (e.g., circle graphs, bar graphs, histograms, stem-and-leaf plots, box plots) based on the type of data provided (e.g., categorical, ordinal, quantitative)

GRAPHS

Data is often summarized and displayed by using one of the following types of graphs:

Circle graphs are used to show how one part relates to the whole by splitting the circle into sectors. The size of each sector is proportional to the amount it represents. For example, a circle graph could be used to show how the household budget is divided up for the various expenses.

Household Budget

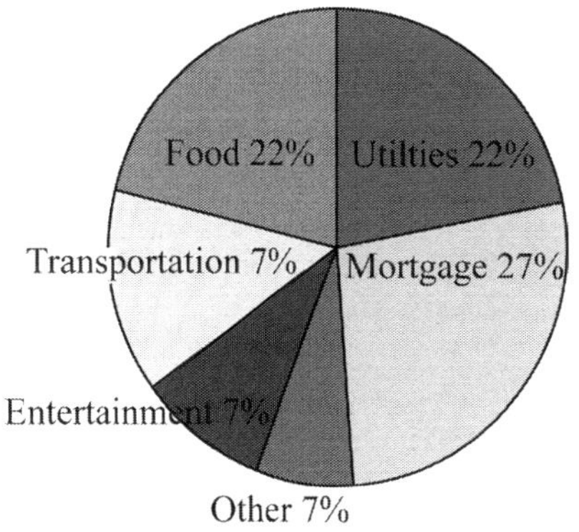

Bar graphs are used to display relative amounts or frequencies for comparable categories. For example, the annual sales of the major auto manufacturers can be compared with a bar graph.

Annual Sales

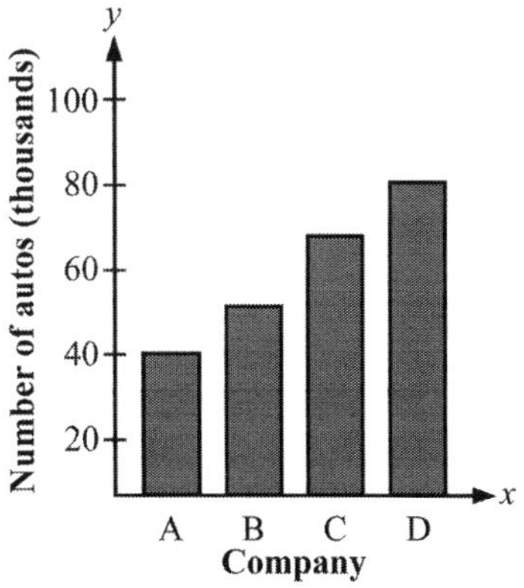

Histograms are used to display relative frequencies of categories of quantitative data. The areas of the bars in a histogram represent the values for each category. For example, frequencies of income categories for all wage earners in Ontario can be compared using a histogram.

Annual Income Frequencies

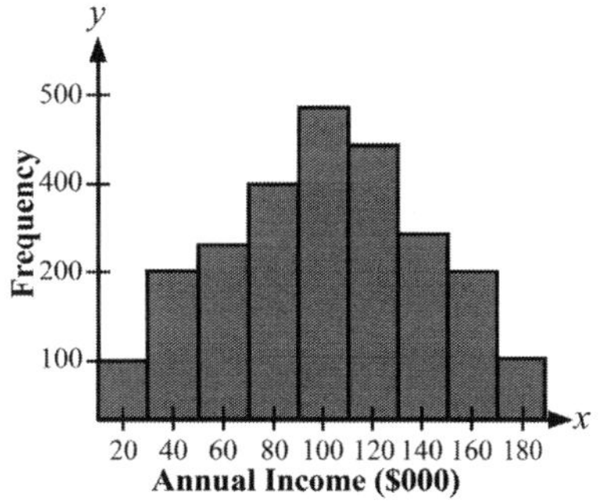

Stem-and-leaf plots show the distribution of data as it is collected. For example, after marking a set of class tests, the teacher can record the scores in a stem-and-leaf plot to see the distribution of the scores.

Test Marks

Stem	Leaf
3	8 8
4	3 5 7
5	0 2 3 8
6	0 0 2 4 4 5 6 7 7
7	0 1 1 2 8 9 9
8	0 2 4 4 5 8
9	0 0 6 8

Box plots are used to summarize the distribution of data by showing the median, the first and third quartiles, and the minimum and maximum data values. For example, the test marks data from the stem-and-leaf plot in the previous example could be summarized using a box plot.

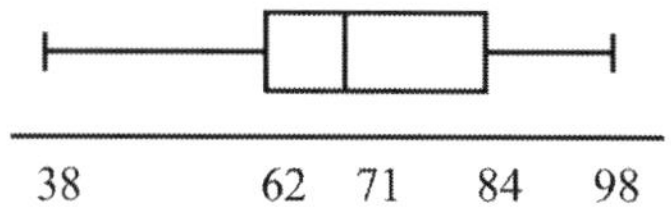

The types of data and the graphs commonly used to display each type are summarized in the following table:

Categorical Data

Description	Types of Graphs
Data values can be put into non-overlapping categories. An example is the number of males and females in a math class.	Circle graphs Bar graphs

Ordinal Data

Description	Types of Graphs
Data values can be ranked, or put in order. The data values can be counted but not measured. For example, a movie rating in which the movie is rated from 1 to 5 stars by a group of moviegoers.	Bar Graphs

Quantatative Data

Description	Types of Graphs
Data that applies to an amount, a quantity, or a range of values. Usually measurement units are associated with the data. For example, the heights of students in the class.	Histograms Stem-and-leaf plots Box plots

Example

A family has a total monthly budget of \$3200. They budget \$650 for groceries. If a circle graph were drawn to display the budget categories, what would be the measure of the central angle of the sector that represents the groceries? Give the answer to the nearest degree.

Solution

The central angle would be a fraction of 360° based on the ratio of the amount spent on groceries to the total budget amount.

$$\text{Central angle} = \frac{650}{3200} \times 360° = 73°$$

Graphing calculators and computer programs can be used to produce the types of graphs discussed here. The following example uses a TI-83 graphing calculator.

Example

The following data represents the vertical jump heights of physical education students at a particular elementary school, rounded to the nearest centimetre. Use a TI-83 graphing calculator to draw a histogram and a box plot for the data.

Height (cm)	**Frequency**
14	2
15	4
16	6
17	9
18	13
19	15
20	14
21	11
22	8
23	7
24	7
25	4

Solution

This data can be entered into a TI-83 graphing calculator and a histogram graphed by using the following procedure:

1. Press 2nd + 4:ClrAllLists ENTER
2. Press STAT 1:Edit and enter the height in L1 and the frequency in L2
3. Press 2nd Y= ENTER
4. Use the arrows to scroll to On, press ENTER, scroll to the histogram icon, press ENTER
5. Scroll to Xlist:, press 2nd 1 to choose L1
6. Scroll to Freq:, press 2nd 2 to choose L2
7. Press ZOOM scroll down to 9:ZoomStat, press ENTER
8. A histogram is displayed, however, the x-scale needs to be adjusted to 1.
9. Press WINDOW, scroll down to Xscl=, press 1
10. Press GRAPH

The following graph should appear:

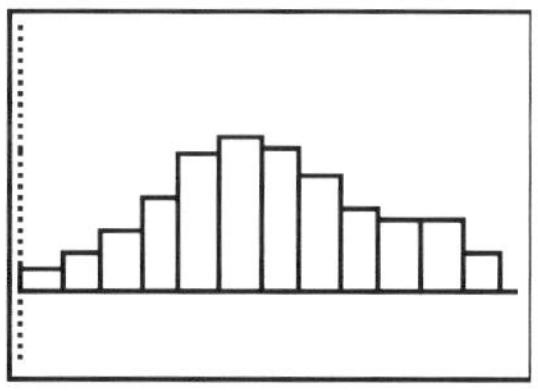

The box plot is the fifth type of graph listed in the STAT PLOT menu.

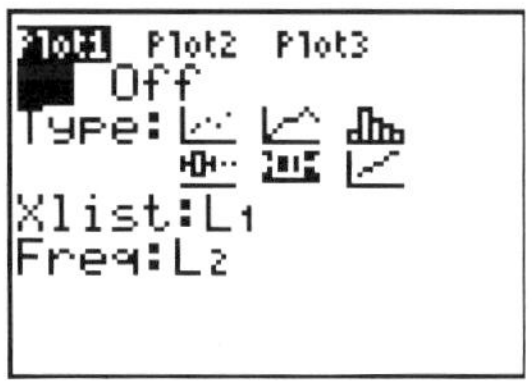

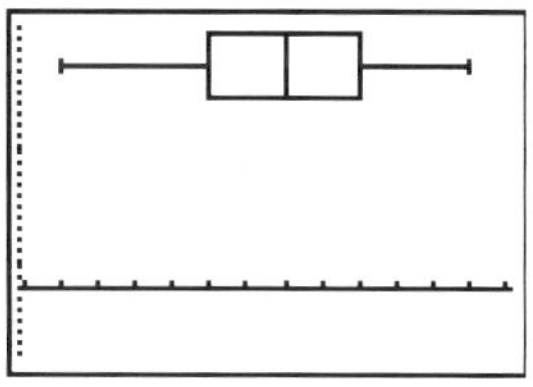

Related Questions: 3, 4

SA1.4 *interpret, for a normally distributed population, the meaning of a statistic qualified by a statement describing the margin of error and the confidence level (e.g., the meaning of a statistic that is accurate to within 3 percentage points, 19 times out of 20), and make connections, through investigation using technology (e.g., dynamic statistical software), between the sample size, the margin of error, and the confidence level (e.g., large sample sizes create higher confidence levels for a given margin of error).*

INTERPRETING THE MEANING OF STATISTICS

When a survey is conducted using a sample of the population, it is unlikely that the sample represents the entire population exactly. If the same survey was conducted on a different sample of the population, the chances are that the results would be at least somewhat different.

The **confidence level** is a measure of how confident the satistician is of the results. A 95% confidence level means that the statistician is 95% confident of the results. The **margin of error** establishes the interval for which the confidence level applies.

Assume a survey was done that reports that 70% of Canadians prefer watching hockey to football on television. The survey states that it is accurate to within 3 percentage points 95% of the time. What does this last statement mean?
It means that if the survey were conducted 100 times, 95 times you would get a result of $70 \pm 3\%$, or between 67% and 73%, of the respondents saying they prefer hockey.

If the sample size in the previous example were 1000 people, and a new survey were done with a sample size of 2 000 people, then the margin of error for the same 95% confidence level would decrease, possibly to 2%. From investigations in this unit, you should have discovered that increasing the sample size has the effect of decreasing the margin of error, but not proportionally, i.e., doubling the sample size does not halve the margin of error.

Dynamic statistical software for a computer, and programs built into some calculators, can efficiently calculate confidence intervals and margins of error, and demonstrate the relationship between the two as the sample sizes change. The following example illustrates the procedure with a TI-83 graphing calculator.

Example

In a survey of 170 students, representing a normally distributed population, it was found that 72 of the students owned a skateboard.

a) If the survey had a 95% confidence level, determine the proportion of students in the represented population who own a skateboard.

b) Determine the margin of error as a percentage to the nearest tenth.

c) Determine the effect on the margin of error if the sample size were increased to 400.

Solution

In order to obtain the answers, follow the given procedure with a TI-83 graphing calculator:

1. Press STAT, scroll to TESTS
2. Scroll down to A:1-PropZint, press ENTER
3. Type 72 after x:, 170 after n:, and .95 after C-level (if it is different)

You should have the following screen:

```
1-PropZInt
 x:72
 n:170
 C-Level:.95
 Calculate
```

4. Scroll the cursor over Calculate and press ENTER.

The result should be:

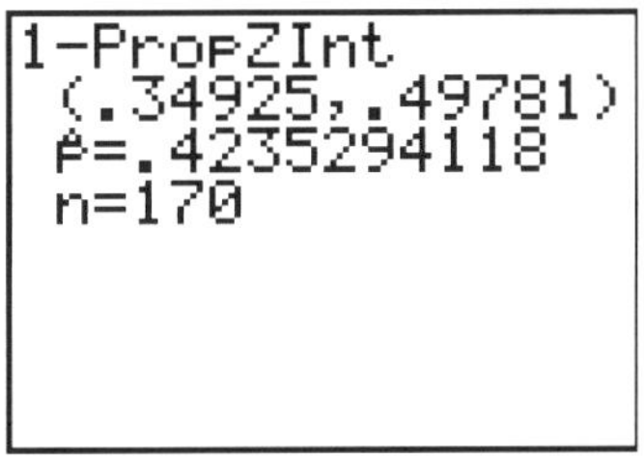

a) The proportion of students who own a skateboard is between 0.34925 to 0.49781, inclusive.

b) The margin of error is $= 0.423529 - 0.34925 = 0.074279 = 7.4\%$

(note that $\hat{p} = \dfrac{72}{170}$).

c) If the sample size were increased to 400, then enter 400 in for the value of n in the calculator and recalculate. The margin of error will then be $0.18 - 0.14235 = 0.03765 = 3.8\%$.

Related Questions: 5, 6

SA1.5 *Interpret statistical summaries (e.g., graphical, numerical) to describe the characteristics of a one-variable data set and to compare two related one-variable data sets (e.g., compare the lengths of different species of trout; compare annual incomes in Canada and in a third-word country; compare Aboriginal and non-Aboriginal incomes); describe how statistical summaries (e.g., graphs, measures of central tendency) can be used to misrepresent one-variable data; and make inferences and make and justify conclusions, from statistical summaries of one-variable data orally and in writing, using convincing arguments.*

UNDERSTANDING STATISTICAL SUMMARIES

The following two graphs compare the sales in a particular year for companies A and B.

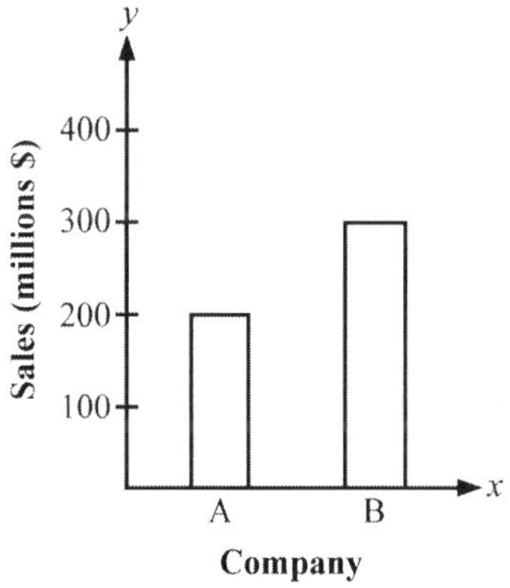

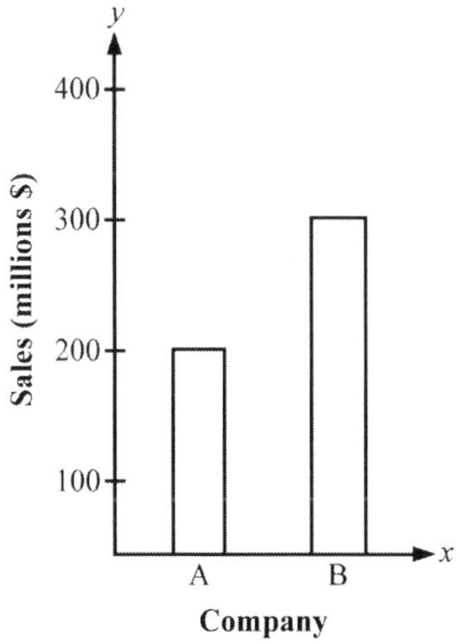

Although the two graphs show the same information, they will make different impressions on readers. In the first graph, it appears that the sales for company B were not much greater than the sales for company A. However, the second graph shows that the sales for company B were significantly greater than the sales for company A.

Company A would likely use the first graph to show that they are competitive with company B. On the other hand, company B would likely use the second graph to show that their sales are far greater than the sales for company A.

The term "average" has a very loose meaning. Although it is usually interpreted as the measure of the mean, it could be used to represent any of the measures of central tendency. The mean is not always the best representation of central tendency, as illustrated in the next example.

Example

> A president of a small company reports that the average annual income of his employees is \$55 000. However, the president does not report the amounts of their salaries, which are \$28 000, \$30 000, \$40 000, \$42 000, \$50 000, \$52 000, \$98 000, and \$100 000. Although the president correctly reported the mean salary, this report is misleading because only two of the eight employees earn more then \$55 000. A better representation of the "average" in this situation would be to use the median salary, which is \$46 000.

Related Questions: 7, 8, OR1

SA2.1 *recognize that the analysis of two-variable data involves the relationship between two attributes, recognize the correlation coefficient as a measure of the fit of the data to a linear model, and determine, using technology, the relevant numerical summaries (e.g., summary tables such as contingency tables; correlation coefficient).*

Analysing Two-Variable Data

In two-variable data, a relationship, or function, exists between the two data sets. For some types of functions, such as a linear function, a correlation coefficient can be used to determine how closely the two data sets fit this particular relationship.

The linear correlation coefficient, denoted by r, measures the fit of two sets of data to a linear model. The value of r can be -1 or $+1$, or any value in between -1 and $+1$ $(-1 \leq r \leq +1)$.

If r is close to $+1$, then there is a strong positive correlation between the variables and the function. This means that one variable will increase as the other variable increases.
If $r = +1$, then the relation is a linear relation with a positive slope.

If r is close to -1, then there is a strong negative correlation between the variables and the function. This means that one variable will increase while the other variable decreases.
If $r = -1$, then the relation is a linear relation with a negative slope.

If $r = 0$, there is no linear correlation between the variables. Generally, if $|r| > 0.8$ then the relationship has a strong correlation, and if $|r| < 0.5$, the relationship has a weak correlation.

Example

A survey was completed to determine the correlation between the amount of time students spent studying mathematics in a week and their math marks. The following table shows a sample of the data collected.

Study time (h)	Math mark (%)
2	52
2.5	60
3	65
3.5	68
4	68
4.5	65
5	72
5.5	75
6	80
6.5	80
7	78
7.5	74

Use a calculator to determine the linear correlation coefficient, *r*, and whether there is a strong positive correlation.

Solution

In order to obtain the answer, follow the given procedure with a TI-83 graphing calculator:

1. Press [2nd] [+] [4:ClrAllLists] [ENTER]
2. Press [2nd] [0], scroll down to [DiagnosticOn], press [ENTER]
3. Press [STAT] [1:Edit] and enter the study time in L1 and the math mark in L2.
4. Press [STAT] ~ to highlight "CALC", then scroll down to [4:linReg(*ax*+*b*)], press [ENTER], [ENTER]

You should see the following screen:

```
LinReg
 y=ax+b
 a=4.032456631
 b=50.76385003
 r²=.7660519478
 r=.8752439362
```

The correlation coefficient is approximately 0.875, which indicates a strong positive correlation.

A **contingency table** can display the frequencies of data elements that are classified by two variables in which the rows of the table represent one variable and the columns of the table represent the other variable.

Example

A sample of 40 patients were randomly given either Drug A or Drug B as part of a pharmaceutical drug trial. The test patients either reacted positively to the drug they were given or they did not react. The results of this medical trial are summarized in the following contingency table, in which the numbers represent the frequencies of results.

Test Reactions for Drugs A and B in Pharmaceutical Trial

	Drug A	Drug B	Row Totals
Positive Reaction	11	16	27
No Reaction	8	5	13
Column Totals	19	21	40

From the contingency table, it appears that Drug B was more effective than Drug A because a greater proportion of the users had a positive reaction. However, more studies would be necessary because it may be that the 11 who reacted positively to Drug A would have no reaction to Drug B, or that the 16 that reacted with Drug B may also react with Drug A.

Related Questions: 9, 10, OR2

SA2.2 *recognize and distinguish different types of relationships between two variables that have a mathematical correlation (e.g., the cause-and-effect relationship between ice cream sales and forest fires over the course of a year; and accidental relationship between the consumer price index and the number of known planets in the universe).*

Relationships Between Two Variables

Example

A study examines the speed limits on various roads in a city and the number of accidents that occur on these roads. The data results in a relationship with a linear correlation coefficient of 0.36. What does this correlation coefficient mean? Are there any other pieces of data that might be significant to help describe the relationship between the speed limits and accidents?

Solution

A correlation coefficient of 0.36 indicates a weak positive correlation between the speed limits and number of accidents that occur. Other data that should be considered includes: data on the seriousness of the accidents, types of accidents (e.g., pedestrian, car, truck, left-turn, etc.), road conditions, and time of day that the accidents occurred.

Related Question: 11

SA2.3 *generate, using technology, the relevant graphical summaries of two-variable data (e.g., scatter plots, side-by-side bo plots) based on the type of data provided (e.g., categorical, ordinal, quantitative)*

Graphical Summaries of Two-Variable Data

Two-variable data that is categorical is often summarized in a contingency table.
Two-variable categorical data may be graphed by using double bar graphs or side-by-side circle graphs.

For example, consider the data summarized in the contingency table below:

	Drug A	**Drug B**	**Row Totals**
Positive Reaction	11	16	27
No Reaction	8	5	13
Column Totals	19	21	40 (Grand Total)

Two-variable data that is ordinal may also be summarized in a double bar graph.

Two-variable data that is quantitative is most often summarized by a scatter plot and a corresponding line (or curve) of best fit.

If one of the variables is categorical and the other is quantitative, side-by-side graphs of various types are possible. Side-by-side box plots are illustrated in the following example.

Statistical software for computers and graphing programs built into calculators provide for quick and accurate graphing.

Example

The following sets of math scores are from students who wrote a test before having a review class and another test after having a review class.

Student	Before review	After review
A	65	84
B	48	65
C	76	98
D	43	67
E	87	86
F	67	76
G	55	44
H	59	68
I	76	87
J	56	78
K	76	66
L	88	89
M	39	58
N	75	54

For the data given in the table above, use a TI-83 (or equivalent) graphing calculator to

a) Draw a scatter plot of the data with the original scores as the independent variable and the scores after the review as the dependent variable.

b) Graph side-by-side box plots of the data.

c) Determine the median and interquartile range for each set of data.

Solution

a) Using a TI-83 graphing calculator the steps are: Press 2nd + 4:ClrAllLists ENTER.
Press STAT 1:Edit and enter the "before review" scores in L1 and the "after review" scores in L2.
Press 2nd Y= ENTER. Use the arrows to scroll to "On", press ENTER, scroll to the first icon (scatter plot), press ENTER

Check that the variables are labelled as Xlist:L1 and Ylist:L2. Change if necessary.
Press ZOOM, scroll down to 9:ZoomStat, press ENTER
You should see the following screen:

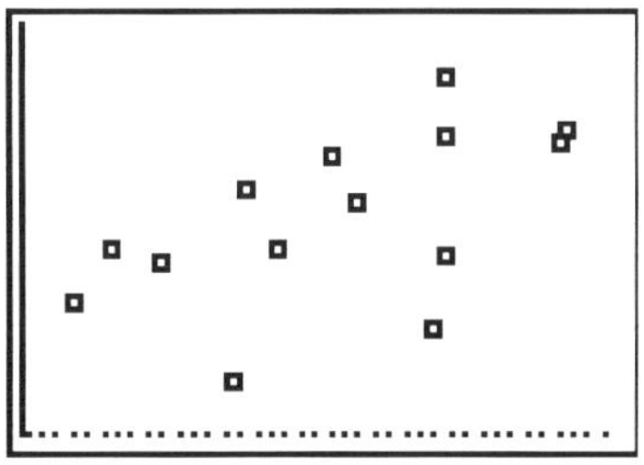

b) Use the arrows to scroll to On, press ENTER, scroll to the fifth icon (second box plot), press ENTER
Scroll to Xlist:, press 2nd 1 to choose L1
Scroll to Freq:, press 2nd 1 to choose L1
Press 2nd Y= ENTER
Press 2 to access Plot 2
Use the arrows to scroll to On, press ENTER, scroll to the 5th icon (2nd box plot), press ENTER
Scroll to Xlist:, press 2nd 2 to choose L2
Scroll to Freq:, press 2nd 2 to choose L2
Press ZOOM scroll down to 9:ZoomStat, press ENTER
You should see the following screen:

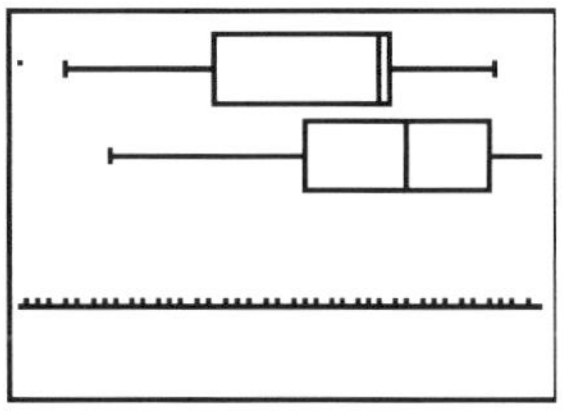

c) Using the TRACE button and the scrolling arrows, you should find that the median for the first set of data is 75, and that the interquartile range is $76 - 56 = 20$.
For the second set of data you should find that the median is 79, and that the interquartile range is $87 - 66 = 21$.

Related Questions: 12, 13

SA2.4 *determine, by performing a linear regression using technology, the equation of a line that models a suitable two-variable data set, determine the fit of an individual data point to the linear model (e.g., by using residuals to identify outliers), and recognize these processes as strategies for two-variable data analysis.*

LINEAR REGRESSION

Generally as indicated in lesson 2.1, if $|r| > 0.8$, the correlation is considered to be strong, if $|r| < 0.5$, the correlation is considered to be weak, and if $r = 0$, there is no correlation. In this lesson, as well as finding the equation of the linear model, which is the line of best fit, you will determine the effect of outliers, which are points that are a significant distance from the line. The vertical distance from an outlier to a line of best fit is called a vertical deviation or **residual**.

An outlier can have a major effect on the value of the regression coefficient, *r*, especially when the number of points is relatively small.
When working with regression models you need to be aware of outliers, their significance, and what may have caused them.

As in previous lessons, this lesson will use the TI-83 graphing calculator to perform the statistical operations and draw the graphs.

Example

The following data was collected about sales of a popular music CD from various Internet sites.

Price per CD ($)	Number sold
7.95	72
8.49	70
8.99	65
9.25	60
9.49	86
9.99	55
10.49	52
10.99	35
11.25	32
11.49	25

Use a TI-83 or similar calculator to

a) determine the linear equation of the line of best fit with the values of *a* and *b* to the nearest tenth.

b) sketch graphs of the scatter plot of points and the line of best fit.

c) determine the residual, rounded to the nearest tenth, for the most extreme outlier.

Solution

a) Press 2nd + 4:ClrAllLists ENTER
Press 2nd 0 , scroll down to DiagnosticOn, press ENTER
Press STAT 1:Edit and enter the price per CD amounts in L1 and the number sold in L2
Press STAT ~ to highlight "CALC", then scroll down to 4:LinReg(ax+b), press ENTER, ENTER
You should see the following screen:

```
LinReg
 y=ax+b
 a=-13.89555602
 b=191.9044801
 r²=.7338903795
 r=-.8566740217
```

You can see that the linear equation is approximately $y = -13.9x + 191.9$.

b) Press [2nd] [Y=] [ENTER]
Use the arrows to scroll to On, press [ENTER], scroll to the 1st icon (scatter plot), press [ENTER]
Check that the variables are labelled as Xlist:L1 and Ylist:L2. Change if necessary.
Press [ZOOM], scroll down to 9:ZoomStat, press [ENTER]
You should see the following screen:

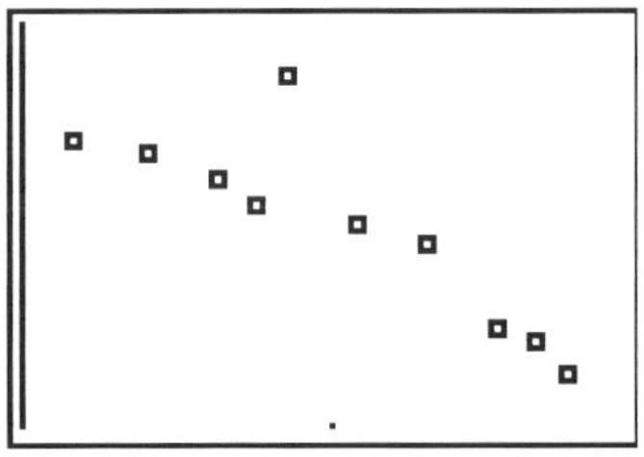

To insert the line of best fit, you have a couple of choices. You can type $-13.9x + 191.9$ into the $Y_1 =$ function, or you can paste the linear regression equation into $Y_1 =$ by the following procedure:
Press [Y=] [VARS] 5:Statistics ~ ~ 1:RegEQ [ENTER]
You should see the following screen:

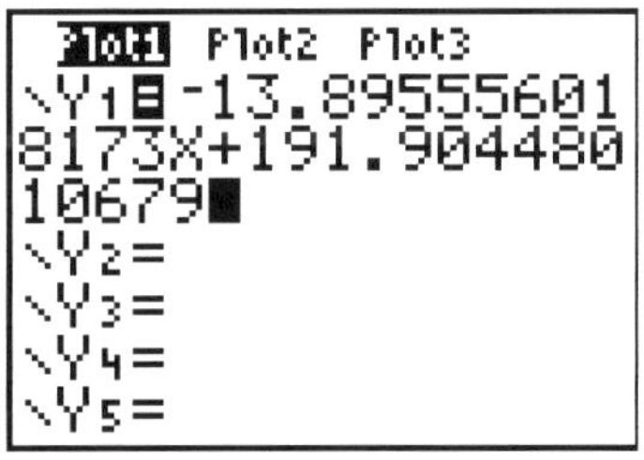

Press [GRAPH] to graph the line of best fit.

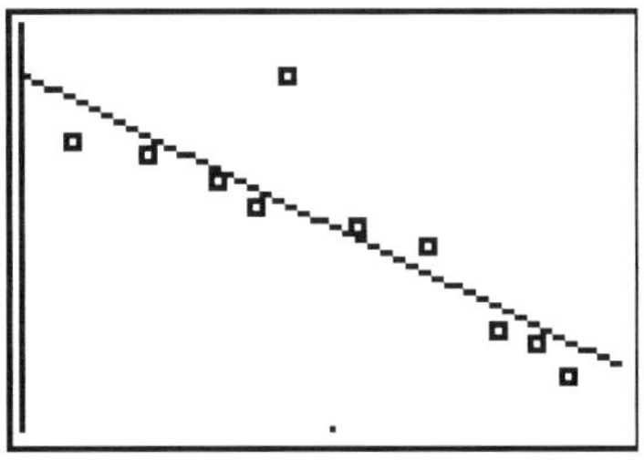

c) The TI-83 calculator has an automatic residual feature. It is in the LIST NAMES menu. You can see the residuals on the main screen or paste them into a number of places. One of the best places is into L3. Press [STAT] [1:Edit] and uses the scrolling arrows to put the cursor on L3. Press [2nd] [STAT], scroll down to 7:RESID, press [ENTER], [ENTER]. The residuals should now appear in L3.

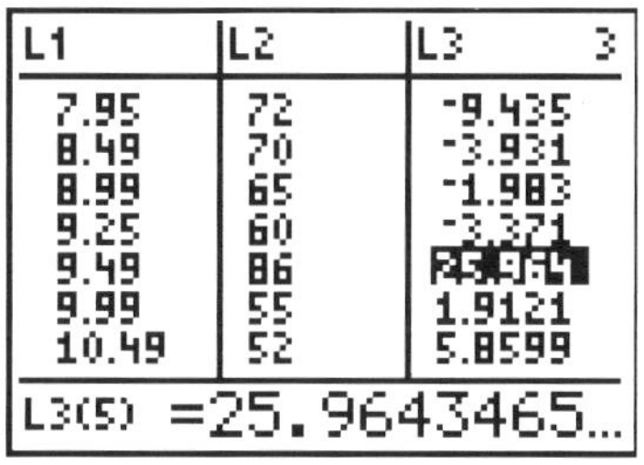

You can see that the residual for the most extreme outlier, which is the 5th point, is approximately 26.0.

Related Questions:14, 15, OR3

SA2.5 *interpret statistical summaries (e.g., scatter plot, equation representing a relationship) to describe the characteristics of a two-variable data set and to compare two related two-variable data sets (e.g., compare the relationship between Grade 12 English and Mathematics marks with the relationship between Grade 12 science and mathematics marks); describe how statistical summaries (e.g., graphs, linear models) can be used to misrepresent two-variable data; and make inferences, and justify conclusions, from statistical summaries of two-variable data orally and in writing, using convincing arguments.*

PRESENTING TWO-VARIABLE DATA

As with other types of data, two-variable data can be presented in various ways and formats that can emphasize different characteristics of the data. Sometimes the presentations are intentionally designed by the author, or by media, to be misleading, and sometimes they are unintentional.

When analyzing two-variable statistical summaries you should be aware of the following factors and techniques that may misrepresent the true relationships between the variables.

1. The sample size is too small to represent the population.
2. The sample is biased so it does not represent the population.
3. A line of best fit is given without a correlation coefficient so there is no way of knowing how well the lie fits the data. The line of best fit may be skewed by one or more extreme outliers.
4. The scales on the axes are stretched or shrunk to show an increased or decreased slope.
5. There are other variables that affect the statistics that are not part of the data.
6. The data may represent an accidental relationship.
7. The data summary does **not** give a comparison to a standard or uninfluenced group (e.g., in the case of drug testing).

Example

Sonia conducted a study to determine if there was a relationship between the average amount of time a student spends on the computer each day and his or her math mark. She surveyed students in her class and obtained data that led to scatter plots with the two lines of best fit shown below.

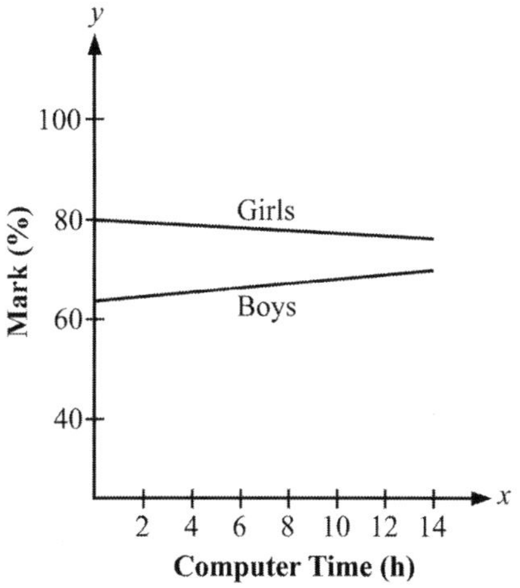

From the results of her study, Sonia makes the claim, "Boys should spend more time on the computer to increase their math marks, and girls should spend less time on the computer."

List at least three things that may make Sonia's claim false.

Solution

Some possible answers are:

1. Because the sample is only one class of students, it is likely very small.
2. No number representing the proportion of boys or girls is given.
3. The correlation coefficient for the line of best fit is not given so it may be skewed by extreme outliers
4. There are likely other variables involved. For example, the boys may spend some of their computer time on math-related activities.
5. The relationship between time spent on the computer and math mark may be completely accidental.

Related Questions: 16, 17

SA3.1 *interpret statistics presented in the media (e.g., the UN's finding that 2% of the world's population has more than half the world's wealth, whereas half the world's population has only 1% of the world's wealth), and explain how the media, the advertising industry, and other (e.g., marketers, pollsters) use and misuse statistics (e.g., as represented in graphs) to promote a certain point of view (e.g., by making a general statement based on a week correlation or an assumed cause-and-effect relationship; by starting the vertical scale at a value other than zero; by making statements using general population statistics without reference to data specific to minority groups)*

SA3.2 *assess the validity of conclusions presented in the media by examining sources of data, including Internet sources (i.e., to determine whether they authoritative, reliable, unbiased and current), methods of data collection, and possible sources of bias (e.g., sampling bias, non-response bias, culture bias in a survey question), and by questioning the analysis of data (e.g., whether there is any indication of the sample size in the analysis) and conclusions drawn from the data (e.g., whether any assumption are made about cause and effect)*

EVALUATING VALIDITY

Often, one- and two-variable statistics can misrepresent the actual situations. This might be accidental, but it can be intentional on the part of the author or presenter. Often these presenters have certain agendas or political points of view that might influence how they present statistics. Even the media, such as newspapers, magazines, radio, and television, may intentionally misrepresent data. There are many techniques that are used to misrepresent or misuse statistics.

When statistics are collected using sampling techniques, the statistician must be very careful to choose a sample that best represents the entire population. Similarly, the reader **must** be equally aware of the sample that was used in order to determine the validity of the statistics. There are numerous methods for selecting a sample that has a particular bias. Some of the most common sample biases are:

1. **Selection bias:** the sample is chosen from a certain part of the population. For example, choosing a sample consisting of particular people whose views are known or suspected.
2. **Non-response bias:** some of the people surveyed do not respond. For example, some responses are not returned in a mail-out survey.
3. **Cultural bias:** the sample targets a particular "culture". For example, conducting a survey of people attending a symphony.
4. **Timing bias:** choosing a sample at a particular time. For example, conducting a survey about people's favourite sport during the Stanley Cup playoffs.
5. **Stratified bias:** a sample chosen by some characteristic of the population. For example, choosing a sample consisting of people between the ages of 20 and 40 inclusively.

Example

A newspaper article states that the average selling price of a home in a particular community within a city dropped by 8.1% over the past 12 months. What are two different reasons that this report may be misleading?

Solution

Sample answers are:

1. The "average" selling price is likely the mean selling price. This value may not represent the central tendency because the selling prices for a few expensive homes may have decreased by large percentages, skewing the average. The remaining houses might not have lost much value, but the reported "average" appears as though they have.

2. There is no indication how many homes were sold or for sale. If only a small number of homes were for sale or sold, the report may not be very meaningful.

Example

A report by political party X claimed that their party was well ahead in the polls before an election. They used the following graph to support their claim.

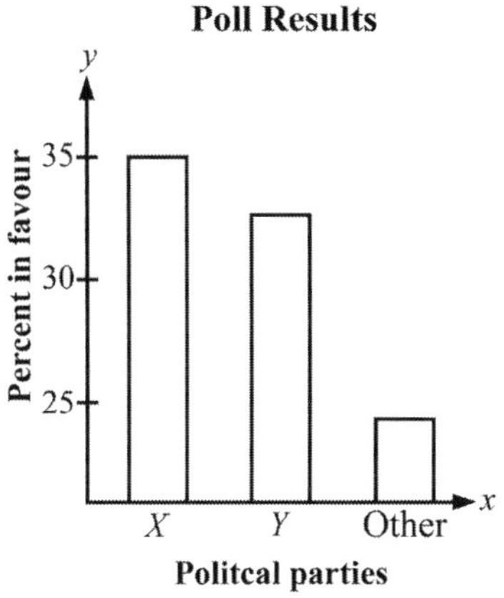

List three reasons that the graph misrepresents the claim by party X.

Solution

Some possible answers are:

1. The scale is drawn so that a difference of only 2% appears to be a significant difference.
2. There is 24% of "Other" which might be another party, or it might include undecided votes that could change the results for party's X and Y.
3. The sum of the figures given is 92%, which means that there is 8% unaccounted for in the results of the poll.
4. The small print reads "Poll results accurate within 3%." This means party X may have as little as 32% and party Y as much as 36% support.

Related Questions: 18, 19, 20, OR4

PRACTICE QUESTIONS—STATISTICAL ANALYSIS

1. If 10 was added to every value in a data set, then the measure that would change is the

   A. range

   B. median

   C. standard deviation

   D. interquartile range

Numerical Response

1. The standard deviation of the data set $\{5, 8, 9, 12, 15, 15, 17, 20, 21, 27\}$ to the nearest hundredth is ____________.

2. Terry had a score of 122 points in a city-wide contest with 3200 participants. There were 473 scores better than Terry's, and 64 scores equal to Terry's. What was Terry's percentile rank in the contest?

   A. 16 **B.** 17

   C. 84 **D.** 85

Numerical Response

2. Karl is 171 cm tall. The mean height of the students in Karl's class is 156 cm, and the standard deviation of their heights is 2.2 cm. If the heights have a normal distribution, then the z-score for Karl's height, to the nearest hundredth, is __________.

3. Which of the following graph types would best display the populations of Canada's ten provinces?

   A. Box plot

   B. Bar Graph

   C. Histogram

   D. Stem-and-leaf plot

Use the following information to answer the next question.

The following graph was obtained by entering one-variable data into a TI-83 graphing calculator.

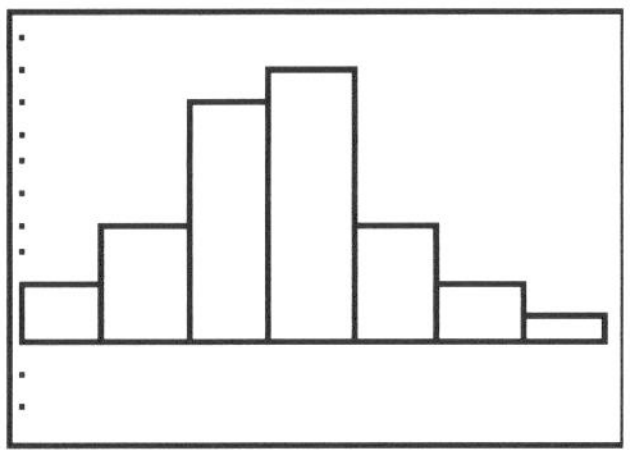

4. Which of the following data sets was **most** likely entered into the calculator to obtain the given graph?

   A. Restaurant ratings on a 10-point scale

   B. Sales of different types of vacuum cleaners

   C. The number of days with specific high temperatures in September

   D. Marks on a math exam compared to amount of time spent studying

5. If the sample size for a normally distributed population were doubled from 200 to 400, then the margin of error for a 95% confidence level will

   A. be exactly half the original margin of error

   B. be exactly double the original margin of error

   C. increase, but it will still be less than double the original margin of error

   D. decrease, but it will still be more than one-half the original margin of error

Use the following information to answer the next question.

The following screen shows information obtained by using the A:1-PropZInt function on a TI-83 graphing calculator.

```
1-PropZInt
 (.07683,.11317)
 p̂=.095
 n=1000
```

6. For the data that has been entered in the A:1-PropZInt function, what is the margin of error for the proportion, to the nearest tenth of a percent?

A. 1.8%

B. 3.6%

C. 7.6%

D. 9.5%

Use the following information to answer the next question.

The following data set represents the number of goals scored by individual players on a professional hockey team during the 2007–2008 season.

$$\left\{\begin{matrix} 51, 50, 35, 22, 21, 16, 8, 7, \\ 6, 6, 6, 3, 3, 2, 2, 2, 1, 1, 1, 0 \end{matrix}\right\}$$

7. The coach of the team reports that the average number of goals scored by his players is more than 12. Which of the following statements is true?

A. The coach reported the mean number of goals, and it is not misleading.

B. The coach reported the median number of goals and it is misleading; the mode would have been a better measure of central tendency.

C. The coach reported the mean number of goals and it is misleading; the median would have been a better measure of central tendency.

D. The coach reported the median number of goals and it is misleading; the mean would have been a better measure of central tendency.

Use the following information to answer the next question.

In preparation for a meeting with shareholders, the president of a company wants to prepare a graph to show that while this year's revenues are less than last year's revenues, they are not much less.

8. Which of the following described graphs would best convey his message?

A. A bar graph using a vertical scale that makes the bar representing this year's revenues slightly shorter than the bar representing last year's revenues.

B. A bar graph using a vertical scale that makes the bar representing this year's revenues much shorter than the bar representing last year's revenues.

C. A circle graph that shows the sector representing this year's revenues smaller than a sector representing last year's revenues.

D. A line graph with a line connecting this year's revenues to last year's revenues.

A calculator or computer with statistical functions is required for this question.

A survey collected data from adult men comparing the amount of time they spent exercising to the number of hours of television they watched on a weekly basis. The following sample of data is from the survey.

Exercising (h)	Television (h)
0	12
0.5	10
1	14
2	10
2.5	10
3	8
3.5	8
4	6
4.5	6
5	5

9. For the data given in the table, the linear correlation coefficient is approximately

A. –0.90

B. –0.81

C. 0.81

D. 0.90

Use the following information to answer the next question.

Two experimental groups of tree seedlings were given either Fertilizer X or Fertilizer Y. They were all planted in the same type of soil, and they received the same amount of water and sunlight. After two months, the heights of the seedlings were measured to see how many were taller or shorter than 20 cm tall, which is the expected height of the seedlings without fertilizer applied. The results of the experiment are shown if the following table.

	Fertilizer X	Fertilizer Y	Row Totals
Above 20 cm	11	13	24
Below 20 cm	14	12	26
Column Totals	25	25	50

10. Which of the following statements best describes the effectiveness of the fertilizers?

A. Both fertilizers stunt the growth of the seedlings.

B. Fertilizer X is significantly more effective than fertilizer Y.

C. Fertilizer Y is significantly more effective than fertilizer X.

D. Neither fertilizer appears to be more effective than the other.

11. Which of the following relationships **most** likely has a linear correlation coefficient of –0.10?

A. The speeds of cars and their stopping distances

B. The amount of cloud cover at night and the number of visible stars.

C. The amount of water applied to a lawn and the outdoor temperature.

D. The price of a cup of coffee and the price of a muffin at numerous coffee shops.

Use the following information to answer the next question.

A survey collected data from golfers comparing the average number of times they played per month to their average scores.

Games per month	Average score
4	98
5	92
6	89
7	90
8	86
9	85
10	82
11	83
12	78
13	78

12. Which of the following statements is **most** accurate?

A. The data is one-variable data and is best graphed by using a box plot.

B. The data is one-variable and is best graphed by using a bar graph.

C. The data is two-variable and is best graphed by using a scatter plot.

D. The data is two-variable and is best graphed by using side-by-side circle graphs.

13. Patrons of a restaurant were asked to fill out a form rating the restaurant on its food and on its service. Both ratings were on a scale of 1 to 5. Which of the following graphing choices would **best** give the owner of the restaurant the best visual summary of the results of the survey?

A. Double bar graph with one bar for each food and one bar for service.

B. Side-by-side circle graphs with one circle for food and one for service.

C. A scatter plot.

D. A histogram.

Use the following information to answer the next question.
A calculator or computer with statistical functions is required for this question.

x	3	7	8	9	12	14	16	19	20	25
y	28	26	25	20	18	17	15	12	11	6

14. For the data in the table above, the line of **best** fit in the form $y = ax + b$ is approximately

A. $y = -1.0x - 1$

B. $y = -1.0x - 31.5$

C. $y = -1.3x + 31.5$

D. $y = -1.0x + 31.5$

Use the following information to answer the next question.

Marco conducted a study with a sample size of 100 where he compared the number of years people spent in post-secondary education to their starting salary. He drew a scatter plot of his results and the corresponding line of best fit, which had a correlation coefficient of 0.98. The line of best fit is shown below.

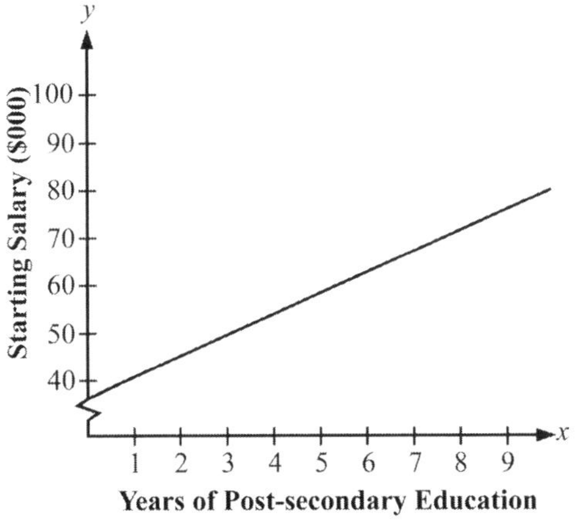

16. If Marco wants to make a change to show that years of post-secondary education do **not** significantly increase the starting salary, he could

A. increase the sample size.

B. eliminate some outliers.

C. stretch the horizontal scale on the graph.

D. stretch the vertical scale on the graph.

17. Rowena wanted to study the relationship between exercise and heart rate. Using the students in her class, she measured their resting heart rates and then had them skip from anywhere between 30 s to 5 min. Immediately after they finished skipping, she recorded their heart rates. Rowena did not get the linear relationship she was expecting. Which of the following reasons is **most** likely for the cause of the non-linear relationship?

A. Students' resting heart rates (before exercise) vary greatly.

B. Some students have trouble skipping.

C. There would be too many extreme outliers.

D. Heart rate as a function of skipping time is not a linear relationship.

Use the following information to answer the next question.

According to a published report in a newspaper, 70% of the students in school district A are honours students, whereas 60% of the students in school district B are honours students.

18. Which of the following statements about the reported statistics is true?

A. School district A had more honours students than school district B.

B. Students in school district A outperformed students in school district B.

C. A larger proportion of the student population in school district B were not honours students than in school district A.

D. The average marks for the honour students in school district A are 10% greater than the average marks of students in school district B.

Use the following information to answer the next question.

The following graph was published to compare the number of cell phone users in a particular region to the number of auto accidents in that region.

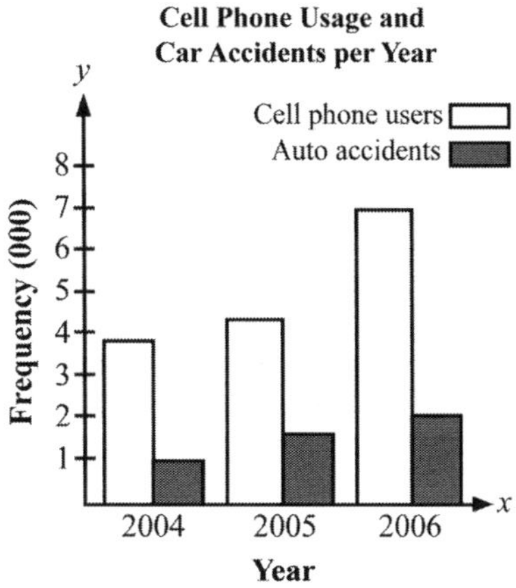

19. Which of the following statements based on the graph is true?

A. Cell phone usage causes accidents.

B. Cell phone usage is positively correlated to the number of auto accidents.

C. Cell phone usage is negatively correlated to the number of auto accidents.

D. Both the number of cell phone users and the number of auto accidents increased.

20. Which of the following sources is **most likely** authoritative, reliable, and unbiased about Canadian military involvement in a foreign country?

A. A documentary on television about the foreign country.

B. A report in the international section of the newspaper.

C. A report published by a federal politician.

D. A report published by Statistics Canada.

15. Which of the following statements regarding outliers is **most accurate**?

A. The effect of outliers on the equation of the line of best fit is always very slight.

B. The effect of outliers on the equation of the line of best fit is always slight when the number of data points is small.

C. The effect of outliers on the equation of the line of best fit may be great when the number of data points is small.

D. The effect of outliers on the equation of the line of best fit is always great when the number of data points is great.

Open Response

Use the following information to answer the next question.

Consider the following headline and pictograph appearing in a newspaper.

A teacher in Canada earns twice as much as a teacher in *XYZ*

OR1. Is the pictograph an accurate representation of the relative teacher earnings? Explain.

A calculator or computer with statistical functions is required for this question.

The following table shows the average wage in each of the ten regions in Canada, as well as the average number of working days lost per worker in each region due to any cause (e.g., illness, injury). The data is adapted from Statistics Canada for 2007.

Average wage ($)	Days lost (days)	
16.91	10.2	A
15.07	9.8	B
17.29	12.0	C
16.58	10.5	D
19.20	12.0	E
21.31	9.3	F
18.39	10.8	G
18.87	10.5	H
22.33	9.0	I
20.37	10.1	J

OR2. Determine the linear correlation coefficient to the nearest hundredth for the relationship between the average wage and the number of days lost per worker. Interpret what this value tells you about the relationship.

A calculator or computer with statistical functions is required for this question.

OR3. The following stopping distances were measured for a particular brand of motorcycle.

Speed (km/h)	Stopping distance (m)
20	5.6
30	7.5
40	9.8
50	13.2
60	17.4
70	21.5
80	25.3
90	28.2

a) Use the data in the given table to determine the equation of a linear regression line of the form $D = ax + b$, where x is the speed of the motorcycle and D is the stopping distance. Give the values of a and b to the nearest hundredth.

b) Use the equation from part **a)** to estimate the stopping distance to the nearest tenth of a metre, when the motorcycle is traveling at 120 km/h.

OR4. Assume that a survey is completed by randomly selecting 2 000 people from the population of Ontario. The survey found that people who ate fruit and vegetables every day had a 50% less chance of having heart problems. Give two reasons that this report may be misleading.

ANSWERS AND SOLUTIONS—STATISTICAL ANALYSIS

1. A	**6. A**	**13. A**	**20. D**
NR1. 6.35	**7. C**	**14. D**	**OR1. See Solution**
2. C	**8. A**	**15. C**	**OR2. See Solution**
NR2. 6.82	**9. A**	**16. C**	**OR3. See Solution**
3. D	**10. D**	**17. D**	**OR4. See Solution**
4. C	**11. D**	**18. C**	
5. D	**12. C**	**19. A**	

1. A

The median is a measure of central tendency. It would increase by 10 when each of the values in the data set increased by 10. The other choices are measures of dispersion, so they do not change because each of the data values is increased by the same amount.

NR1. 6.35

Follow the following steps using a TI-83 calculator:

1. Press [2nd] [+] [4:ClrAllLists] [ENTER]
2. Press [STAT] 1:Edit and enter the data in L1
3. Press [STAT] ~ to highlight "CALC", then [1:1-Var Stats], [ENTER]

You should see the following screen:

```
1-Var Stats
 x̄=14.9
 Σx=149
 Σx²=2623
 Sx=6.690789689
 σx=6.347440429
↓n=10
```

The standard deviation (σ), shown to the nearest hundredth, is 6.35.

2. C

The number of scores below Terry's is $3200-(473+64)=2663$.

The number of scores equal to Terry's is 64.

$$\text{Terry's percentile rank } = \frac{B+\frac{1}{2}E}{n}\times 100$$

$$= \frac{2663+\frac{1}{2}(64)}{3200}\times 100$$

$$= \frac{2695}{3200}\times 100$$

$$= 84$$

NR2. 6.82

Karl's z-score can be determined using $z=\frac{x-\mu}{\sigma}$, where $x=171$, $\mu=156$, and $\sigma=2.2$

$$z=\frac{171-156}{2.2}$$

$$=\frac{15}{2.2}=6.82$$

3. **D**

The data is categorical, so the bar graph is the best choice. The other given graphs are not used to show categorical data.

4. **C**

Since the graph is a histogram, the data is quantitative. The number of days (frequency) with specific temperatures (quantitative data) would be appropriately displayed by a histogram. The sales figures for different types of vacuum cleaners are categorical data, restaurant ratings are ordinal data, and the marks on a math exam compared to the amount of time spent studying are two-variable data.

5. **D**

The margin of error will definitely decrease, but not to half of what it was. From your investigations, you should have discovered that increasing the sample size decreases the margin of error, but not proportionally, i.e., when the sample size is doubled, the margin of error is not halved.

6. **A**

The margin of error for the proportion is $= 0.095 - 0.07683 = 0.018 = 1.8\%$ (note that $\hat{p} = \frac{95}{1000}$).

7. **C**

The mean number of goals is 12.15, so that is the measure of central tendency that the coach reported. This is misleading because only 6 of the 20 players scored more than 12 goals. The median, which is 6, is a better indication of the central tendency of the data.

8. **A**

Since the president intends to compare the revenues for only the past two years, the data set is one-variable data so a bar graph would be appropriate. As well, since the purpose is to show only a slight loss in revenues, a vertical scale that results in the bars being closer in height should be used. A circle graph is only appropriate for showing how one thing, or amount, is partitioned. For example, it could show the different factors that contributed to one year's revenues. A line graph would not be appropriate because more relationships between the year and the revenues would be required to create a correlation that can be represented by the line.

9. **A**

In order to obtain the answer, follow the given procedure with a TI-83 calculator:

1. Press [2nd] [+] [4:ClrAllLists] [ENTER]

2. Press [2nd] [0], scroll down to [DiagnosticOn], press [ENTER]

3. Press [STAT] [1:Edit] and enter the exercising time in L1 and the television time in L2.

4. Press [STAT] ~ to highlight "CALC", then scroll down to [4:linReg(ax+b)], press [ENTER], [ENTER]

You should see the following screen:

```
LinReg
 y=ax+b
 a=-1.492424242
 b=12.78030303
 r²=.8066051461
 r=-.8981119897
```

The correlation coefficient is approximately –0.90, which indicates a strong negative correlation.

10. **D**

Since the number of seedlings growing above 20 cm is close to 12.5, which is half of the seedlings in each group, neither fertilizer appears to be more effective than the other. However, since approximately half of the seedlings exceeded the expected 20 cm height, it cannot be concluded that the either fertilizer stunts the growth of the seedlings either.

11. **D**

A correlation coefficient of –0.10 suggests a very slight negative correlation. However, since the coefficient is very close to 0, the coefficient suggests that there is almost no correlation. The price of a cup of coffee and the price of a muffin are probably unrelated, but there may be a slight correlation, negative or positive. The speeds of cars and their stopping distances have strong positive correlations, as does the amount of water applied to a lawn and the outdoor temperature. The amount of cloud cover at night and the number of visible stars has a strong negative correlation.

12. **C**

The data is two-variable and quantitative. A scatter plot would be an appropriate graph. Choice **D** would be inappropriate because the data does not apply to how one thing is partitioned.

13. **A**

Since the data is ordinal data, the bar graphs with the heights of the bars determined by the frequencies would be the best visual summary.

14. **D**

Using a TI-83 calculator, the procedure is
Press [2nd] [+] [4:ClrAllLists] [ENTER]
Press [2nd] [0] , scroll down to [DiagnosticOn], press [ENTER]
Press [STAT] [1:Edit] and enter the x-values in L1 and the y-values in L2.
Press [STAT] ~ to highlight "CALC", then scroll down to [4:LinReg(ax+b)], press [ENTER], [ENTER]
You should see the following screen:

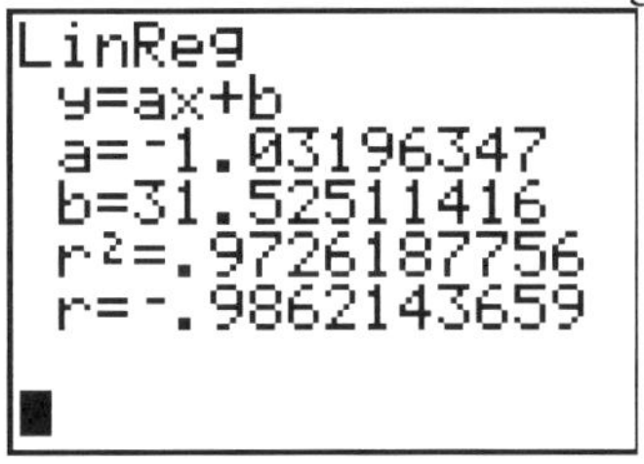

You can see from the values of *a* and *b* that the linear equation is approximately $y = -1.0x + 31.5$.

15. **C**

When the number of data points is small, each outlier has a greater influence on the line of best fit, and consequently, on its equation.

16. **C**

Stretching the horizontal scale on the graph would make it appear that the slope of the line is not as great and thus, giving the impression that the increase in salary is not as great for each year of increase in post-secondary education. Choice **D** would have the opposite effect. Choice **A** is incorrect because the effect of a larger sample size is unknown. Choice **B** is incorrect because the correlation coefficient is given as 0.98, which means the relation is very close to linear and that the outliers are having little effect.

17. **D**

Generally, heart rates would reach a maximum before 5 minutes of skipping and then remain relatively constant, so there would not be linear relationship. Choice **C** would likely be the case if she drew a scatter plot and line of best fit, but there is no indication that she did so.

18. **C**

Since 60% of the students in the school district B were honours students, 40% were not, whereas only 30% of the students in school district A were not honours students. Therefore, a larger proportion of the student population in school district B were not honours students than in school district A.
It cannot be determined from the statistics given that there are more honours students in school district A than school district B because you don't know the number of students in each district. As well, the actual performance of the students in the districts is unknown because the districts may have different standards for honours, or perhaps many of the students in district A barely achieved honours, while most of the honours students in district B achieved very high standards. While 10% more students were honours students in district A, this does not mean their grades were 10% higher, because you do not know the marks of any students.

19. **A**

Although both the cell phone usage and the accidents increased, you cannot say for sure that one caused the other. Therefore, it cannot be concluded that the two data sets are correlated in any manner.

20. **D**

Statistics Canada reports should be the best of the given choices. Statistics Canada has the legal power to ensure their sampling techniques are representative of the population they represent. For example, surveys from Statistics Canada must be completed and returned. It is illegal to not do so.

OR1.

The pictograph is not an accurate representation of the relative teacher earnings. Although the relative heights of the two bags are correct, the taller bag is also wider. Because the taller bag is also twice as wide, the pictograph shows a larger money bag that would hold approximately $2 \times 2 = 4$ times the amount of money. Therefore, the pictograph is showing that the teacher in Canada makes 4 times as much money as the teacher in country XYZ, not twice as much as the headline states.

OR2.

In order to obtain the answer, follow the given procedure with a TI-83 calculator:

1. Press [2nd] [+] [4:ClrAllLists] [ENTER]
2. Press [2nd] [0], scroll down to [DiagnosticOn], press [ENTER]
3. Press [STAT] [1:Edit] and enter the average wage in L1 and the days lost in L2.
4. Press [STAT] ~ to highlight "CALC", then scroll down to [4:linReg(ax+b)], press [ENTER], [ENTER]

You should see the following screen:

```
LinReg
 y=ax+b
 a=-.1670518441
 b=13.53250996
 r²=.1432400549
 r=-.378470679
```

The correlation coefficient is approximately –0.38, which indicates a weak negative correlation. This means that there is a weak relationship between higher wages and fewer days lost per worker.

OR3.

Using a TI-83 calculator, the procedure is

Press [2nd] [+] [4:ClrAllLists] [ENTER]

Press [2nd] [0], scroll down to [DiagnosticOn], press [ENTER]

Press [STAT] [1:Edit] and enter speed values in L1 and the stopping distances in L2.

Press [STAT] ~ to highlight "CALC", then scroll down to [4:LinReg(ax+b)], press [ENTER], [ENTER]

You should see the following screen:

```
LinReg
 y=ax+b
 a=.3410714286
 b=-2.696428571
 r²=.9886403424
 r=.9943039487
```

You can see from the values of *a* and *b* that the linear equation is approximately $D = 0.34x - 2.70$.

Substitute $x = 120$ into $D = 0.34x - 2.70$ and solve for D.

$D = 0.34(120)) - 2.70$

$D = 40.8 - 2.70$

$D = 38.1$

Thus the stopping distance when travelling 120 km/h is approximately 38.1 m.

OR4.

Possible answers are:
The sample size of 2 000 for Ontario is relatively small.
The survey says "ate fruit and vegetables every day," which would likely be a small number of people.
There is no indication of the numbers of people who replied that they eat fruit and vegetables, or the number of people with heart problems.
There is no definition of "heart problems."
What does 50% less mean? For example, if 2/100 is reduced to 1/100, is that 50% less?

STATISTICAL ANALYSIS—UNIT TEST

1. Which of the following data sets would be classified as one-variable data?
   A. The lengths of a tree's shadow at various times of the day.
   B. Goals scored by a hockey team in each of the games last season.
   C. The stopping distances for a car travelling with various initial speeds.
   D. Marks on a mathematics test by various students compared to their hours of study.

Numerical Response

1. The interquartile range for the data set $\{6.8, 9.2, 3.1, 7.5, 8.0, 5.5, 9.3, 3.7, 3.6, 2.8\}$ is ____________.

2. The marks for a math test had a normal distribution with a mean of 52% and a standard deviation of 8. The teacher decided to raise the mean of the marks to 64% and change the standard deviation to 12 by not including the value of one of the difficult questions on the test. If Matthew's original mark was 58% before the adjustment, what was his mark after the teacher made the adjustment?
   A. 66
   B. 70
   C. 73
   D. 76

Numerical Response

2. The mean temperature at 12:00 P.M. in 68 cities across Canada was 22.4°C on a particular day in June. The temperature in Thunder Bay was 21.0°C. If there were 35 cities warmer than Thunder Bay and two cities with the same temperature, the percentile rank of the temperature in Thunder Bay, to the nearest whole number, was ____________.

3. Greg surveyed 134 students from his school to determine what mode of transportation they used to get to school. He then drew a circle graph to display these results. If the circle graph had a sector representing bike transportation with a central angle of 51°, then how many students in the survey used bike transportation to get to school?
   A. 19 **B.** 38
   C. 51 **D.** 137

Use the following information to answer the next question.

A teacher attempted to draw a box plot for the distribution of math marks in her class using her TI-83 calculator. She used the following steps to draw a box plot graph.

Step 1 Press [2nd] [+] [4:ClrAllLists] [ENTER]
Step 2 Press [STAT] [1:Edit] and enter the height in L1 and the frequency in L2.
Step 3 Press [2nd] [Y=] [ENTER]
Step 4 Use the arrows to scroll to On, press [ENTER], scroll to the second box plot icon, press [ENTER]
Step 5 Scroll to Xlist:, press [2nd] [1] to choose L1
Step 6 Press [ZOOM], scroll down to 9:ZoomStat, press [ENTER]

4. The histogram that the calculator produced did not correctly represent the given data. Which of the given steps used by the teacher was incorrect?

   A. Step 2

   B. Step 3

   C. Step 4

   D. Step 5

A calculator or computer with statistical functions is required for this question.

5. A political party surveyed 2500 people and reported that 56% of the potential voters in a riding preferred their candidate. The political party wanted to know how accurate their survey was. If the population of voters was normally distributed, then the margin of error for the reported confidence level should be

   A. 1%

   B. 2%

   C. 3%

   D. 4%

Use the following information to answer the next question

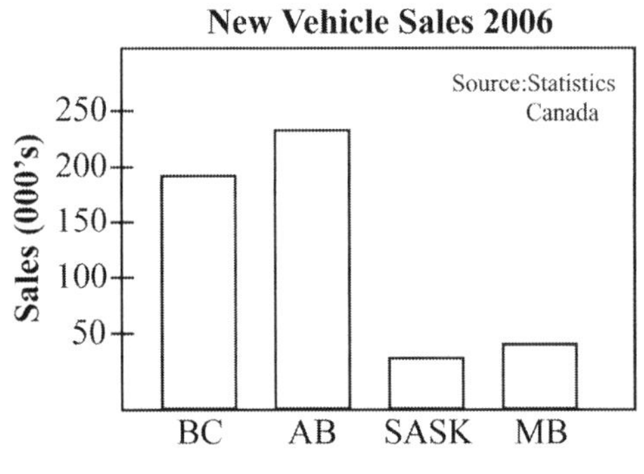

6. Which of the following statements is based on the information in the graph?

   A. In 2006, there were more trucks in Alberta than in Manitoba.

   B. The population of British Columbia in 2006 was greater than the population of Saskatchewan.

   C. In 2006, more new vehicles were sold in British Columbia than in Saskatchewan and Manitoba combined.

   D. Fewer new vehicles were sold in Saskatchewan than in Alberta because more new vehicles were sold in Saskatchewan in 2005.

Use the following information to answer the next question.

The following table illustrates the sample data collected in a study comparing the purchase price of automobiles by one manufacturer in 1980 to the number of kilometres they were driven before requiring major mechanical repair (i.e., engine, transmission, or suspension repairs).

Purchase price ($)	**Kilometres driven (× 1000)**
10 000	190
12 000	180
14 000	290
16 000	240
18 000	280
20000	240
22 000	300
24 000	280

7. Which of the following statements best describes the quality of the correlation between the variables?

   A. There is a strong positive correlation between the purchase price and the kilometres driven.

   B. There is a strong negative correlation between the purchase price and the kilometres driven.

   C. There is a moderate positive correlation between the purchase price and the kilometres driven.

   D. There is a moderate negative correlation between the purchase price and the kilometres driven.

8. The relationship between the number of people barbecuing and the time of sunset would most likely have a linear correlation coefficient that is closest to

   A. –0.8

   B. –0.4

   C. 0

   D. 0.5

Use the following information to answer the next question.

Jennifer is using a TI-83 calculator to draw a scatter plot of two variable data that she has collected. She follows the following steps

Step1 Press [2nd] [+] [4:ClrAllLists] [ENTER]

Step2 Press [STAT] [1:Edit] and enter the dependent variable values in L1 and the independent variable values in L2.

Step 3 Press [2nd] [Y=] [ENTER]

Step 4 Use the arrows to scroll to "On", press [ENTER], scroll to the 1st icon (scatter plot), press [ENTER]

Step 5 Ensure that the variables are labelled as Xlist:L1 and Ylist:L2.

9. Jennifer made her first mistake in

   A. Step 1

   B. Step 2

   C. Step 3

   D. Step 4

10. When data in two variables is compared by drawing side-by-side box plots, then it is easy to see the

    A. frequencies of individual data values.

    B. mean of the two data sets

    C. relationships between individual data values

    D. medians of the two data sets

A calculator or computer with statistical functions is required for this question.

x	y
38	18
41	17
45	14
49	12
52	10
54	9
57	7
61	4
65	3
70	2

11. When a line of best fit is drawn for the data shown in the table above, the most extreme outlier has an x-value of

    A. 0.76

    B. 1.5

    C. 41

    D. 70

Use the following information to answer thee next question.

An experimental farm studied the effects of two different fertilizers, **A** and **B**, on wheat production. They applied Fertilizer **A** to 100 separate plots of one acre each and applied the same amount of Fertilizer **B** to a different 100 one-acre plots. The farm summarized and reported the results of the study with the following set of box plots.

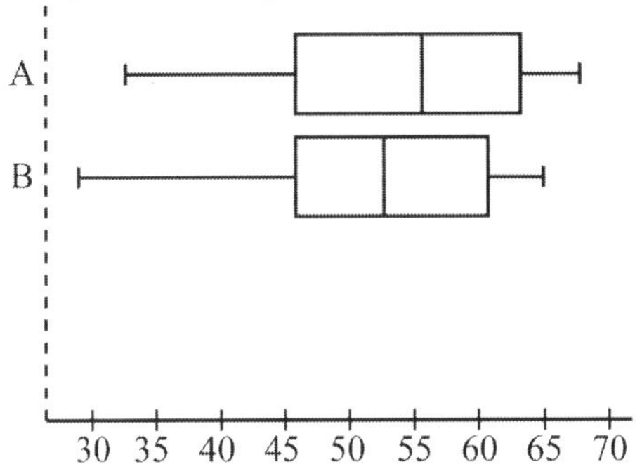

12. Which of the following statements **cannot** necessarily be made from the information summarized by the graphs of the box plots?

A. Fertilizer **A** outperformed Fertilizer **B**.

B. The median for Fertilizer **A** production is higher than for Fertilizer **B** production.

C. The interquartile range for Fertilizer **A** production is greater than for Fertilizer **B** production.

D. Both Fertilizer **A** and Fertilizer **B** increased production.

13. A city council advertises that it increased the police force by 10% in the previous year. They claimed that the crime rate in the city dropped by 6% as a result. This is an example of

A. an assumed cause-and-effect relationship

B. an accidental relationship

C. a inverse linear correlation

D. a direct linear correlation

Use the following information to answer the next question.

Assume that a company did a taste test survey using four different brands of coffee. The participants were asked to rate each coffee on a scale of one to five. After the survey was completed and the mean of the scores for each brand of coffee were calculated, the following summary was reported:

Coffee Brand	Average Rating
A	4.2
B	3.8
C	3.1
D	2.1

14. Which of the following conclusions can be made based on the summary?

A. Coffee brand A received the most scores of 5.

B. Coffee brand A is twice as good as coffee brand D.

C. More drinkers gave brand D a score of 1 or 2 than a score of 5.

D. More people drink coffee brands A and B than coffee brands C and D.

15. Before manufacturing a CD of 1960s music hits, a recording company surveys potential customers. If they want to choose a sample that would have the greatest number of potential customers for the CD, then they would **most likely** choose a sample with a

A. timing bias

B. cultural bias

C. stratified bias

D. non-response bias

Open Response

A calculator or computer with statistical functions is required for this question.

OR1. A golf equipment company claims that 50% of all players use their brand of golf ball. They also state they are 95% confident of this claim.

a) If the company's statement is correct, determine the margin of error, to the nearest tenth of a percent, for sample sizes of 200, 400, 800, and 1600 golfers, from a population with normal distribution.

b) Using the results from part **a)**, determine the amount of change in the margin of error each time the sample size doubled: from 200 to 400, 400 to 800, and 800 to 1600.

c) From the results from part **b)**, what affect does doubling the sample size have on the margin of error?

A calculator or computer with statistical functions is required for this question.

x	16	20	24	28	32	36	40	44
y	18	21	24	27	40	33	36	39

OR2. For the data given in the table above, determine the amount of change in the slope of the line of best fit when the outlier is removed. Give the answer to the nearest hundredth.

OR3. The owner of a gasoline service station recorded the following data regarding the price of gasoline and the number of daily sales.

Gasoline Price ($/L)	Number of Daily Sales
1.05	320
1.09	270
1.14	250
1.19	245
1.24	140
1.29	132

a) Determine the linear equation of the line of best fit in the form $N = ap + b$ where N is the number of daily sales and p is the price ($/L). Round values of a and b to the nearest whole number.

b) Use your calculator to draw a scatter plot and the line of best fit for the data.

c) Use the linear equation from a) to predict the price of gasoline when the number of sales is 100.

d) The owner claims that he will not be able to keep the station open when the number of daily sales is less than 100. Based on the scatter plot and line of best fit, give a reason why the predicted price from part **c)** is unreasonable.

Open Response

Use the following information to answer the next question.

A magazine publisher surveys the readership of its magazine about the likely results of an upcoming election. The results of the survey give a prediction that Johnson will beat White in the election. On Election Day, White beats Johnson by a wide margin.

OR4. What is the **most likely** reason for the incorrect prediction?

ANSWERS AND SOLUTIONS—UNIT TEST

1. B	**5. D**	**10. D**	**14. C**
NR1. 4.4	**OR1. See solution**	**11. D**	**15. C**
2. C	**6. C**	**OR2. See solution**	**OR4. See solution**
NR2. 47	**7. C**	**12. D**	
3. A	**8. D**	**OR3. See solution**	
4. D	**9. B**	**13. A**	

1. **B**

There is no indication that the goals scored in the hockey games are related to any other data. Therefore, this data is one-variable. All the other choices are examples of two-variable data because they involve a relationship between two different attributes (shadow length vs. time, stopping distance vs. speed, math marks vs. hours of study).

NR1. **4.4**

Follow the following steps using a TI-83 calculator:
Press [2nd] [+] [4:ClrAllLists] [ENTER]
Press [STAT] [1:Edit] and enter the data in L1
Press [STAT] ▷ to highlight "CALC", then [1:1-Var Stats], [ENTER]
Press the downward arrow several times to view the following information.
You should see the following screen:

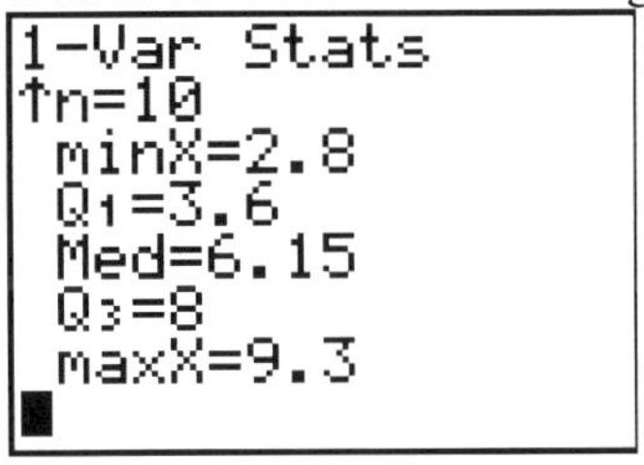

The interquartile range
$= Q_3 - Q_1 = 8 - 3.6 = 4.4.$

2. **C**

Matthew's rank in the class would not change after the adjustment, so his z-score remains the same. His z-score from his original mark of 58 was

$$z = \frac{58-52}{8} = \frac{6}{8} = 0.75.$$

You can now calculate his new score, x, with the new mean of 64 and new standard deviation of 12.

$$0.75 = \frac{x-64}{12}$$
$$0.75(12) = x - 64$$
$$9 = x - 64$$
$$73 = x$$

Therefore, Matthew's adjusted mark was 73%.

NR2. **47**

Since there were 35 cities warmer and two with the same temperature, there were $68-(35+2)=31$ with lower temperatures.
Thunder Bay's percentile rank

$$= \frac{B + \frac{1}{2}E}{n} \times 100$$
$$= \frac{31 + \frac{1}{2}(2)}{68} \times 100$$
$$= \frac{32}{68} \times 100$$
$$= 47$$

3. **A**

The fraction of students who used bike transportation was $\frac{51}{360}$. The number of students who used bike transportation was $\frac{51}{360} \times 134 = 19$ (to the nearest whole number).

4. **D**

In Step 5, the teacher must be sure that L2 is entered as the frequency (beside Freq:).

5. **D**

In order to obtain the answers, follow the given procedure with a TI-83 calculator:
Press STAT, scroll to TESTS
Scroll down to A:1-PropZint, press ENTER
Enter x:1400 (which is 0.56×2500), n:2500, and C-Level:95
Scroll to Calculate and press ENTER.
You should see the following screen:

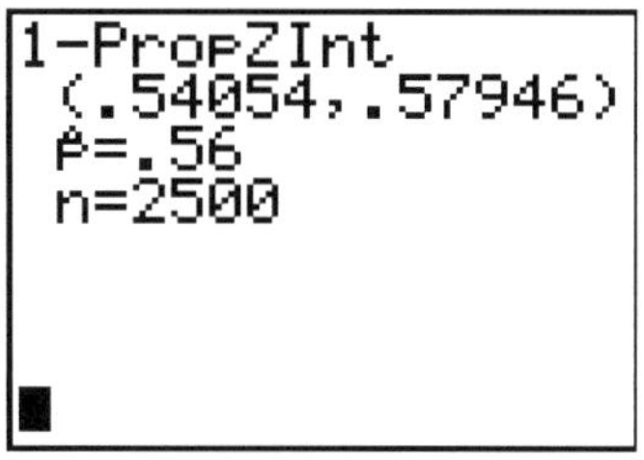

The margin of error $= 0.56 - 0.54054 = 0.01946 = 1.9\%$.
Therefore, the margin of error for the reported confidence level should be 2%.

6. **C**

The new vehicle sales for Saskatchewan and Manitoba were less than 50 000 for each, so their combined total sales were less than 100 000. The new vehicle sales for British Columbia were close to 200 000. Therefore, the statement that more new vehicles were sold in British Columbia than in Saskatchewan and Manitoba combined is true.
While there might have been more trucks in Alberta than in Manitoba in 2006, this is not represented on the graph. As well, the graph does not show any information about population, so the statement that British Columbia has a larger population than Saskatchewan is not based on the graph.

7. **C**

First, determine the value of the linear correlation coefficient (*r*). Follow the given procedure with a TI-83 calculator:

1. Press 2nd + 4:ClrAllLists ENTER
2. Press 2nd 0, scroll down to DiagnosticOn, press ENTER
3. Press STAT 1:Edit and enter the purchase price in L1 and the kilometres driven in L2.
4. Press STAT ~ to highlight "CALC", then scroll down to 4:linReg(ax+b), press ENTER, ENTER

The value of *r* according to the calculator should be approximately 0.72, which indicates a moderate positive correlation.

8. **D**

There is likely more people barbecuing during the summer when the time of sunset is later, although the relationship is likely not real strong. Therefore, the relationship likely has a moderate positive correlation. Of the given alternatives, the coefficient that best represents a moderate positive correlation is 0.5.

9. **B**

Jennifer should have entered the independent variable value in L1 and the dependent variable values in L2.

10. **D**

The medians of the two data sets are clearly visible on the box plots. The characteristics stated in the other choices are not visible.

11. **D**

Using a TI-83 calculator, the procedure is
Press [2nd] [+] [4:ClrAllLists] [ENTER]
Press [2nd] [0] , scroll down to [DiagnosticOn], press [ENTER]
Press [STAT] [1:Edit] and enter the x-values in L1 and the y-values in L2.
Press [STAT] ~ to highlight "CALC", then scroll down to [4:LinReg(ax+b)], press [ENTER], [ENTER]
Press [STAT] [1:Edit] and uses the scrolling arrows to put the cursor on L3. Press [2nd] STAT, scroll down to 7:RESID, press [ENTER], [ENTER]. The residuals should now appear in L3. When you scroll through the residuals you find that the one with the larges absolute value is the one that occurs when the value of x is 70, as shown.

L1	L2	L3 3
49	12	.11519
52	10	-.2528
54	9	-.1648
57	7	-.5328
61	4	-1.357
65	3	-.1808
70	2	1.5392

L3(10) =1.53922789...

12. **D**

There is no indication of what the wheat production would be without the fertilizer. The other choices are clearly correct from the graphs. Because the median is higher for fertilizer A production, you know that the top half of these plots outperformed the top half of the fertilizer B plots. The lowest score, highest score, lower quartile, and third quartile are all as good or better for the fertilizer A plots. Therefore, it is clear that fertilizer A outperformed fertilizer B.

13. **A**

It is assumed that increasing the police force decreased the crime rate. However, there are not enough ordered pairs to draw a conclusion about a linear relationship.

14. **C**

If one-half of the coffee drinkers rated brand **D** a 5 and the other half rated brand **D** a 1, then the expected mean would be a 3 $\left(\frac{5+1}{2}=3\right)$. Therefore, more drinkers had to give brand **D** a score less than 3 than a score of 5.

Coffee brand **A** may not have more scores of 5 (it must have some) than brand **B**, because brand **B** might have had more 5s and more lower scores (1s and 2s, for example) than brand **A**. This would result in a lower mean score, even though brand **B** had more 5s.

It cannot be determined if brand A is "twice as good" as brand **D** as there is no measure for goodness. It can only be understood that brand **A** scored a mean twice that of the mean for brand **D**. It cannot be determined from the summary how many coffee drinkers drink which brand.

15. **C**

The recording company would likely choose a stratified sample based on age, possibly people between people between 50 and 70, because they were likely fans of the 60s music.

OR1.

a) Using a TI-83 calculator and the A:1-PropZInt function, the calculated margin of error for each of the sample sizes is:
Sample size = 200:
Calculator screen:

```
1-PropZInt
 (.4307,.5693)
 p̂=.5
 n=200
```

Margin of error
$= 0.5 - 0.4307 = 0.0693 = 6.9\%$.
Sample size = 400:
Calculator screen:

```
1-PropZInt
 (.451,.549)
 p̂=.5
 n=400
```

Margin of error
$= 0.5 - 0.451 = 0.049 = 4.9\%$.
Sample size = 800:
Calculator screen:

```
1-PropZInt
 (.46535,.53465)
 p̂=.5
 n=800
```

Margin of error
$= 0.5 - 0.46535 = 0.03465 = 3.5\%$.
Sample size = 1 600:
Calculator screen:

```
1-PropZInt
 (.4755,.5245)
 p̂=.5
 n=1600
```

Margin of error
$= 0.5 - 0.4755 = 0.0245 = 2.5\%$.

b) The amounts of change in the margin of error for each instance that the sample size doubled are:
For sample size change from 200 to 400, the change in the margin of error is $4.9 - 6.9 = -2.0$ percentage points.
For sample size change from 400 to 800, the change in the margin of error is $3.5 - 4.9 = -1.4$ percentage points.
For sample size change from 800 to 1600, the change in the margin of error is $2.5 - 3.5 = -1.0$ percentage points.

c) Doubling the sample size reduces the margin of error, but as the sample size increases the significance of the effect diminishes.

OR2.

By examining the data it is clear that the point (32, 40) is the outlier. For every consecutive pair of points not including (32, 40), a change of 4 in the *x*-value results in a change of 3 in the *y*-value. Thus, without (32, 40), the line of best fit would have a slope of $\frac{3}{4} = 0.75$.

To determine the slope of the line with (32, 40) included, you can use a graphing calculator.
Using a TI-83 calculator, the procedure is
Press [2nd] [+] [4:ClrAllLists] [ENTER]
Press [2nd] [0] , scroll down to DiagnosticOn, press [ENTER]
Press [STAT] 1:Edit and enter the x-values in L1 and the y-values in L2.
Press [STAT] ~ to highlight "CALC", then scroll down to [4:LinReg(ax+b)], press [ENTER], [ENTER]
You should see the following screen:

```
LinReg
 y=ax+b
 a=.7797619048
 b=6.357142857
 r²=.824611984
 r=.9080814854
```

The slope is the a-value, which is approximately 0.80. Thus, the change in slope by removing the outlier would be from 0.80 to 0.75, which is –0.05.

OR3.

a) Press 2nd + 4:ClrAllLists ENTER
Press 2nd 0 , scroll down to DiagnosticOn, press ENTER
Press STAT 1:Edit and enter the gasoline price in L1 and the number of sales in L2.
Press STAT ~ to highlight "CALC", then scroll down to 4:LinReg(ax+b), press ENTER, ENTER
You should see the following screen:

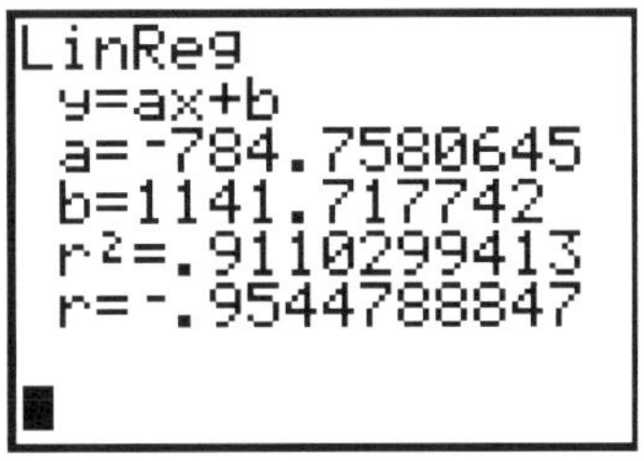

You can see that the linear equation is approximately $N = -785p + 1142$.

b) Press 2nd Y= ENTER
Use the arrows to scroll to On, press ENTER, scroll to the 1st icon (scatter plot), press ENTER
Check that the variables are labelled as Xlist:L1 and Ylist:L2. Change if necessary.
Press Y= VARS 5:Statistics ~ ~ 1:RegEQ ENTER
Press ZOOM, scroll down to 9:ZoomStat, press ENTER
You should see the following screen:

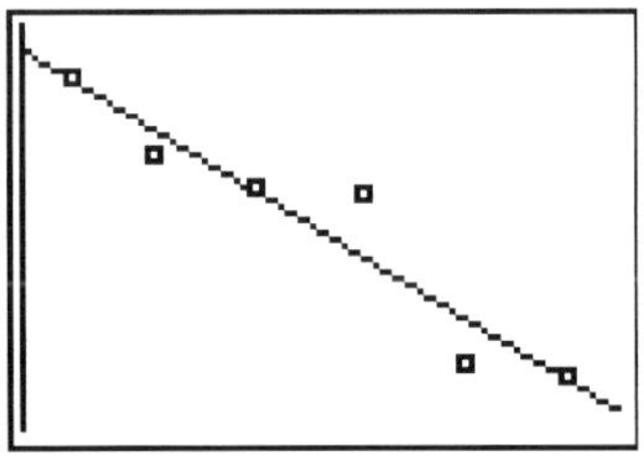

c) Substitute $N = 100$ into $N = -785p + 1142$ and solve for p.

$100 = -785p + 1142$

$785p = 1042$

$p \approx 1.33$

d) It appears that when the price gets to a certain level, a change of \$0.05 in the price does not affect the number of customers in a direct linear fashion. For example, notice that when the price changed from \$1.24 to \$1.29 there was a loss of only 8 customers.

OR4.

The most likely reason that the prediction was incorrect is that the readership is a biased sample of the electorate. The magazine likely appeals to a certain culture or interest group.

NOTES

Culminating Data Management Investigation

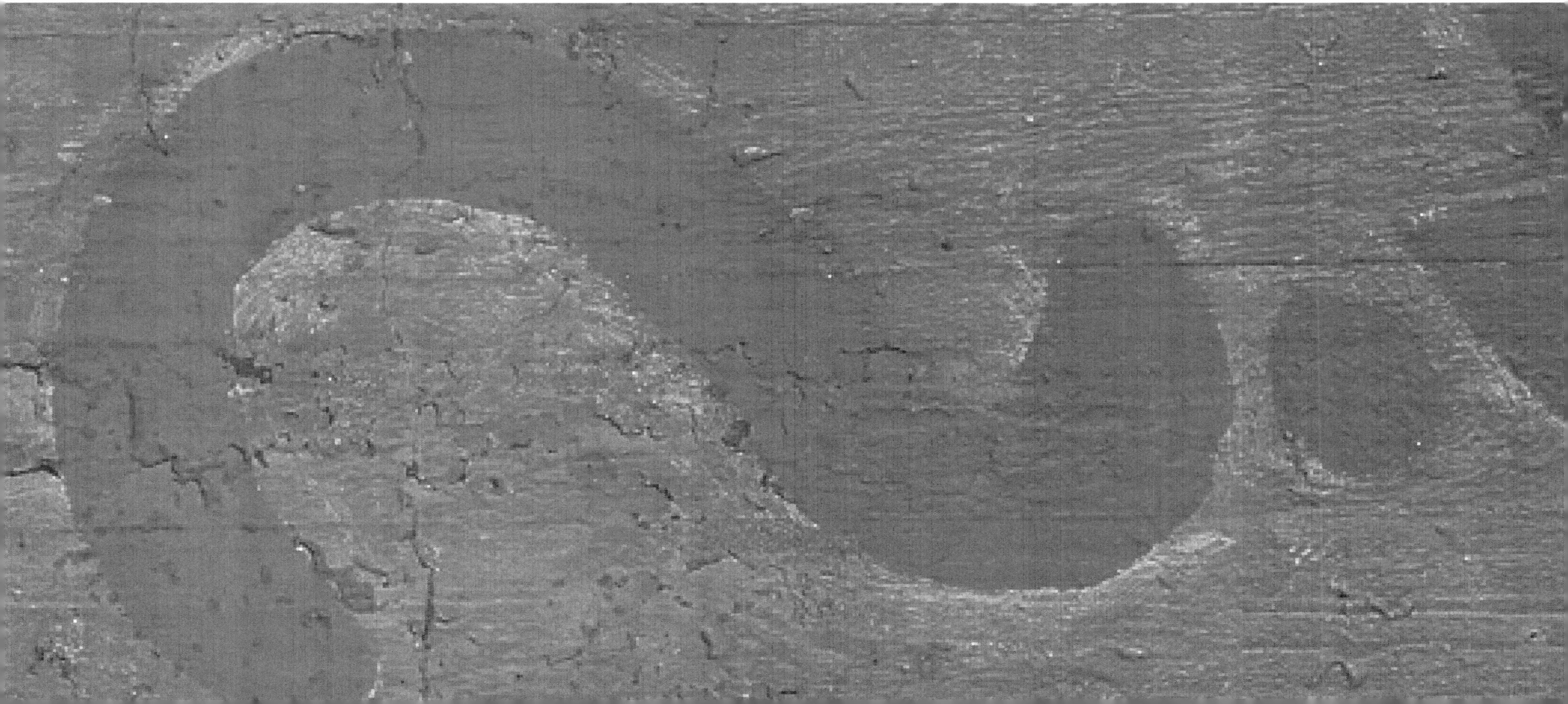

CULMINATING DATA MANAGEMENT SAMPLE INVESTIGATION

DESIGN AND CARRY OUT AN INVESTIGATION

The concepts and skills acquired in Data Management can be used to study and analyse a variety of topics. In order to analyse a topic using your data management skills, you will need to:

- identify a topic
- design a survey
- identify a sample size
- collect the data
- present the data graphically

SAMPLE INVESTIGATION

Use your understanding of data management to create an investigation based on the following question:

"Is there a relationship between the number of hours spent on homework per week and the number of hours worked part-time per week?"

SURVEY DESIGN AND SAMPLE SELECTION

Begin your investigation by designing a procedure for the investigation. In this case, a survey could be used to collect the data required. Design a student survey that will obtain the following information from each participant:

i) Grade level of the participant
ii) Average number of part-time hours worked per week
iii) Actual courses currently taken
v) Average number of hours spent on homework per week for each course.

After designing the survey, select a representative sample of Grade 11 and 12 students from your school population that work part-time. Ensure that the sample size .

Design and administer a teacher survey to determine the number of expected hours of homework per week that the teacher for each course suggests.

DATA COLLECTION AND ORGANIZATION

Collect the necessary data from each student and teacher according to the survey design. Organize the data into the following tables:

- Number of hours of part-time work/week.
- Average number of hours of homework per course $= \dfrac{\text{Total homework hours/week}}{\text{Number of courses/week}}$

Organize the data into two frequency tables—one for each of the categories shown above. The frequency categories should be appropriately sized so that the number of categories for each table is between 5 and 10.

GRAPHICAL REPRESENTATION OF DATA

In order to display the data, construct the following graphs:

- Use the frequency tables to construct overlapping histograms for each of the two grade levels. One histogram will represent the number of hours of part-time work per week; the other will represent the average number of hours of homework per week.
- Construct a double bar graph to representing the average hours of homework per week for each selected course. One bar should represent the students' values and the second bar should represent the teachers' values.
- Make a scatter plot of the number of hours of homework per course per week (vertical axis) compared to the number of part-time hours worked per week (horizontal axis). Use all of the individual student data values.

Data Analysis and Calculations

1. Choose three courses taken at each grade level and find the following:
   a) Average hours of homework per week per selected course
   b) Expected hours of homework per week per selected course
2. Analyse the data represented by the scatter plot:
   a) Decide if there appears to be a positive correlation, a negative correlation, or no correlation at all.
   b) Carry out a linear regression on the data. Enter the data used for the scatter plot as lists L_1 (number of part-time hours per week) and L_2 (number of hours of homework per week). Determine the linear correlation coefficient for the data and a linear function of the form $y = mx + b$ where y represents the number of hours of homework and x represents the number of hours of part-time work per week.
   c) Determine the average (mean) values of all student results for the number of part-time hours worked per week and the number of homework hours per course per week. Round the answers to the nearest tenth.
   d) Use the regression equation to predict the number of hours spent on homework per course per week for three values for hours of part-time work per week that are greater than the largest value in the data set.
3. Use the values in L_1 to determine the mean $\left(\overline{X}\right)$ and the standard deviation $\left(\sigma_x\right)$ for the number of part-time hours worked per week. Round the answers to the nearest tenth.
4. Assuming a normal distribution, determine the:
   a) number of hours worked per week above 1σ of the mean, rounded to the nearest tenth.
   b) percentage of students that exceeded the answer from **a)**, to the nearest tenth of a percent.
5. Assume that the homework hours per course per week represents a binomial distribution and that 40% of the students in the sample spend the expected number of hours on homework per week per course. What is the probability that 5 out of 10 students from a random sample would meet this expectation?

Conclusion

What conclusions can you reach regarding hours of part-time work and time spent on homework?

Address the following results and factors:

1. Graphs and scatterplot you constructed
2. Correlations you found
3. Calculations you performed
4. Strength of the evidence
5. Sampling methods you used
6. Sample size
7. Sample bias
8. Unexpected factors or limitations that have or may have influenced results

Suggest a possible follow-up study that may help understand the relationship between hours of part-time work and performance at school.

NOTES

Key Strategies for Success on Tests

KEY STRATEGIES FOR SUCCESS ON TESTS

THINGS TO CONSIDER WHEN TAKING A TEST

It is normal to feel anxious before you write a test. You can manage this anxiety by using the following strategies:

- Think positive thoughts. Imagine yourself doing well on the test.
- Make a conscious effort to relax by taking several slow, deep, controlled breaths. Concentrate on the air going in and out of your body.
- Before you begin the test, ask questions if you are unsure of anything.
- Jot down key words or phrases from any instructions your teacher gives you.
- Look over the entire test to find out the number and kinds of questions on the test.
- Read each question closely, and reread if necessary.
- Pay close attention to key vocabulary words. Sometimes, these words are **bolded** or *italicized*, and they are usually important words in the question.
- If you are putting your answers on an answer sheet, mark your answers carefully. Always print clearly. If you wish to change an answer, erase the mark completely, and ensure that your final answer is darker than the one you have erased.
- Use highlighting to note directions, key words, and vocabulary that you find confusing or that are important to answering the question.
- Double-check to make sure you have answered everything before handing in your test.
- When taking tests, students often overlook the easy words. Failure to pay close attention to these words can result in an incorrect answer. One way to avoid this is to be aware of these words and to underline, circle, or highlight them while you are taking the test.
- Even though some words are easy to understand, they can change the meaning of the entire question, so it is important that you pay attention to them. Here are some examples.

all	always	most likely	probably	best	not
difference	usually	except	most	unlikely	likely

Example

1. Which of the following expressions is **incorrect**?

A. $3 + 2 \geq 5$

B. $4 - 3 < 2$

C. $5 \times 4 < 15$

D. $6 \times 3 \geq 18$

Test Preparation and Test-Taking Skills

Helpful Strategies for Answering Multiple-Choice Questions

A multiple-choice question gives you some information and then asks you to select an answer from four choices. Each question has one correct answer. The other choices are distractors, which are incorrect.

The following strategies can help you when answering multiple-choice questions:

- Quickly skim through the entire test. Find out how many questions there are, and plan your time accordingly.
- Read and reread questions carefully. Underline key words, and try to think of an answer before looking at the choices.
- If there is a graphic, look at the graphic, read the question, and go back to the graphic. Then, you may want to underline the important information from the question.
- Carefully read the choices. Read the question first and then each choice that goes with it.
- When choosing an answer, try to eliminate those choices that are clearly wrong or do not make sense.
- Some questions may ask you to select the best answer. These questions will always include words like *best*, *most appropriate*, or *most likely*. All of the choices will be correct to some degree, but one of the choices will be better than the others in some way. Carefully read all four choices before choosing the answer you think is the best.
- If you do not know the answer, or if the question does not make sense to you, it is better to guess than to leave it blank.
- Do not spend too much time on any one question. Make a mark (*) beside a difficult question, and come back to it later. If you are leaving a question to come back to later, make sure you also leave the space on the answer sheet, if you are using one.

- Remember to go back to the difficult questions at the end of the test; sometimes, clues are given throughout the test that will provide you with answers.
- Note any negative words like *no* or *not*, and be sure your answer fits the question.
- Before changing an answer, be sure you have a very good reason to do so.
- Do not look for patterns on your answer sheet, if you are using one.

HELPFUL STRATEGIES FOR ANSWERING WRITTEN-RESPONSE QUESTIONS

A written response requires you to respond to a question or directive indicated by words such as explain, predict, list, describe, show your work, solve, or calculate. The following strategies can help you when answering written-response questions:

- Read and reread the question carefully.
- Recognize and pay close attention to directing words such as *explain*, *show your work*, and *describe*.
- Underline key words and phrases that indicate what is required in your answer, such as *explain*, *estimate*, *answer*, *calculate*, or *show your work*.
- Write down rough, point-form notes regarding the information you want to include in your answer.
- Think about what you want to say, and organize information and ideas in a coherent and concise manner within the time limit you have for the question.
- Be sure to answer every part of the question that is asked.
- Include as much information as you can when you are asked to explain your thinking.
- Include a picture or diagram if it will help to explain your thinking.
- Try to put your final answer to a problem in a complete sentence to be sure it is reasonable.
- Reread your response to ensure you have answered the question.
- Ask yourself if your answer makes sense.
- Ask yourself if your answer sounds right.
- Use appropriate subject vocabulary and terms in your response.

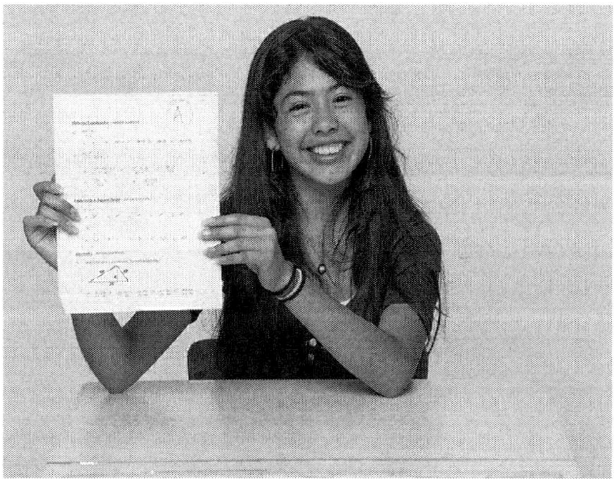

About Mathematics Tests

What You Need to Know about Mathematics Tests

To do well on a mathematics test, you need to understand and apply your knowledge of mathematical concepts. Reading skills can also make a difference in how well you perform. Reading skills can help you follow instructions and find key words, as well as read graphs, diagrams, and tables. They can also help you solve mathematics problems.

Mathematics tests usually have two types of questions: questions that ask for understanding of mathematics ideas and questions that test how well you can solve mathematics problems.

How You Can Prepare for Mathematics Tests

The following strategies are particular to preparing for and writing mathematics tests:

- Know how to use your calculator, and, if it is allowed, use your own for the test.
- Note taking is a good way to review and study important information from your class notes and textbook.
- Sketch a picture of the problem, procedure, or term. Drawing is helpful for learning and remembering concepts.
- Check your answer to practice questions by working backward to the beginning. You can find the beginning by going step by step in reverse order.
- Use the following steps when answering questions with graphics (pictures, diagrams, tables, or graphs):
  1. Read the title of the graphic and any key words.
  2. Read the test question carefully to figure out what information you need to find in the graphic.
  3. Go back to the graphic to find the information you need.
  4. Decide which operation is needed.
- Always pay close attention when pressing the keys on your calculator. Repeat the procedure a second time to be sure you pressed the correct keys.

TEST PREPARATION COUNTDOWN

If you develop a plan for studying and test preparation, you will perform well on tests.

Here is a general plan to follow seven days before you write a test.

COUNTDOWN: 7 DAYS BEFORE THE TEST

1. Use "Finding Out about the Test" to help you make your own personal test preparation plan.
2. Review the following information:
   - Areas to be included on the test
   - Types of test items
   - General and specific test tips
3. Start preparing for the test at least seven days before the test. Develop your test preparation plan, and set time aside to prepare and study.

COUNTDOWN: 6, 5, 4, 3, 2 DAYS BEFORE THE TEST

1. Review old homework assignments, quizzes, and tests.
2. Rework problems on quizzes and tests to make sure you still know how to solve them.
3. Correct any errors made on quizzes and tests.
4. Review key concepts, processes, formulas, and vocabulary.
5. Create practice test questions for yourself, and answer them. Work out many sample problems.

COUNTDOWN: THE NIGHT BEFORE THE TEST

1. Use the night before the test for final preparation, which includes reviewing and gathering materials needed for the test before going to bed.
2. Most importantly, get a good night's rest, and know you have done everything possible to do well on the test.

TEST DAY

1. Eat a healthy and nutritious breakfast.
2. Ensure you have all the necessary materials.
3. Think positive thoughts, such as "I can do this," "I am ready," and "I know I can do well."
4. Arrive at your school early, so you are not rushing, which can cause you anxiety and stress.

SUMMARY OF HOW TO BE SUCCESSFUL DURING A TEST

You may find some of the following strategies useful for writing a test:

- Take two or three deep breaths to help you relax.
- Read the directions carefully, and underline, circle, or highlight any important words.
- Look over the entire test to understand what you will need to do.
- Budget your time.
- Begin with an easy question or a question you know you can answer correctly rather than follow the numerical question order of the test.
- If you cannot remember how to answer a question, try repeating the deep breathing and physical relaxation activities. Then, move on to visualization and positive self-talk to get yourself going.
- When answering questions with graphics (pictures, diagrams, tables, or graphs), look at the question carefully, and use the following steps:
    1. Read the title of the graphic and any key words.
    2. Read the test question carefully to figure out what information you need to find in the graphic.
    3. Go back to the graphic to find the information you need.
- Write down anything you remember about the subject on the reverse side of your test paper. This activity sometimes helps to remind you that you do know something and are capable of writing the test.
- Look over your test when you have finished, and double-check your answers to be sure you did not forget anything.

NOTES

Practice Test

PRACTICE TEST

Tables of Correlations

	Specific Expectation	Practice Test
CP1.1	*recognize and describe how probabilities are used to represent the likelihood of a result of an experiment and the likelihood of a real-world event*	1
CP1.3	*determine the theoretical probability, Pi (i.e., a value from 0 to 1), of each outcome of a discrete sample space, recognize that the sum of the probabilities of the outcomes is 1 (i.e., for n outcomes, P(1) + P(2) + P(3) + ... + P(n) = 1), recognize that the probabilities Pi form the probability distribution associated with the sample space, and solve related problems*	NR1
CP1.5	*recognize and describe an event as a set of outcomes and as a subset of a sample space, determine the complement of an event, determine whether two or more events are mutually exclusive or non-mutually exclusive, and solve related probability problem using a variety of strategies*	2
CP1.6	*determine whether two events are independent or dependent and whether one event is conditional on another event, and solve related probability problems using a variety of strategies*	OR1
CP2.1	*recognize the use of permutations and combinations as counting techniques with advantages over other counting techniques, distinguish between situations that involve the use of permutations and those that involve the use of combinations, and make connections between, and calculate, permutations and combinations*	3, 4
CP2.2	solve simple problems using techniques for counting permutations and combinations, where all objects are distinct, and express the solutions using standard combinatorial notation	5, 6
CP2.3	*solve introductory counting problems involving the additive counting principle and the multiplicative counting principle*	NR2, NR3
CP2.4	*make connections, through investigation, between combinations (i.e., n choose r) and Pascal's triangle*	7
CP2.5	*solve probability problems using counting principles for situations involving equally likely outcomes*	8
PROBABILITY DISTRIBUTIONS		
PD1.1	recognize and identify a discrete random variable X (i.e., a variable that assumes a unique value for each outcome of a discrete sample space, such as the value x for the outcome of getting x heads in 10 tosses of a coin), generate a probability distribution [i.e., a function that maps each value x of a random variable X to a corresponding probability, P(X = x)] by calculating the probabilities associated with all values of a random variable, with and without technology, and represent a probability distribution numerically using a table	9
PD1.2	calculate the expected value for a given probability distribution [i.e., using $E(X) = \Sigma xP(X = x)$], interpret the expected value in applications, and make connections between the expected value and the weighted mean of the values of the discrete random variable	OR2, OR3 a
PD1.3	represent a probability distribution graphically using a probability histogram (i.e., a histogram on which each rectangle has a base of width 1, centred on the value of the discrete random variable, and a height equal to the probability associated with the value of the random variable), and make connections between the frequency histogram and the probability histogram	OR3 b, c

PD1.5	recognize conditions that give rise to a random variable that follows a hypergeometric probability distribution, calculate the probability associated with each value of the random variable, and represent the distribution numerically using a table and graphically using a probability histogram	10
PD1.6	compare, with technology and using numeric and graphical representations, the probability distributions of discrete random variables	NR4
PD1.7	solve problems involving probability distributions, including problems arising from real-world applications	11
PD2.1	recognize and identify a continuous random variable (i.e., a variable that assumes values from the infinite number of possible outcomes in a continuous sample space), and distinguish between situations that give rise to discrete frequency distributions and situations that give rise to continuous frequency distributions	12
PD2.2	recognize standard deviation as a measure of the spread of a distribution, and determine, with and without technology, the mean and standard deviation of a sample of values of a continuous random variable	NR5
PD2.5	recognize that theoretical probability for a continuous random variable is determined over a range of values, that the probability that a continuous random variable takes any single value is zero, and that the probabilities of ranges of values form the probability distribution associated with the random variable	13
PD2.6	recognize that the normal distribution is commonly used to model the frequency and probability distributions of continuous random variables, describe some properties of the normal distribution, and recognize and describe situations that can be modelled using the normal distribution	14
PD2.7	make connections, through investigation using dynamic statistical software, between the normal distribution and the binomial and hypergeometric distributions for increasing numbers of trials of the discrete distributions	15
PD2.8	recognize a z-score as the positive or negative number of standard deviations from the mean to a value of the continuous random variable, and solve probability problems involving normal distributions using a variety of tools and strategies, including problems arising from real-world applications	NR6
ORGANIZATION OF DATA		
DA1.3	distinguish different types of statistical data (i.e., discrete from continuous, qualitative from quantitative, categorical from numerical, nominal from ordinal, primary from secondary, experimental from observational, microdata from aggregate data) and give examples	OR4
DA2.2	explain the distinction between the terms population and sample, describe the characteristics of a good sample, explain why sampling is necessary, and describe and compare some sampling techniques	16
DA2.3	describe how the use of random samples with a bias or the use of non-random samples can affect the results of a study	OR5
DA2.4	describe characteristics of an effective survey, and design questionnaires or experiments for gathering data	17
DA2.5	collect data from primary sources, through experimentation, or from secondary sources, and organize data with one or more attributes to answer a question or solve a problem	18
STATISTICAL ANALYSIS		
SA1.1	recognize that the analysis of one-variable data involves the frequencies associated with one attribute, and determine, using technology, the relevant numerical summaries (i.e., mean, median, mode, range, interquartile range, variance, and standard deviation)	19
SA1.2	determine the positions of individual data points within a one-variable data set using quartiles, percentiles, and z-scores, use the normal distribution to model suitable one-variable data sets, and recognize these processes as strategies for one-variable data analysis	NR7
SA1.3	generate, using technology, the relevant graphical summaries of one-variable data based on the type of data provided	20

SA1.5	interpret statistical summaries to describe the characteristics of a one-variable data set and to compare two related one-variable data sets; describe how statistical summaries can be used to misrepresent one-variable data; and make inferences, and make and justify conclusions, from statistical summaries of one-variable data orally and in writing, using convincing arguments	OR6
SA2.1	recognize that the analysis of two-variable data involves the relationship between two attributes, recognize the correlation coefficient as a measure of the fit of the data to a linear model, and determine, using technology, the relevant numerical summaries	21
SA2.2	recognize and distinguish different types of relationships between two variables that have a mathematical correlation	22
SA2.3	generate, using technology, the relevant graphical summaries of two-variable data based on the type of data provided	23
SA2.4	determine, by performing a linear regression using technology, the equation of a line that models a suitable two-variable data set, determine the fit of an individual data point to the linear model, and recognize these processes as strategies for two-variable data analysis	OR7
SA2.5	interpret statistical summaries to describe the characteristics of a two-variable data set and to compare two related two-variable data sets: describe how statistical summaries can be used to misrepresent two-variable data; and make inferences, and make and justify conclusions, from statistical summaries of two-variable data orally and in writing, using convincing arguments	24
SA3.2	assess the validity of conclusions presented in the media by examining sources of data, including Internet sources (i.e., to determine whether they are authoritative, reliable, unbiased, and current), methods of data collection, and possible sources of bias, and by questioning the analysis of the data and conclusions drawn from the data	25

PRACTICE TEST

Use the following information to answer the next question.

There are 10 000 households in the city of Rosetown, which has three local newspapers. Of the 10 000 households, 4809 subscribe to the Daily News, 430 subscribe to Paper View, and 275 subscribe to Gossip News.

1. Based on these statistics, what is the probability that the next family to move to Rosetown will **not** subscribe to a local paper?

A. 0.4486

B. 0.4809

C. 0.5191

D. 0.5514

Numerical Response

1. Kylie chose, without looking, one marble from a bag containing 3 red marbles and 4 green marbles. What is the probability, to the nearest thousandth, that she chose a red marble? _____

Use the following information to answer the next question.

The given Venn diagram indicates the number of students taking a computer course (C), the number of students taking a data management course (D), and the number of students taking neither course.

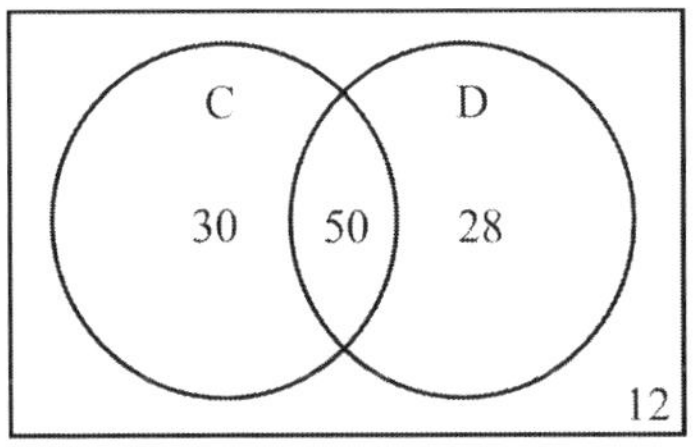

2. A student is chosen at random from the entire group. If $P(\mathrm{C})$ represents the probability that the student is taking the computer course and $P(D)$ the probability that the student is in the data management course, then which of the following probabilities is **not** correct?

A. $P(\mathrm{C}) = \frac{80}{120} = \frac{2}{3}$

B. $P(\bar{\mathrm{D}}) = \frac{42}{120} = \frac{7}{20}$

C. $P(\mathrm{C \text{ or } D}) = \frac{108}{120} = \frac{9}{10}$

D. $P(\mathrm{C \text{ and } D}) = \frac{108}{120} = \frac{9}{10}$

3. Which of the following problems can be solved by using permutations?

A. Determine the number of quadrilaterals that can be formed using the vertices of an octagon.

B. Determine the number of 4-member committees that can be selected from a group of 12 people.

C. Determine the number of 5-letter arrangements of the letters in the word **COUNTRY.**

D. Determine the number of 5-card hands that can be made using a standard deck of 52 cards.

4. Which of the following problems is solved by using combinations?

A. Determine the number of different 3-topping pizzas that can be made if 9 toppings are available.

B. Determine the number of ways in which 8 different fruits can be distributed among 7 students.

C. Determine the number of arrangements of 3 different plays if a football team has 6 basic plays.

D. Determine the number of ways in which 2 adults and their 3 children can be arranged in a line to have their picture taken.

5. The number of ways in which a group of 7 students can be seated 5 at a time in a row of 5 desks is

A. $5!$

B. $7!$

C. $5! \times 2!$

D. $\frac{7!}{2!}$

6. After everyone had shaken hands once with everyone else in a room, there were a total of 66 handshakes. How many people were in the room?

A. 11

B. 12

C. 33

D. 67

Numerical Response

2. How many 3-letter arrangements consisting of 1 vowel followed by 2 consonants are possible using the letters in the word WEALTH?

____

3. Blake's rural high school has fifteen Grade 12 students and ten Grade 11 students. His principal wants to choose students to form a 5-member planning committee for the school's year-end trip to Ottawa. How many different groups of 5 students can the principal choose for the committee if at least one Grade 11 student **must** be on the committee?

____

Use the following information to answer the next question.

The given figure represents a street map.

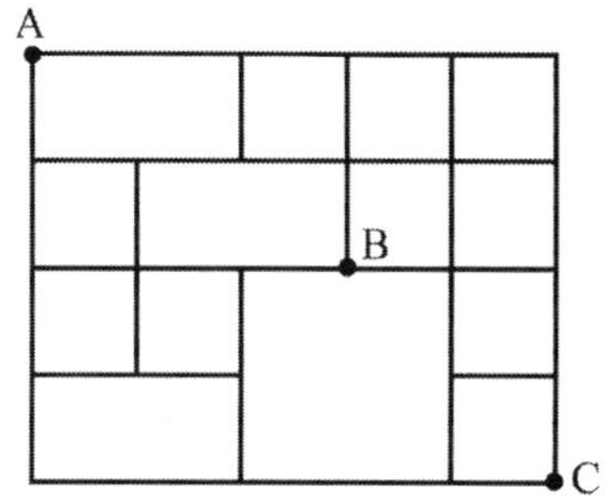

7. If Seamus can travel only west to east or north to south on the streets, how many different routes could he take from point A to point C that pass through point B?

A. 5 **B.** 8

C. 15 **D.** 38

8. There are 6 red balls and 7 black balls in a bag. If two balls are randomly chosen, without replacement, from the bag, what is the probability that both balls are red or that both balls are black?

A. $\frac{6}{13}$

B. $\frac{2}{35}$

C. $\frac{85}{169}$

D. $\frac{35}{676}$

Use the following information to answer the next question.

Suppose you flipped 3 coins. The theoretical probabilities for the possible outcomes for the coin landing heads can be represented in the following table.

Number of Heads Showing, x	$P(x)$
0	i
1	ii
2	iii
3	iv

9. To complete the table, the probabilities represented by i, ii, iii, and iv, respectively, are

A. $\frac{1}{4}, \frac{1}{4}, \frac{1}{4}, \frac{1}{4}$

B. $\frac{1}{8}, \frac{2}{8}, \frac{3}{8}, \frac{4}{8}$

C. $\frac{1}{8}, \frac{3}{8}, \frac{3}{8}, \frac{1}{8}$

D. $\frac{1}{6}, \frac{2}{6}, \frac{2}{6}, \frac{1}{6}$

10. Which of the following conditions is required for a hypergeometric probability distribution?

A. The probability of success does not change as each trial is made.

B. The probability distribution involves a series of independent trials.

C. There are exactly 2 outcomes—success or failure.

D. The probability of success is equal to the probability of failure.

Numerical Response

4. In a group of 8 printers, only 6 work. If a sample of 4 printers is randomly chosen, then the probability that exactly 3 of these 4 printers work, to the nearest hundredth, is

____

11. How many of the following experiments would produce binomial distributions?

i. Drawing names out of a hat without replacement and recording the number of names that begin with a vowel.

ii. Counting the number of spades in a hand of 13 cards dealt from a well-shuffled deck.

iii. Asking all students in a class whether they prefer cola or ginger ale.

iv. Selecting the winning ticket in a lottery.

v. Predicting the expected number of heads when flipping a coin 100 times.

vi. Predicting the number of boys among five children randomly selected from a group of eight boys and six girls.

A. 1 **B.** 2

C. 3 **D.** 4

12. Which of the following statements is **not** a characteristic of a continuous random variable?

A. Continuous random variables have graphs that are smooth curves.

B. Continuous random variables can take fractional or decimal values.

C. Continuous random variables can be determined using counting principles.

D. Continuous random variables arise from situations that involve measurement.

Numerical Response

5. The scores for a class of math students on a recent quiz worth 10 marks are as follows: 5, 7, 9, 6, 5, 10, 8, 2, 10, 8, 7, 7, 6, 9, 5, 8. What is the standard deviation of the scores to the nearest hundredth? _____

Use the following information to answer the next question.

Salty Potato Chips produces bags of potato chips with a labelled mass of 355 g. In reality, not all the bags have a mass of exactly 355 g, but they must be within a reasonable range of 355 g to maintain their business licence. Therefore, the company must perform regular quality testing to ensure that the bags have close to 355 g. One hundred bags are randomly selected and their masses are recorded. The probability histogram shown below indicates the percentage of the randomly selected bags of chips whose masses fell within a particular range.

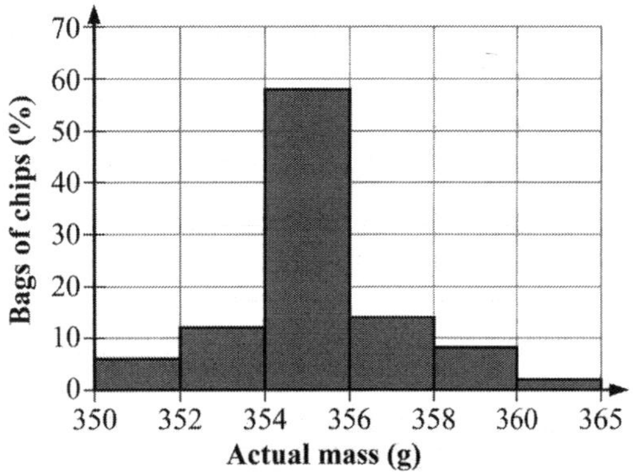

13. Which of the following conclusions can be determined from the given histogram?

A. The percentage of the randomly chosen bags of chips with a mass between 354 g and 357 g.

B. The percentage of the randomly chosen bags of chips with a mass greater than 355 g.

C. The probability that a randomly chosen bag of chips will have a mass of exactly 356 g.

D. The probability that a randomly chosen bag of chips will have a mass less than 356 g.

14. The strength of a female athlete is normally distributed with a mean of 50 and a standard deviation of 10. In which interval do the middle 68% of the female athletes score?

A. 30 to 70

B. 40 to 60

C. 30 to 50

D. 50 to 70

Use the following information to answer the next question.

Tom is doing a study of the predominance of left-handedness in his hometown, which has a population of 850 000. Statistics show that about 9.8% of the population are left-handed.

15. The mean, to the nearest whole number, and the standard deviation, to the nearest hundredth, for the population of left-handed people in his hometown are, respectively,

A. $\mu = 83\ 300$ people,
$\sigma = 274.11$ people

B. $\mu = 83\ 300$ people,
$\sigma = 7513.66$ people

C. $\mu = 833\ 000$ people,
$\sigma = 274.11$ people

D. $\mu = 766\ 700$ people,
$\sigma = 7513.66$ people

Numerical Response

6. The marks on a final exam in Statistics are normally distributed. Susan scored 68%, which is equivalent to a *z*-score of 1.25. If the standard deviation of the Statistics test is 4%, then the mean, correct to the nearest percent, is _____%.

Use the following information to answer the next question

The owners of an amusement park would like to determine what percentage of patrons are returning customers. The customers enter the park one at a time and pass an attendant who takes their tickets. A suitable survey question could be asked at that time. Not every customer would be asked because the attendant wants to keep the line moving at a steady rate.

16. The sampling method that would likely be used is

A. simple random sampling

B. convenience sampling

C. volunteer sampling

D. systematic sampling

17. Which of the following characteristics is found in an effective survey?

A. The questionnaire is designed to avoid bias.

B. The random sampling technique is well designed and the sample represents the population.

C. The wording of the question takes into account privacy laws.

D. All of the above.

Use the following information to answer the next question.

A survey of downtown workers vs. non-downtown workers was conducted in answer to the question "How do you usually travel to work?" The results are summarized in the following tables.

Downtown Workers			
Mode of Transportation	**Women (%)**	**Men (%)**	**All (%)**
Car	45.1	41.8	43.5
Bus	31.6	31.7	31.7
Rail	19.5	20.9	20.2
Cycle	2.7	3.1	2.9
Walk	0.6	1.9	1.2
Other	0.5	0.6	0.5
Non-Downtown Workers			
Mode of Transportation	**Women (%)**	**Men (%)**	**All (%)**
Car	39.0	36.4	37.7
Bus	31.6	31.8	31.7
Rail	27.8	24.8	26.36
Cycle	1.4	5.3	3.4
Walk	0.1	1.1	0.7
Other	0.1	0.6	0.2

18. Which of the following conclusions about the given data is correct?

A. Most downtown workers regularly bus to work.

B. The percentage of men who come to work in a car is less than the percentage of women who come to work in a car.

C. Bicycling to work is not common but the percentage of this means of transportation is higher for women.

D. The percentage of women who cycle, walk, or have other means of transportation is higher than men.

19. Which of the following measures will definitely **not** change if a data set were increased by adding an extra smallest value and an extra largest value to the set?

A. Only the mean

B. Only the median

C. Only the mean and the median

D. The mean, median, and standard deviation

Numerical Response

7. The lifetimes for a certain brand of light bulb are normally distributed with a mean lifetime of 700 hours and a standard deviation of 20 hours. If a light bulb has a z-score of -1.6, then its lifetime, to the nearest hour, will be __________.

20. Individual hockey players were timed as they skated one lap around the ice rink. The coach sat in the stands with a stopwatch and recorded the time for each player. Which of the following graphs should the coach use to get a quick distribution of the times of the players?

A. Box plot

B. Histogram

C. Circle graph

D. Stem-and-leaf plot

21. A research company studied the effectiveness of a cold remedy by giving the remedy to a group of 50 cold sufferers and giving a placebo (sugar pill) to a different group of 50 cold sufferers. After one week, the researchers recorded the number of people for each group who reported an improvement in their symptoms and the number for each group who reported no improvement. Which type of graph will the research company **most likely** use to display their results?

A. Histogram

B. Circle graph

C. Contingency table

D. Stem-and leaf plot

22. Which of the following relationships would **most likely** have a linear correlation coefficient near zero?

A. The amount of tread on a tire and the distance it has travelled.

B. The interest rates for bank loans and the amounts of the loans.

C. The number of tickets sold in a lottery and the price of homes in a city.

D. The time of day based on a 24-hour clock and the number of people watching television.

Use the following information to answer the next question.

When cooking a roast in the oven, Thomas recorded the following data regarding time in the oven and temperature of the roast:

Time (min)	Temperature (°C)
20	45
40	85
60	110
80	135
100	140
120	185
140	195
160	205
180	210
200	210

Thomas used his TI-83 calculator to draw a scatter plot of the data he collected.

23. Which of the following would be the scatter plot he obtained if he used the 9:ZoomStat window?

A.

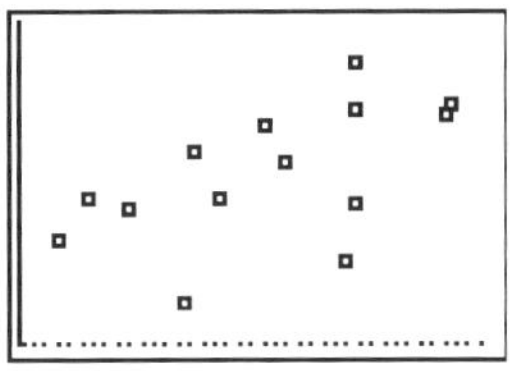

B.

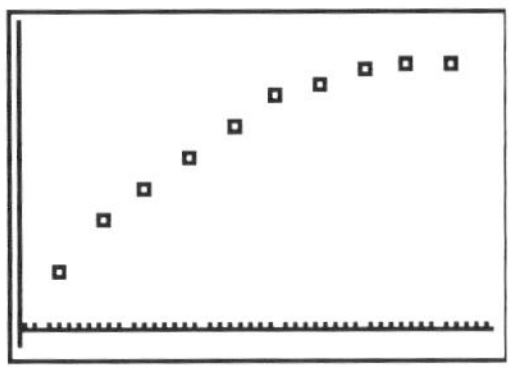

C.

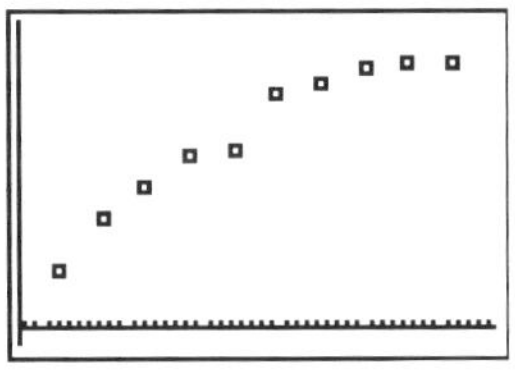

D.

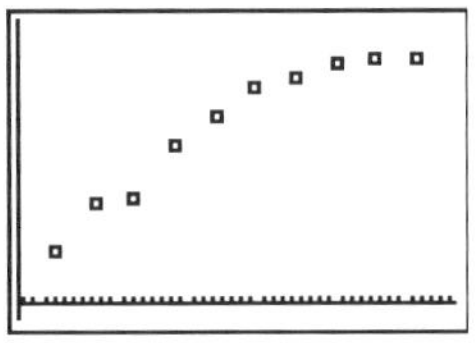

Use the following information to answer the next question.

A study was done to predict the number the number of college hockey players that would play professional hockey. The results of the study are shown in the following table:

Year	Number that Played Professionally
1995	82
1996	80
1997	90
1998	94
1999	97
2000	99
2001	98

24. Based on the data, a reason why a linear model of the data could not be used to predict the number of ex- college players that played professional hockey in 2005 is

A. The sample is too small

B. Other players are not included in the study.

C. A linear model is inappropriate to make the prediction.

D. The data values are likely inaccurate.

Use the following information to answer the next question.

The headline that accompanies the following graph reads "Big Decrease in Credit Card Interest Rate."

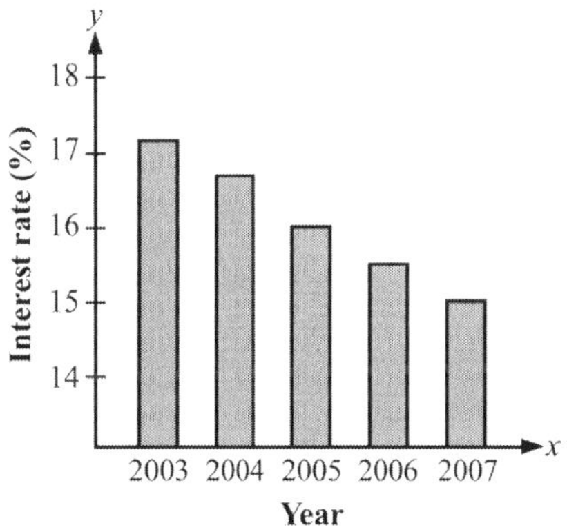

25. Which of the following changes to the graph should be made to **best** represent the change in the interest rate?

A. Reduce the space between the bars.

B. Connect the midpoints of the tops of the bars.

C. Switch the variables on the horizontal and vertical axes.

D. Change the scale on the vertical axis so that it starts at 0.

Open Response

OR1. Marcie owns a candy shop. Her most popular product is a box of 30 assorted chocolates, 5 of which contain nuts.

a) Marcie selects two chocolates at random from the box. Determine the following probabilities:

i) Both of the chocolates contain nuts

ii) Neither of the chocolates contains nuts

iii) Only one of the chocolates contains nuts

b) The chocolates with nuts are popular with Marcie's customers, so she plans to double the number of chocolates with nuts in each box. She claims that if 10 rather than 5 of the 30 chocolates contain nuts, then the probability that one or both of the two randomly selected chocolates will contain nuts doubles. Do you agree with her claim? Support you answer with probability calculations.

OR2. James has designed a board game that requires a 10-sided die numbered 1 to 10. If the die lands with an odd number showing, a player moves forward double that number of squares. However, if the die shows an even number, the player moves back one-half that number of squares.

a) What is the expected move per roll of the die?

b) Is the rule fair in terms of movements forward and back? Explain.

OR3. The table of data below gives the number of people of a given age group who purchased a particular type of vehicle over a given month

Age (rounded to the nearest 5 years)	20	25	30	35	40	45	50
Number of People (Total = 211)	7	27	31	75	39	23	9

a) Complete the probability distribution for the data, giving the probabilities to the nearest hundredth.

Age	20	25	30	35	40	45	50
Probability	$\frac{7}{211} \approx 0.03$						

b) Draw the probability histogram, using decimal notation on the vertical axis.

c) Based on the data, determine the probability that a person under the age of 30 will purchase this type of vehicle. Round the answer to the nearest hundredth.

OR4. A teacher collected data from her students on the amount of homework that each student completed over the week. She used a scale from 0 to 10 where 0 meant none of the homework was completed and 10 meant that all of the homework was completed.

a) Would the data be discrete or continuous? Explain.

b) Would the data be ordinal data or nominal data? Explain.

c) Is the data primary or secondary? Explain.

d) Is the data quantitative or qualitative? Explain.

Use the following information to answer the next question.

You have recently dined at a new restaurant in town and the owner hands you a card with a question to determine how your meal was. He asks you to check your rating as

☐ **scrumptious**	☐ **really good**
☐ okay	☐ bland

OR5. State how this survey is biased and suggest how the bias could be avoided.

OR6. The directors of company B presented the following graph to the shareholders of the company representing the company's net earnings or losses over a three-year period.

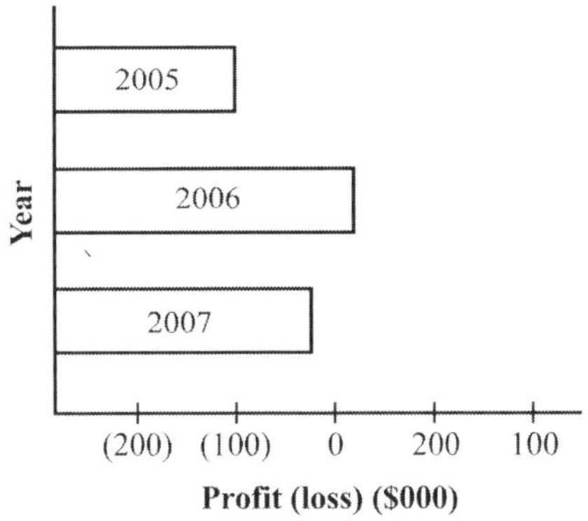

Some of the shareholders complained that the graph was misleading. Explain two possible complaints about the graph and corresponding fixes that would improve the graph.

OR7. A line of best fit is given by $y = 4x - 1$. What is the residual of an outlier point (x, y) that has coordinates (3, 7)?

ANSWERS AND SOLUTIONS—PRACTICE TEST

1. A	**5. D**	**8. A**	**12. C**	**NR6. 63**
NR1. 0.429	**6. B**	**9. C**	**NR5. 2.06**	**OR1 ****
2. D	**NR2. 72**	**10. C**	**13. D**	**OR2. ****
3. C	**NR3. 50 127**	**NR4. 0.57**	**14. B**	**OR3. ****
4. A	**7. C**	**11. B**	**15. A**	**See solution**

1. **A**

Newspaper	Number of Households Subscribed
Daily News	4809
Paper View	430
Gossip News	275
None	4486
Total	10 000

$$P(\text{None}) = \frac{4\ 486}{10\ 000} = 0.4486$$

NR1. 0.429

It is equally likely that Kylie chose any marble in the bag. Since there are 3 red marbles in the bag,

$$P(\text{choosing a red marble}) = \frac{3}{7} \approx 0.429$$

2. **D**

A is Correct.

$$P(\text{C}) = \frac{\text{Number of students in circle C}}{\text{Total number of students}} = \frac{30+50}{30+50+28+12} = \frac{80}{120} = \frac{2}{3}$$

B is Correct.

$$P(\bar{\text{D}}) = 1 - P(\text{D}) = 1 - \frac{50+28}{120} = 1 - \frac{78}{120} = \frac{42}{120} = \frac{7}{20}$$

C is Correct.

$$P(\text{C or D}) = P(\text{C}) + P(\text{D}) - P(\text{C and D}) = \frac{80}{120} + \frac{78}{120} - \frac{50}{120} = \frac{108}{120} = \frac{9}{10}$$

D is **not** correct.

The outcomes in C and D are in the region where the two sets overlap. Thus,

$$P(\text{C and D}) = \frac{50}{120} = \frac{5}{12}$$

3. **C**

"Determining the number of 5-letter arrangements of the letters in the word COUNTRY" is the only problem in which order is important. Different arrangements of the 5 letters form different "words."

4. **A**

"Determine the number of different 3-topping pizzas that can be made if 9 toppings are available" is the only problem in which the order of the objects is not important when the selection is made.

5. **D**

In this problem, 5 students out of 7 are chosen and arranged. Since the order in which the students are seated is important, this is a permutations problem. The number of permutations of 7 objects taken 5 at a time is

$${}_7P_5 = \frac{7!}{(7-5)!} = \frac{7!}{2!}$$

6. B

Let n be the number of people in the room. Since it takes 2 people to shake hands and order is not important, the number of handshakes is the number of combinations of n objects taken 2 at a time. The number of handshakes is 66, so

$$\begin{aligned} {}_nC_2 &= 66 \\ \frac{n!}{(n-2)!2!} &= 66 \\ \frac{n(n-1)(n-2)!}{(n-2)!2!} &= 66 \\ \frac{n(n-1)}{2} &= 66 \\ n^2 - n &= 132 \\ n^2 - n - 132 &= 0 \\ (n-12)(n+11) &= 0 \\ n = 12 \text{ or } n &= -11 \end{aligned}$$

Because n must be a positive number, $n = 12$.

NR2. 72

Before you can arrange the three letters, you first have to select the one vowel and two consonants that are to be arranged. There are ${}_2C_1$ ways of choosing one vowel from the 2 vowels and ${}_4C_2$ ways of selecting the two consonants from the 4 consonants. Finally you must arrange the three letters which can be done in 3! different ways. Since you must perform all three operations the number of different 3-letter arrangements is the product:

$$\begin{aligned} {}_2C_1 \times {}_4C_2 \times 3! &= 2 \times 6 \times 6 \\ &= 72 \end{aligned}$$

NR3. 50 127

This is a combinations of problems because there are no specified positions on the committee, so the order in which students are chosen is not important.

The number of different groups of 5 with at least one Grade 11 student is equal to the total number of different five member groups minus the number of different five member groups with no Grade 11 students:

$$\begin{aligned} &{}_{25}C_5 - {}_{15}C_5 \times {}_{10}C_0 \\ &= 53\ 130 - 3\ 003 \\ &= 50\ 127 \end{aligned}$$

7. C

The given figure illustrates the solution to this pathway problem.

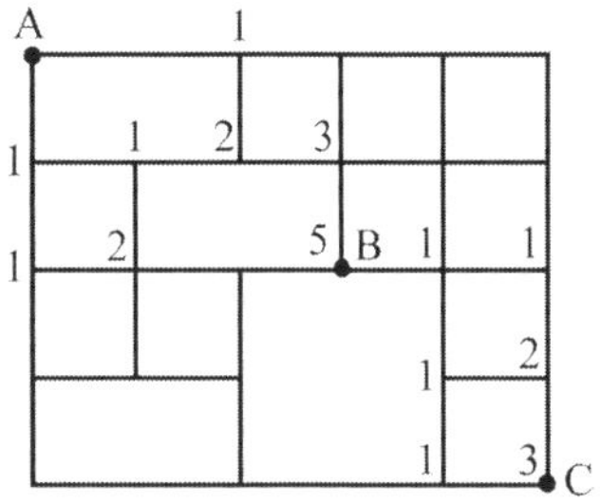

Since there are 5 paths from A to B and 3 paths from B to C, by the multiplicative counting principle, there are $5 \times 3 = 15$ possible routes from point A to point C that travel through point B.

8. A

Since the order in which the balls are chosen is not considered, this is a combinations problem. You can consider the balls as being chosen at the same time.

The number of different selections of 2 balls from the 13 in the bag is ${}_{13}C_2$.

The number of different selections of 2 red balls from 6 is ${}_6C_2$.

The number of different selections of 2 black balls from 7 is ${}_7C_2$.

The number of different selections of 2 red or 2 black balls is ${}_6C_2 + {}_7C_2$.

Thus,

$$\begin{aligned} P(\text{both red or both black}) &= \frac{{}_6C_2 + {}_7C_2}{{}_{13}C_2} \\ &= \frac{15+21}{78} = \frac{36}{78} = \frac{6}{13} \end{aligned}$$

9. C

The following tree diagram can be used to determine the sample space for tossing 3 coins.

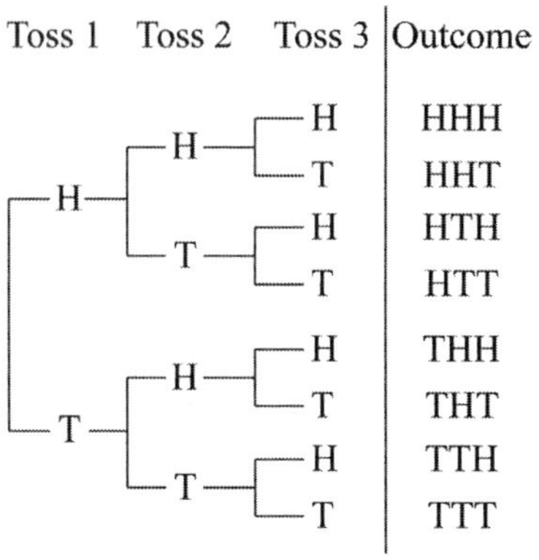

As shown, there are 8 equally likely outcomes. Only one outcome shows 0 heads (TTT) so, $P(0 \text{ heads}) = \frac{1}{8}$. Three of the outcomes show 1 head, so $P(1 \text{ head}) = \frac{3}{8}$, Three of the outcomes show 2 heads, so $P(2 \text{ heads}) = \frac{3}{8}$. One outcome shows 3 heads (HHH) so $P(3 \text{ heads}) = \frac{1}{8}$.

10. C

A hypergeometric probability distribution has two outcomes: success or failure, which is the same as a binomial probability distribution. Choices A and B apply to a binomial probability distribution but not to a hypergeometric probability distribution. Choice **D** is not a necessary condition for either a binomial or hypergeometric distribution.

NR4. 0.57

Since the probability changes as soon as one printer is selected for the sample, a hypergeometric probability must be calculated.

$$P(3 \text{ work}) = \frac{{}_6C_3 \times {}_2C_1}{{}_8C_4} \approx 0.57$$

11. B

Experiments (iii) and (iv) produce binomial distributions because the trials are independent and there are 2 outcomes.

Experiment (iv) is a uniform distribution. Each ticket has the same chance of being the winning ticket.

Experiments (i), (ii), and (vi) are hypergeometric distributions.
In hypergeometric distributions, the probability of success changes for each trial. Therefore, the trials are dependent.

12. C

Discrete random variables are determined using counting principles.

NR5. 2.06

The standard deviation of a set of numbers can be done on the calculator by listing the scores in L_1 then using 1-Var Stats to determine the standard deviation, σx, for the population.

13. D

For choices **A** and **B**, to find the percentage of randomly chosen bags within a given range of masses, the intervals must be as shown on the histogram and cannot fall within the given intervals.

For choice **C**, in grouped data, the probability that a continuous random variable takes any single value cannot be determined.

14. B

Since 68% of the data in a normal distribution lies within 1 standard deviation of the mean, the interval needed is the mean $\pm 1\sigma = 50 \pm 10$

$50 - 10 = 40$ and $50 + 10 = 60$. The interval where 68% of the female athletes scored is from 40 to 60.

15. A

To determine the mean and standard deviation of the data provided in this scenario, use the formulas for the normal approximation to a binomial distribution:

$$\begin{aligned}\mu &= np\\ &= (850000)(0.098)\\ &= 83300\\ \sigma &= \sqrt{np(1-p)}\\ &= \sqrt{(850000)(0.098)(1-0.098)}\\ &\approx 274.11\end{aligned}$$

NR6. 63

Use the z-score formula to determine the mean.

$$\begin{aligned}z &= \frac{x-\mu}{\sigma}\\ 1.25 &= \frac{68-\mu}{4}\\ 1.25(4) &= 68-\mu\\ 5 &= 68-\mu\\ \mu &= 68-5 = 63\%\end{aligned}$$

16. D

In order to keep the line moving, the attendant may pose the question to every fifth person, for example. This would be systematic sampling.

17. D

An effective survey must avoid bias that will affect the data. This includes the selection of the sample and the way the survey question is worded. The sample must represent the population and be randomly selected. The wording of the question must not lead the respondent to an answer and privacy laws must be taken into account when recording the answers.

18. B

The percentage of men who come to work in a car is 41.8 + 36.4 = 78.2%. The percentage of women who come to work in a car is 45.1 + 39.0 = 84.1%.

19. B

The median will not change because the middle value, or values, will remain the same when an extra value is added to both extremes of the data set. The value of the mean will change if the added values are not symmetrical about the mean. The standard deviation will increase because the set of data will be more spread out due to the inclusion of the two extreme values.

NR7. 668

The bulb's lifetime can be determined using $z = \frac{x-\mu}{\sigma}$, where $z = -1.6$, $\mu = 700$, and $\sigma = 20$.

$$\begin{aligned}-1.6 &= \frac{x-700}{20}\\ -32 &= x-700\\ 668 &= x\end{aligned}$$

The bulb's lifetime will be 668 hours.

20. D

Since the coach wanted a quick distribution, he should use a stem-and-leaf plot so the times are recorded in the form of a distribution.

21. C

The data fits the requirements for a contingency table: there are two variables (the treatments and the effects) and the frequencies are known.

The other alternatives are graphs used to display one-variable data.

22. C

When a relationship has a linear correlation coefficient of zero, it means that there is no linear correlation. The number of lottery tickets sold and the price of homes may have a minor correlation, but if so, it would be very slight. Therefore, it likely has a correlation coefficient of zero.

The amount of tread on a tire and the distance the tire has travelled should have strong negative correlation, as should the relationship between the interest rates for bank loans and the amounts of the loans. The relationship between the time of day and the number of people watching television should have a strong positive correlation.

23. **C**

From the data values you can see that the fifth pair of values has a y-value of 140, which is only 5 greater than the y-value in the previous ordered pair. Thus, the plotted point for this ordered pair is slightly lower than the trend of the others. This lower fifth point is visible in choice **C**.

24. **C**

It appears from the data that the number of professional players is levelling off at around 100. A linear model would not allow for this levelling off. None of the other choices are statements that can definitely be made from the given data.

25. **D**

Starting the vertical scale at 0 would adjust the vertical scale to de-emphasize the amount of change in the interest rates. Also, all of the bars would be relatively tall, showing that the interest rate remained high, so the change in rate is not that significant.

OR1.

a) The events of drawing two chocolates randomly from the box are dependent.

i) $P(\mathrm{N}_1 \text{ and } \mathrm{N}_2) = P(\mathrm{N}_1) \times P(\mathrm{N}_2|\mathrm{N}_1)$

$$= \frac{5}{30} \times \frac{4}{29}$$

$$= \frac{20}{870} = \frac{2}{87}$$

ii) $P(\overline{\mathrm{N}_1} \text{ and } \overline{\mathrm{N}_2}) = P(\overline{\mathrm{N}_1}) \times P(\overline{\mathrm{N}_2}|\overline{\mathrm{N}_1})$

$$= \frac{25}{30} \times \frac{24}{29}$$

$$= \frac{600}{870} = \frac{20}{29}$$

iii)

$$P(\mathrm{N}_1 \text{ and } \overline{\mathrm{N}_2}) + P(\overline{\mathrm{N}_1} \text{ and } \mathrm{N}_2)$$

$$= P(\mathrm{N}_1) \times P(\overline{\mathrm{N}_2}|\mathrm{N}_1) + P(\overline{\mathrm{N}_1}) \times P(\mathrm{N}_2|\overline{\mathrm{N}_1})$$

$$= \frac{5}{30} \times \frac{25}{29} + \frac{25}{30} \times \frac{5}{29}$$

$$= \frac{125}{870} + \frac{125}{870}$$

$$= \frac{250}{870} = \frac{25}{87}$$

b) To determine most efficiently the probability that one or both of the chocolates selected contain nuts, use the concept of complementary events.

$P(\text{one or both chocolates contain nuts})$

$= 1 - P(\text{neither chocolate contains nuts})$

For the box of 30 chocolates with 5 chocolates that contain nuts,

$P(\text{one or both chocolates contain nuts})$

$= 1 - P(\text{neither chocolate contains nuts})$

$= 1 - P(\overline{\mathrm{N}_1} \text{ and } \overline{\mathrm{N}_2})$

$= 1 - P(\overline{\mathrm{N}_1}) \times P(\overline{\mathrm{N}_2}|\overline{\mathrm{N}_1})$

$$= 1 - \frac{25}{30} \times \frac{24}{29}$$

$$= 1 - \frac{600}{870}$$

$$= \frac{870}{870} - \frac{600}{870}$$

$$= \frac{270}{870} = \frac{27}{87} = \frac{9}{29}$$

For the box of 30 chocolates with 10 chocolates that contain nuts:

$P(\text{one or both chocolates contain nuts})$

$= 1 - P(\text{neither chocolate contains nuts})$

$= 1 - P(\overline{\mathrm{N}_1} \text{ and } \overline{\mathrm{N}_2})$

$= 1 - P(\overline{N_1}) \times P(\overline{N_2} | \overline{N_1})$

$= 1 - \frac{20}{30} \times \frac{19}{29}$

$= 1 - \frac{380}{870}$

$= \frac{870}{870} - \frac{380}{870}$

$= \frac{490}{870} = \frac{49}{87}$

Since $\frac{49}{87} \neq 2 \times \frac{27}{87}$, Marcie's claim is incorrect.

You can also calculate the probability without using the concept of complementary events by considering the possible cases that one or both of the chocolates contain nuts.

OR2.

a) Complete a table that shows the probability distribution for each number showing on the die.

Number	Movement, x	$P(x)$
1	2	$\frac{1}{10}$
2	–1	$\frac{1}{10}$
3	6	$\frac{1}{10}$
4	–2	$\frac{1}{10}$
5	10	$\frac{1}{10}$
6	–3	$\frac{1}{10}$
7	14	$\frac{1}{10}$
8	–4	$\frac{1}{10}$
9	18	$\frac{1}{10}$
10	–5	$\frac{1}{10}$

Observe that the sum of the probabilities is 1 and that the probability of each outcome is the same. This is a uniform distribution.

The expected move, E, per roll of the die is

$$E = 2\left(\frac{1}{10}\right) - 1\left(\frac{1}{10}\right) + 6\left(\frac{1}{10}\right) - 2\left(\frac{1}{10}\right) + 10\left(\frac{1}{10}\right) - 3\left(\frac{1}{10}\right) + 14\left(\frac{1}{10}\right) - 4\left(\frac{1}{10}\right) + 18\left(\frac{1}{10}\right) - 5\left(\frac{1}{10}\right)$$

$E = 3.5$

The expected move is 3.5 squares forward.

b) This rule is not fair. For the rule to be fair, it cannot be weighted in favour of one direction. That is, the expected value would be 0 if the rule were fair.

OR3.

a)

Age	Probability
20	$\frac{7}{211} \approx 0.03$
25	$\frac{27}{211} \approx 0.13$
30	$\frac{31}{211} \approx 0.15$
35	$\frac{75}{211} \approx 0.36$
40	$\frac{39}{211} \approx 0.18$
45	$\frac{23}{211} \approx 0.11$
50	$\frac{9}{211} \approx 0.04$

b)

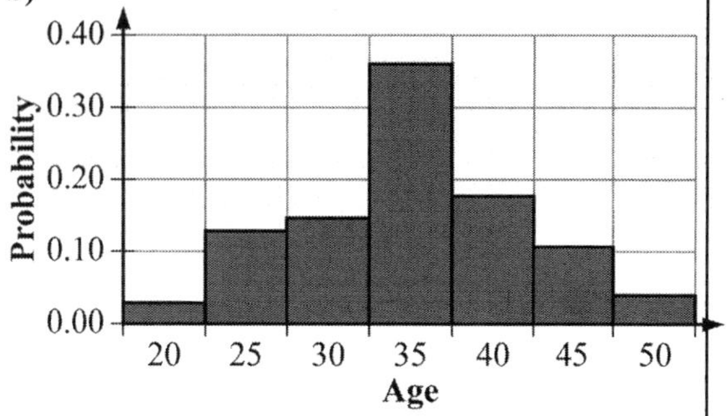

c) $P(\text{under } 30) = P(20) + P(25)$

$$= \frac{7}{211} + \frac{27}{211} = \frac{34}{211} \approx 0.16$$

OR4.

a) The correct answer here depends on the explanation.
If the assumption is made that students will answer with a whole number, then the data will be discrete. However, if students may answer with any real number between 0 and 10 inclusive, so they could give fractional or decimal answers, then the data would be continuous.

b) The reason the data is ordinal is that there is a logical order to the data.
The closer the response is to 10, the more homework the student completed.

c) The reason the data is primary is that the teacher is the researcher and is collecting the data firsthand.

d) This is considered quantitative data because the data is measured numerically.

OR5.

Response bias. Scrumptious is in larger print and the use of bold font will influence peoples' responses.

An unbiased version of the question would be to remove the bold font and use the same size font for all the alternatives.

OR6.

Possible answers:

1. The bars point in a positive direction, even though for two of the years there was a net loss. To correct this, the bars should start in the centre of the graph and move left for a loss and right for a profit. As well, they could switch the scales so that the bars move up for a profit and down for a loss.
2. The bar for profit appears to be wider than the other two. They should be the same size.
3. The amounts of profit and loss are not clearly shown. It would be better to label the bars with the amounts of profit or loss, which should be the emphasis, rather than the year.

OR7.

When $x = 3$, the y-value of the line of best fit is $y = 4(3) - 1 = 11$. The y-value of the outlier is 7. Therefore, the residual is $7 - 11 = -4$. The residual is negative because the outlier lies below the line of best fit.

Appendices

DATA TABLES

The following information may be useful in writing an examination.

GRAPHING CALCULATOR WINDOW FORMAT

$x:[x_{\min}, x_{\max}, x_{scl}]$

$y:[y_{\min}, y_{\max}, y_{scl}]$

EXPONENTS, LOGARITHMS, AND GEOMETRIC SERIES

$A = P(1+i)^n$

$\log_a(m \times n) = \log_a m + \log_a n$

$\log_a\left(\frac{m}{n}\right) = \log_a m - \log_a n$

$\log_a m^n = n\log_a m$

$\log_b c = \frac{\log_a c}{\log_a b}$

TRIGONOMETRY

arc length $a = r\theta$

$\csc x = \frac{1}{\sin x}$

$\sec x = \frac{1}{\cos x}$

$\cot x = \frac{1}{\tan x}$

$\cot x = \frac{\cos x}{\sin x}$

$\tan x = \frac{\sin x}{\cos x}$

$\sin^2 x + \cos^2 x = 1$

$1 + \tan^2 x = \sec^2 x$

$1 + \cot^2 x = \csc^2 x$

$\sin(A+B) = \sin A\cos B + \cos A\sin B$

$\sin(A-B) = \sin A\cos B - \cos A\sin B$

$\cos(A+B) = \cos A\cos B - \sin A\sin B$

$\cos(A-B) = \cos A\cos B + \sin A\sin B$

$\sin(2A) = 2\sin A\cos A$

$\cos(2A) = \cos^2 A - \sin^2 A$

CREDITS

Every effort has been made to provide proper acknowledgement of the original source and to comply with copyright law. However, some attempts to establish original copyright ownership may have been unsuccessful. If copyright ownership can be identified, please notify Castle Rock Research Corp so that appropriate corrective action can be taken.

Some images in this document are from www.clipart.com, © 2013 Clipart.com, a division of Getty Images.

NOTES

NOTES

NOTES

NOTES

NOTES

NOTES

NOTES

Student Notes and Problems
Workbook
Ordering Information

Student Notes and Problems (SNAP) Workbooks contain complete explanations of curriculum concepts, including examples and practice exercises

SNAP Workbook—$29.95 each plus applicable sales tax

Ontario SNAP Titles
Physics 12, University Preparation (SPH4U)
Physics 11, University Preparation (SPH3U)
Math 10, Academic, Principles of Mathematics (MPM2D)
Math 9, Academic, Principles of Mathematics (MPM1D)
Math 9, Applied, Foundations of Mathematics (MFM1P)

Total Cost

SOLARO Study Guides Ordered ________

SNAP Books Ordered ________

Cost Subtotal ________

Shipping and Handling
Please call for current rates ________

GST ________

Order Total ________

Payment and Shipping Information

Name ________________

School ________________

Telephone ________________

SHIP TO:

School Code ________________

School Name ________________

Address ________________

City: ________________

Postal Code: ________________

PAYMENT OPTIONS:

☐ By Credit Care VISA/MC

Name on Card: ________________

Number: ________________

Expirely Date: ________________

☐ By Enclosed Cheque

☐ Invoice School

PO Number: ________________

To order books, please visit
www.castlerockresearch.com

Volume pricing is available. Contact us at orders@castlerockresearch.com